Land of the
Cloud Warriors

by Jackie McGuire

Published by Amazon KDP

Cover art by Jackie McGuire,

with technical assistance from Dan Farnsworth

Printed in the United States of America

Dedication

Many thanks to those who helped me by reading and giving me their impressions and advice. My son Dan, husband Gene, and friend Diane Z. Special appreciation goes to my friend, Gretchen Brunk, without whose long hours of difficult research and beta reading this book might have lacked some fantastic color and discoveries. To the Ash Creek Too critique group: Tony L., Sue A., Don S., and Barbara L., who encouraged me through the first drafts and revision, and made our weekly meetings feel like a family adventure.

Please remember that this is a fiction story, even though many background details are true. Some of the story was originally inspired by the book *Wurd Amerika in der Antike entdeckt?* by Hans Giffhorn, an in-depth scientific study of a mysterious and controversial subject which ignited our curiosity and imagination.

Foreword

Lila Darrow, formerly Lila Winters, had married handsome detective Amzi Darrow, and moved with him to Cuzco, Peru, where he worked as a detective and security agent with the Antiquities Department and the Cuzco Museum. During their life at the hacienda, Lila learned of fascinating mysteries in the history of the high Andes.

The most intriguing was the origin of the Cloud Warriors. They seemed different from all the other Andean natives: taller, some with Nordic features, and many were blonde or red-haired. They wanted only to be left alone to live in peace, yet were known as the fiercest of fighters in protection of their walled cities in the lofty heights of the Andes. The Incas feared them, calling them "White Warriors of the Clouds." *Chachapoyas.*

Controversies have raged back and forth, some saying they came from somewhere in Europe, others that this idea was impossible and ridiculous. Who can find the answer?

It's now 20 years later, and the children of Lila and Amzi are coming into adulthood at the family home, Spurwink Manor, in Maryland. The most studious of the four is Amzi Jr, known as "AJ" Darrow. He returns to Cuzco, Peru, to study the history, and mystery, of the Chachapoyas.

Table of Contents

Map of the Ancient World by Dan Farnsworth
Chapter 1: The Darrows Return 1
Chapter 2: Old Haunts; Moving Mummies 11
Chapter 3: Ships in the Mountains 22
Chapter 4: The Sea of Atlantis 28
Chapter 5: Kuelap 41
Chapter 6: Kidnapped 49
Chapter 7: Daisy and the Shining Path 57
Chapter 8: Old Carmella...62
Chapter 9: The New World...68
Chapter 10: Kanmi's Axe..76
Chapter 11: Amzi Comes for Daisy 87
Chapter 12: Qhawa: Intrepid to the Last 94
Chapter 13: Fly Away to Spurwink 101
Chapter 14: AJ Returns to Cuzco...107
Chapter 15: 1 BC in the Amazon...113
Chapter 16: Exploring the West: 121
Chapter 17: AJ meets Umayo 130
Chapter 18: The Cave and the Earthquake.........................137
Chapter 19: Canaanites 144
Chapter 20: Ancient Writings..152
Chapter 21: Tanitay and Time Travel.....................................159
Chapter 22: Traitors at Kuelap 168
Chapter 23: AJ's Mission to the Amazon 176
Chapter 24: Queen of the Amazon and the Madeira Maid........185
Chapter 25: Finding Kanmi's Axe...195
Chapter 26: Aife's Escape, and the Pink Emerald 201
Chapter 27: Secrets of Atahuaqa 210
Chapter 28: Fall of Atahuaqa 218
Chapter 29: Grief Shared; Heading for Spurwink...................228
Chapter 30: Home on the Amazon..235
Glossary 245
The Author...263
About This Book 265

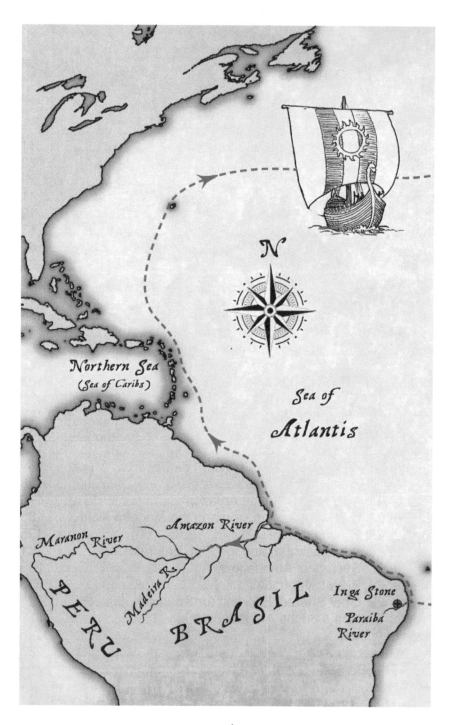

Northern Sea
(Sea of Caribs)

Sea of
Atlantis

Maranon River

Amazon River

Madeira R.

PERU

BRASIL

Inga Stone

Paraiba River

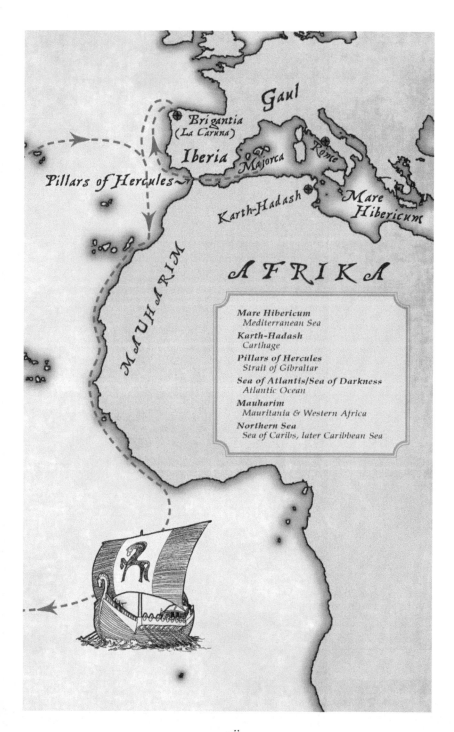

Gaul

Brigantia
(La Caruna)

Iberia

Majorca

Rome

Pillars of Hercules

Karth-Hadash

Mare
Hibericum

AFRIKA

MAUHARIM

Mare Hibericum
  Mediterranean Sea

Karth-Hadash
  Carthage

Pillars of Hercules
  Strait of Gibraltar

Sea of Atlantis/Sea of Darkness
  Atlantic Ocean

Mauharim
  Mauritania & Western Africa

Northern Sea
  Sea of Caribs, later Caribbean Sea

Land of the
Cloud Warriors

(Sequel to *Gem of the Andes*) by Jackie McGuire

Chapter 1

Late June, 2013. High in the Andes, a soft wind swirls through the snowy peaks, flowing down jungle canyons where no human had trod for hundreds of years, whispering over the vine-covered tops of ancient ruined cities known only to monkeys and condors, and the occasional wild llama.

Far below, a guttural murmur answers the soft soughing of the wind. Deep in the earth, off the coast of Peru, a fractured edge of the Nazca Tectonic Plate stirs, straining to slide under the opposing South American Plate until it breaks free, sending shock waves through the crust of the Earth, up through the flanks and crags of the mountains.

Along the western edge of the continent, people feel the temblors. Disquieting, but not as terrifying as others had been. Some lose homes or outbuildings, some find cracks across roads or pastures. A few are injured by falling rocks or pieces of structures. They take familiar measures to repair and rebuild. Earthquakes are common in Peru.

The shifting fault disturbs places where no people live, as well. One hillside above the ancient city of Atahuaqa becomes unstable, but does not slide.

Still, it is cause for concern.

The Darrows Return

"Do you think we could all go back?" Lila had perceived that Amzi was thinking more about Peru recently. It was early July, 2013, and their children were now young adults. Lila and Amzi had only made a couple of quick trips back to Cuzco since they'd escaped from their burning hacienda that night in 1993, just ahead of the *Sendero Luminoso*. The Shining Path terrorists might still be carrying a deadly grudge.

Amzi, and by association his family, had become a target, because he had worked for the Peruvian government in Cuzco for many years as a detective and security agent with the Antiquities Department and the museum in Cuzco. He had worked mostly with smuggling cases, but had been instrumental in foiling some of the terrorists' subversive activities. Would there be any danger now?

He and Lila had met in 1990 in Maryland, while Amzi was investigating the theft and disappearance of two rings. The rings held the severed halves of a mystical pink emerald that had belonged, originally, to an ancient priestess, Tica, in the lost city of Atahuaqa, high in the Andes of Peru. Lila had, by chance, found one of the rings, lost by her cousin Elfie, and secretly kept it safe in her room at Spurwink, her family's home, while everyone else was searching for it and its twin. Amzi and Lila had realized, after collaborating to retrieve and protect the rings, that they were of allied minds, and had found they enjoyed working together, and had grown to love each other. They soon married, and moved to Peru to return the rings.

After Amzi and his young family had lived a few years at their hacienda at Cuzco, the terrorists had begun to turn their attention toward him, the *nortéamericano* intruder who was working with the despised Peruvian government, gumming up the works of their plans. Lila and Amzi had only two small children at that time, Danny, 2-1/2, and Daisy, just a few months old. They had escaped, looking back at the

2

light of their burning home, that November night in 1993. Danny vaguely remembered the experience, and their journey through the mountains, but especially the helicopter ride to safety. Daisy didn't remember any of it.

Danny had often regaled his siblings with tales of Peruvian adventures—embellished from his point of view and limited memories of hacienda life. Even though he had been too young at the time to participate in the grownups' activities, he and his siblings had heard their dad tell the stories over and over, giving their mother a far-away gaze as she listened.

Now, she and the kids wanted to go back with Amzi and see for themselves what it was like after all these years. One place that Lila particularly missed being able to visit was the land of the *Chachapoyas*, the Cloud Warriors of the high Andes. "Some day we'll go," she had said. That was shortly before the Shining Path had forced their sudden departure and nearly caught up with the family in their flight from the hacienda. In the years since, Lila often wondered if they would ever be able to go safely back to Cuzco and then to see ancient Kuelap, the high Andes fortress of the mysterious Chachapoya tribe. Her curiosity about the Cloud People had grown through the years, as she discovered more references to them in articles and books.

Amzi Jr., (whom they had nicknamed "AJ" to avoid confusion with his dad) had, in his studies, taken special interest in them, too, and was beginning to gather information for a paper about them as his college thesis at Yale.

He had uncovered facts and opinions that often seemed at war with one another. Some archaeologists ridiculed the theory, the belief, that the Chachapoyas had come to the high Andes from far away to the east—possibly somewhere in Europe. It seemed ludicrous, on the one hand. Yet they could not deny that ancient artifacts had been found in Peru, and in Brazil, raising fascinating questions.

It was an exciting idea. Was it true? The Cloud People, or Cloud Warriors, were recognized as fierce fighters, experts with the sling, in defense of their

3

settlements . Yet they were known to be a peace-loving race, gentle in nature. According to 16th century records of the Conquistadors, they were taller than the Spanish, light-skinned, and were often found to have red or blonde hair. The Incas feared them, even though they finally conquered them after many years. "Chachapoya" was a name the Incas had given them. What did they call *themselves?* No one seemed to know.

Daisy was not as intrigued with mummies and tombs as were her parents and AJ. She did, however, find the ancient Peruvian architecture interesting, along with the native food and clothing.

She and her Aunt Elfie were close, sharing many interests like design and fashion. This sometimes gave Lila a tinge of jealousy, but the inherited personality traits were magnetic and undeniable.

At 20, Daisy was a captivating red-haired temptress. She had her father's deep blue eyes, a trait she shared with the two older boys. She had put off college for a while, having grown tired of the academic life, but she had finally applied at the Maryland Institute of Art, following her Aunt Elfie's example.

Benjamin, their youngest brother, had talents for art and music. He also shared a closeness and understanding of animals with his elder brother, Dan.

Danny, aged 22 ½, was majoring in horticulture and animal husbandry at a nearby agricultural college, while 19-year-old AJ had begun a study of ancient history and languages after his first year at Yale, concentrating especially on Pre-Columbian Peru through independent study. These were natural choices, given the involvement of their father in that country's ancient relics, and their mother's interest in its flora, fauna, and history.

AJ looked more like his father every day, and the two older boys' youthful blonde hair had darkened to brown. Lila suspected that their hair might turn prematurely silver, like their father's, now snowy white. Ben, 18, was a sandy blonde, with gray eyes, like his mother.

They were an interesting mixture, those Darrows.

Qhawa, the Peruvian hairless dog, was now over twenty years old. He had joined the family as a pup at the hacienda in Cuzco, and returned in a mysterious manner, along with Missy, Lila's cat, when the family escaped the Shining Path that November night. Later, he had helped find and rescue Amzi from the deep hole he'd fallen into during an investigation in the old warehouse in Maryland. In the years since, he'd been a faithful companion and protector of the growing children, especially Daisy. Now he was slowing down, his muzzle whitening, just getting old, sleeping a lot. Missy had died at 19, well into seniority for a cat, in 1996.

Dan and Ben each had a dog, Bartleby and Lionel, both corgis. Bart had the black, tan and white color combination and Lionel was golden brown and white. They happily shared the family with Qhawa, even enticing him to play now and then.

Lila enjoyed her children. She had regularly assembled them up in the cupola at Spurwink Manor through the years, and made it their special story-time retreat, where she read books aloud to them, and then they took turns reading to each other as they grew able. When the kids were older, they spent part of the time in discussions about people in faraway places—especially Peru. Lila and the kids delighted in talking about the events of that night in 1990, when the rings were found and Amzi had proposed marriage to her right there in the cupola before whisking her away to Peru.

Little Daisy had thought it so romantic, how Lila had discovered and used the cupola for a hiding place, accessible only by secret brick steps that went up the side of the chimney of the old house. It was fun for Lila, igniting the imagination of the children, and they begged to hear the stories again and again.

Elfie's kids began to join them in the cupola, too. The twins, Nathan and Nick, liked the action-adventure stories, while their sister, Tamara, was entranced by the lost cities in the Andes, the jewelry, Priestess Tica, and the ancient writings in the tombs. "Some day, I want to go there," she'd declared, but she was even more drawn to follow her parents in their interior design work.

Nick and Nathan were now 18, just graduated from high school, along with their cousin Ben, and Tamara was 17. The boys were not heavily into sports, but they did enjoy basketball and baseball. Tamara was a popular cheerleader, and a proficient player on the volleyball team.

Lila sometimes wondered if Danny would decide to change back to his real first name, Angus. Uncle Angus had passed away in late 2001, at the well-seasoned age of 102. He had been such a fixture in the family—even though not related—it seemed strange not to see him around. His health had always been good, though, and one morning his housekeeper found him, lying peacefully as in sleep, in his bed. She had called the family at Spurwink right away, as soon as the coroner was on his way. The family came immediately to his home in Wexford, to help and comfort his longtime staff and make arrangements, since they were the nearest to kin he'd ever had in America.

"That's the way to go," Lila had said, tears filling her eyes. "I think Angus and Grampa Cornelius are together— somewhere." She wasn't sure why she thought that, but it was comforting.

~*~*~*~*~*~*~

Amzi was, indeed, thinking about Peru again, as Lila had perceived. He'd had a dream about Umayo, his friend and guide in the Andes. Amzi mentioned that, in the dream, Umayo seemed to be beckoning, imploring him to come. "Maybe I was just thinking about him, and it caused my dream," he'd said to Lila. "I have no reason to think anything is going on down there."

An earthquake, fairly large at 6.9 magnitude, had shaken the country recently. It was centered near the Madre de Dios region, not far to the east of Cuzco. But no one had contacted Amzi with any mention of distress.

6

A few days after his dream, Amzi received a phone call from Umayo: "Hello, my friend. It's been a long time."

"Yes," Amzi stepped into the study and closed the door. "I've been thinking of you for several days. I hope all is well with you and your family in Vilcatambo?"

"Yes, we are all right. No real damage here from the earthquake. But...could you come? I've been thinking about calling you. I know it's such a long way to travel."

"What's wrong? Is there trouble with the Shining Path? How can I help?"

"No, no, not the Sendero Luminoso. Ahhh... I've had some dreams of...Tica..."

"What is it? Did something happen? Atahuaqa? Huaqueros? The earthquake?"

"Yes, it does have something to do with the quake, but, well... Can you come? It's something that wouldn't take long. I can tell you more when you get here."

Amzi knew that Umayo must have something important to tell him, but not on the phone. "I was thinking just recently of coming to Peru. My wife never got to see the homeland of the Chachapoyas. My children would like to come, too. I could let them stay at the hotel in Cuzco while you and I work out this...project."

"That sounds like a good idea," said Umayo. "It's been pretty quiet around here, and it would only take a few days. You are the only one who can help."

When Amzi broke the news to the family that they were indeed going to Peru, they were all ecstatic. "I knew it!" said Lila. "I could feel your thoughts gathering about going back, and then when Umayo called, right after your dream— well, that clinched it. How soon do we leave?"

"Hold on! We have preparations to make, decisions and itineraries to figure out. Umayo wants me to help him with something, so that will be a consideration, too."

"What does he need?"

"Actually, I don't know yet, but I'll have to see how things are going down there, you know, with the Shining Path."

"Oh. I know, it may be dangerous. Do you think there's really much threat?" Lila saw that look in his eyes. Even after all these years, the grudge might still be in effect.

"I wish I knew. I don't want to put any of us in danger. And there could be."

~*~*~*~*~*~*~

A couple of weeks later, the Darrow family deplaned at the Cuzco Airport. Excitement crackled in the air among them. Amzi still couldn't tell them much about his and Umayo's "project," but it was exciting enough just to be in Peru together, at last.

Lila could hardly contain her curiosity about Amzi's plans. *Why is it such a secret? Does it have anything to do with Tica?*

Umayo had asked Amzi not to talk about it until he had filled him in on the details. "I want to be sure it is okay with you, and how much to tell your family," he had said.

"I'm not sure what it's all about yet myself," Amzi told them, "or if there's any danger, but maybe I'll be able to give you more details after my meeting with Umayo."

They piled into a van-taxi with their luggage and excitedly viewed the local sights on the way to their hotel in Cuzco. *Not much has changed here*, thought Lila.

When the family checked in at their hotel, Amzi repeated his instructions that he had discussed with them before leaving Maryland. "First, I'll go with you to some of the places your mom and I felt were really special, and then I have to help Umayo for a few days. If you stay with the main tourist crowds, you should be fine going on the guided sightseeing trips. You can go to Machu Picchu, and tours to Rainbow Mountain, the Sacred Valley, and Saqsaywaman. Those should fill up several days. I've asked the police for an escort, too, wherever you go."

Amzi had worked with the police, as well as the Department of Antiquities and museum officials, when he had lived for many years in Cuzco, helping guard against grave robbers and smugglers. The older members of the police force remembered him.

Amzi called his friend as soon as his family was settled in their hotel suite. "Umayo, you said you'd had dreams of Tica. What did you mean?"

"I'm sorry I couldn't go into detail before. The spy is gone for today, so I can tell you a little more. The earthquake has disturbed the ground above Atahuaqa, the place up the hill, where Tica and Maupi were buried in that ancient quake. She wants her and Maupi's remains to be moved. We are the only ones that know about her, and our special skills will be needed."

"Skills?"

"After you and your family left, I was hired for a job at the Leymebamba Museum, constructing replicas of those famous sarcophagi of the Chachapoyas—you know, the ones that stand up on the high bluffs? I will need to make two of them, and you can help me. You have watched the archaeologists move mummies, so Tica trusts that you will know how to do it respectfully."

"Chachapoyan sarcophagi?" said Amzi. "What..."

"I'll tell you more when we're alone. Too many ears around here. I'll see you—in a few days?"

"That sounds good. I want to be with my family when we go to some of our old favorite places and some restaurants and the marketplace. See you soon." Amzi put down the phone and came back into the main room.

"Okay! Who's up for dinner?" He rubbed his hands together.

"We thought you'd never ask," said Danny. "These two are about to chew my arm off!" The three young men jostled each other in fraternal horseplay as they made for the door.

Daisy grinned, exchanging a knowing look with Lila. *Brothers!*

Lila watched Amzi, questioning with her eyes for some sign, some indication of what the phone conversation had been about, but he only raised an eyebrow at her, meaning, *wait 'til later.*

They went to the restaurant where Amzi had taken Lila when they'd first arrived in Peru. Even after so many years, it was much the same. The aromas of Peruvian cooking permeated the air with familiar spices and specialties. Lila ordered the same thing she'd had that day, "Just for old time's sake," she said, *Lomo Saltado*, a dish made with beef cooked in soy sauce with tomatoes and other vegetables and served with French fries and rice. The boys and Daisy shared a large combination platter of tasty *ceviche*, trout, paired with *juanes*—rice seasoned with turmeric and cumin, stuffed with a little chicken, egg and olives and wrapped in a green *bijao* leaf, and spicy little shish kebabs called *anticuchos*.

"This is like what you make at home," said Daisy to Lila, as she savored the juanes in small bites. "But I think I like yours just a bit better."

Lila felt a warm swell of love for her only daughter as they smiled across the table.

Lila noticed that Amzi was preoccupied, eating his tamales and rice with a far-away look in his eyes. "What is it?" she asked. "What is Umayo asking of you? Is there something more that I should know? Why the secrecy?"

"Sorry, I really can't tell you more until I know, myself. It *is* something about Tica. I hope you'll be able to come, too. I know you feel that connection." Something Umayo had said kept swirling in his mind – *Tica wanted interment in a Chachapoyan sarcophagus? Why?... does that mean....*

Amzi's reticence to discuss the subject only served to pique Lila's curiosity even more. *I guess I'll just wait and see....* She sighed, and opened the dessert menu.

Dessert was ice cream, with Lila's favorite South American cookies, *alfajores*, and coffee. Then they headed back to their suite to plan their next day's activities. First on the list was the marketplace, with lunch at another favorite restaurant.

~*~*~*~*~*~*~

10

Chapter 2: Old Haunts; Moving Mummies

Lila and Amzi and their kids sat in their second-floor Cuzco hotel suite, peering out the window as the evening came on, at a sea of red tile rooftops that seemed to fill the little valley.

"Well, where should we go tomorrow?" Lila unfolded some brochures and turned on an overhead light.

AJ spoke up first: "What about the museum you keep talking about? I've heard about it all my life. *Got* to see that! Do they have a current dig open, where the public can see some of it?"

"Yes, we should be able to see the museum, and I'm sure my old friends will let us see a dig." Amzi looked over Lila's shoulder. "I think there's one open now."

"One thing *we* want to see is the marketplace." Lila held up a picture postcard. "Daisy wants to see the ceramics and jewelry, and get a poncho. I want to get another jug or two for myself, and one each for Aunt Melanie and your grandma Lorna back home. How about you guys?"

"We can tag along wherever you go," said Danny. "It's all interesting, and maybe later we can find some llamas or alpacas. I'd like to see them close up and see how they take care of them and train them."

"Me too," said Ben. "Dad, do they have farms around here where they raise those kinds of animals? I saw some donkeys, too."

"Yes, I'm sure they do." Amzi seemed preoccupied, smiling and nodding, enjoying his family's interest in his adopted country, yet deep in thought.

The hotel offered a free breakfast, an appetizing layout of eggs, bread and jam, tamales, coffee, and piles of exotic fruit. They also had breakfast humitas: the sweet kind, fresh-ground corn mixed with lard, sugar, raisins and cinnamon, and steamed in corn husks. It provided a hearty start to the day.

After breakfast, the Darrows started their tour with the marketplace. Some of the people there remembered Amzi. A very elderly Peruvian lady in a faded shawl looked approvingly at his family, and whispered something to him. He smiled and nodded.

Tables and racks were piled high with colorful rugs, ponchos and chullos, the knitted, pig-tailed hats of the Andes, and in another area hung row upon row of silver jewelry, which Daisy pored over lovingly. Lila gravitated toward the ceramics, and found some treasures to take home.

The boys were beginning to suspect they'd been brought along as beasts of burden.

The family made several stops to gather lunch items at the food vendors', then found a table and benches in a nearby park where they could eat. They had collected an assortment of several treats so all of them could sample some: Savory humitas, like small tamales wrapped in corn husks with queso fresco; Peruvian-style empanadas, pastry dough folded around a filling of meat, with cheese and olives, and a bag of boiled quail eggs with seasoning. They had picked out several kinds of Peruvian drinks to share, too – new flavors the kids hadn't seen in the States.

Amzi savored the sight of his family getting so much enjoyment from their shopping. But he was also looking around, constantly observing the crowd.

Lila noticed, but didn't say anything. *Does he think there might be someone here with ulterior motives? Does the Shining Path hold a grudge this long? I don't want to spoil the fun, but I'll watch, too.*

12

They toured the city, looking at ancient buildings in the town square, especially the Spanish missions, courtyards, and fountains, stopping to watch people in brightly colored costumes putting on dances for the tourists.

"We could go on that tourist hike to see Ollantay-tambo, if you want," said Amzi.

Lila looked at him. He smiled, a little sadly. "It's all right. I think I've come to terms with it. Maybe I need it as closure."

Lila knew he had avoided that place where his first wife had become fatally ill from an insect bite. "We could do that," she said. "We'll see how things go." They embraced, and watched their children enjoying the festivities.

Later, they found another restaurant to check out. "I want to try their *papa rellena*," said Danny, reading from the menu, "I see it's a little different from what you make at home, Mom. It's made of mashed Peruvian potato stuffed with meat, onions, egg, and olives, then deep-fried until the outer part is golden brown. And maybe I'll have some choclo with it." Peruvian corn, *choclo*, is a special treat, with fatter, shorter cobs and very large kernels—just corn, but Danny had never been able to try any in the States.

AJ and Daisy ordered *ceviche*, trout marinated in lime juice, along with the Andean cream soup, lawa, made with fresh ground corn, and potatoes, cheese and eggs, and seasoned with turmeric.

Ben and Lila chose *escabeche*, cooked chicken pickled in vinegar with a variety of vegetables: onions, cauliflower, carrots and peas, garnished with chopped parsley.

Amzi had his favorite *causa*, mashed yellow potato layered with meat and vegetables, and a side of choclo.

The next day, the family toured some museums, including the Choco Museo, offering an exhibition of how chocolate is grown, harvested and made into wonderful desserts. Afterward, they enjoyed hot chocolate and chocolate mousse in the adjoining cafe. Then they found a textile museum that gave a detailed presentation of how the local fabrics were made, the traditions of weaving, the various materials and dyes, and the meanings of the woven designs. Of course, the one museum they really looked forward to visiting was the one where Amzi had worked for so many years. His old friends and colleagues were delighted to see him and complimented him on his fine family. The Darrows were allowed special viewing of the latest excavations at a nearby dig. AJ paid particular attention to everything the archaeologists said.

Early the following day, Amzi called Umayo, to let him know he had arrived and would come out to talk. He had asked Lila to do some local activities with the kids until he found out what Umayo was concerned about. He found Rafa, his trusted driver from the old days, to take him out to Vilcatambo, reminiscing during the couple hours' drive to get there.

"Hello, mi amigo," said Amzi, as Umayo came out to meet him. They embraced briefly, with a friendly slap on the back each. "I see the road out here is as atrocious as before."

"All the better. We like our privacy here."

"Yes, I can certainly understand that. I think I have my family safely ensconced in Cuzco. They're going to go on some short sightseeing trips, with a police escort, while I'm gone this morning. I told them to stay with the crowds and not get isolated."

"Good advice. We haven't had anything happen for a year or more, but..." Umayo smiled grimly and shrugged.

"So. Now...what's this all about?"

"Let's take a walk." Umayo headed for the road. "Better for talking. I think there is a person or two in my village who don't think the same way we do."

Amzi raised one eyebrow. "Oh? Someone dangerous to Tica's interests?"

"It could be. Or maybe it's my imagination. I just have a feeling. I wanted to tell you all about it, but with no possibility of being overheard."

"You said you had a dream—of Tica—asking for help?"

14

"Yes. Her resting place, with Maupi, is becoming unstable from the earth tremors. She always wanted to rest with her ancestors, but had never asked."

"She's asking now."

"Yes."

"And what do we do? How do we help?"

"As I mentioned on the phone, I was employed near Kuelap, the great Chachapoyan fortress in the high Andes, to make some replicas of the Cloud People's sarcophagi, to decorate the museum there, at Leymebamba. The originals were once brightly painted, you know, and the people at the museum thought it would be a wonderful enhancement to the place."

"So they hired you?"

"Yes, they advertised for applicants, and I received special training. I've always been pretty good with my hands."

"How does this relate to our accommodating Tica's request?"

"I have been working on some of the parts and materials," said Umayo, "We can take them to Atahuaqa. I have to look at the placement to see how to move them. We can take a path up the hill from the temple to get the mummies. It shouldn't be too difficult."

"Umayo, may I request that Lila come along? She already has special feelings toward Tica, and she knows this has something to do with her."

"What about your children? Will they be safe by themselves in Cuzco?"

"I am a little concerned about that. I don't know about them coming along here, though. They should be safe enough if they stay on guided tours, going to Machu Picchu and touring Saqsaywaman, but I've asked for some chaperone help from the police, just to be sure."

"Well, if you feel they are careful enough...I remember when your wife came with us, to return the emerald. She seemed very intuitive and involved. Yes, I know she would be okay to come along."

15

"I'll return for her now, then, and I'll double-check to make sure my sons and daughter know where they can go. I don't know if the Sendero Luminoso knows we are here."

"They very well may know by now. They have spies everywhere." He rolled his gaze back toward his village.

"We should be able to travel a little faster through the mountains this time, without so many people as before."

"Yes, that time was enjoyable, was it not? But no embellishments this time. He smiled. You have a good, strong wife, so loyal and supportive."

Amzi returned his gaze, remembering that last trip. "I know she'll be fine."

Amzi returned to Cuzco that evening, and found his family at the hotel. He outlined the plan briefly to Lila, and asked if she wanted to go, and if she thought the young people would feel safe on their own for a few days.

Lila wrung her hands and wiped her palms on her clothes. "I wish I could say whole-heartedly that I'll just jump right into this and go with you. I'm trying not to worry about the Shining Path, but they scared me so much back then."

"I understand, and if you feel you shouldn't...."

"I'll go. You talk to the kids and make sure they understand. They are all around the age I was when you brought me here, and I think they are pretty level-headed. And I'm glad the policemen will be escorting them, too."

Amzi could tell that Lila was still struggling within herself, but wanting badly to go. "Okay," he said, "I'll give them a very serious talking-to. We leave early tomorrow morning."

At dawn, Lila hugged her children and went with Amzi, Rafa driving. The morning mists were still swirling about when their car arrived at Vilcatambo. Umayo and one porter, his son, Pacay, waited out front with four llamas carrying large packs. There was also a donkey, saddled for Lila to ride.

"Oh, I can walk." Lila petted the donkey. "I did it last time."

16

"I'm still taking the donkey," said Amzi. "You never know; we might need it." He looked at the packs on the llamas, wondering what would be revealed on this trip.

They started up the trail. Lila felt one of those old familiar shivers of excitement as she caught glimpses of familiar landmarks -- snowy, rocky peaks looking close enough to touch. They were walking just a bit faster this time than what she remembered, but she didn't object. They wanted to get back to their children as soon as possible.

The first day was long and arduous, and Lila was beginning to look with yearning at the donkey, when Umayo said, "I think this would be a good place to camp tonight. It's farther than we went that other time." It was starting to get dark, and Umayo and Pacay began setting up and getting a fire started.

Lila could hardly wait to sink to the ground. *Am I getting old, or what?*

Amzi came over and started massaging her shoulders and caressing her. "You did really great today, Love. I hope it isn't too hard on you?"

"I'm just not used to it, I think. Out of shape! Phew!"

"Sit and relax," said Umayo. "We'll have something to eat, and get some sleep. Early rising tomorrow." This time there was only basic food, no singing or playing music, no story-telling. But Lila was glad to sleep.

Amzi had to nudge her awake the next morning.

"Ohhhh, maybe I *am* getting old." Lila groaned, and massaged her leg muscles.

"Not old, just old*er*," said Amzi sympathetically. "I feel it, too. We've been letting ourselves go."

"What about your leg?" said Lila. "Maybe *you* should ride the donkey."

Amzi had lost a leg years before when he was a detective in Maryland, and had been injured from falling into a deep hole, stuck for days before being rescued. "I'll let you know if it gets bad, but really, it hasn't hurt. I just think of that mountain climber who climbed Mt. Everest with *two* prosthetic legs."

17

After a quick, simple breakfast, they went on. They were glad to see the faint paths had overgrown, and it only slowed them a little, while still concealing their passing. They were able to shave considerable time off the trip, and arrived at Atahuaqa at the end of two days. The men set up camp in a little space a short distance from the massive stone gateway. It was still covered in vines and mosses, the evening mist clouding the narrow entrance at times, then wafting away. It was a relief to finally rest and eat.

"I'm so glad no huaqueros have found this place," said Lila. "Well, except the Gerards, back in 1852. But if they hadn't, we'd never have known about the pink emerald."

In 1852, Orrin Gerard had found the pink emerald as a bead, in a necklace along with two green emeralds, where it had been buried with Tica and her maiden assistant, Maupi, in an earthquake hundreds of years before. He gave the pink one to his wife, Donna, and it ended up broken, half in each of two rings, separated, and setting off a long story of mystery before being reunited with Tica in 1990, thanks to Amzi and Lila.

"I had no idea what an adventure would unfold when I found that ring," mused Lila as they sat at the campfire. "Or where it would lead us, changing our lives forever."

"And you and I would never have met," said Amzi, giving her a squeeze. "So some good came of it, and Tica got her gem back, too. I hope we can do this one last thing for her now."

Lila was energized with excitement now, and forgot how tired she was. She sat on an ancient squared stone nearby and watched as the three men unpacked the supplies that Umayo would use to put together the sarcophagi. It seemed ages ago that she and Amzi, back at the hacienda, had speculated about Atahuaqa, the Pahuaca tribe, and the similarities they shared with the Chachapoyas. It was then just a passing notion, and no one had written about that association because no one but Donna Gerard had studied the place before. Now Lila wondered again—could it be? Were Tica and Atahuaqa Chachapoyan?

Lila was anxious to see the caskets. She had seen pictures of the famous ones on the high cliffs near Kuelap. Would these look similar? The ones at Kuelap were constructed to stand upright, with large, flat, oval faces attached at the top. Sometimes a warrior's coffin would have the skull of his enemy suspended above it. They had been mostly white, with geometric designs painted a certain way on them to look a little like stylized clothes and jewelry, mostly in gold ochre, red, black and dark brown pigments. The paints had faded, but were still visible. They stood lined up on a high, hollowed-out cliff face, looking out over the deep chasm of the Utcubamba River.

After setting up camp and organizing the parts and supplies, they turned in for the night. Umayo went to work on the new caskets after a quick breakfast early the next morning. Lila and Amzi sat at a respectful distance to watch. Umayo had brought for each coffin a bamboo frame, bent and molded into shape to make the shell. He used clay mixed with straw for covering, and it had dried hard. These were of strong construction, but totally different from the heavy stone sarcophagi of the Egyptians.

Now, he laid out the pieces and painted the designs on them. Lila found it interesting that he used paints he had made himself, from jungle materials. The sarcophagi did, indeed, look just like the ones in the pictures she had seen, only new. Lila's pulse was racing, and one look at Amzi told her that he had been thinking this, too. She appreciated the special designs Umayo painted on each coffin. They were like the ones she'd seen, yet a little different, very pretty, like highly stylized representations of necklaces and feathered cloaks over a dress. It looked to her like a labor of love. *Umayo has feelings for Tica, too*, she thought. *What is his connection?*

After the paint dried, they were ready to go up the hill to bring the mummies down. Umayo prepared each of two llamas with a carrying receptacle. Pacay stayed with the other llamas and the donkey, guarding the camp and the sarcophagi shells as they lay ready to receive the mummies.

Amzi had brought a small shovel and other tools, carefully chosen so as not to compromise anything pertaining to the delicate bodies. He was not sure what to expect, because Tica's and Maupi's bodies had been spontaneously mummified, from the effects of the ancient earthquake and hundreds of years of natural burial, not prepared by skilled hands.

They came to the depression by the trail. Lila gasped. She remembered passing by there that November night in 1993, seeing that place, having a definite feeling of some kind—but then they had seen the terrorists below and she was distracted as they hurried to hide themselves. Now, she watched in fascination.

Amzi and Umayo carefully prodded the ground and began to dig in a certain spot that seemed to beckon to them. They began to find bones, and remnants of rotted fabric, and worked even more carefully.

Lila could imagine, from what she was seeing, the scene unfolding, how the two girls had looked that night, huddled together in their hiding place. They had instinctively reached for each other as the quake began and the cave collapsed upon them, so they were leaning close together. Orrin Gerard, back in 1852, had disturbed the remains a bit, searching for more jewels, but did not intentionally desecrate them otherwise. He had put things back in place before covering them up again.

Poor frightened little girls, she thought sadly, *that's all they really were. But close friends, together in death, as well.* Tears trickled down Lila's face.

"The Chachapoyas had a little different way of preparing a body, unlike the Incas or other tribes," Umayo explained. "They usually buried it for about a year, until only bones were left, and then carefully brought it out and reassembled the body in something like a fetal position, with forearms crossed in front of the knees, and the hands over the face. Then they wrapped it in soft cotton cloth before placing it in the sarcophagus. The earlier ones were actually more like a skeleton than a mummy, before they refined their methods of preservation."

20

Amzi remembered seeing Inca mummies, some dressed in traditional clothing of fine textiles and wearing golden jewelry and different hairstyles, showing their place in life, such as chief, priest, or similar high-ranking occupation. Of course others didn't have as much finery, but were often interred with tools of their trade or fine pottery. In Inca tradition, they were taken out from time to time and paraded to participate in ceremonies, and were offered food and drink. At different times, a variety of preservative methods were used, most anciently with simple salt, but using more sophisticated techniques in subsequent ages, also depending partly on the cold, dry desert air to achieve freeze-drying.

Different, yes.

Umayo had laid out the carrying receptacles on the ground nearby. The two men worked very carefully and respectfully to separate each body, wrap it in the correct position, and place it into a receptacle for the short trip down the hill.

Lila sat quietly, understanding that she had been invited there to witness the process. She was happy that Umayo (and Tica) seemed to value her presence.

They loaded the precious burdens on the llamas and started down toward their camp, where Pacay waited to help. Umayo had seen how the ancient mummies were placed inside the old sarcophagi at Kuelap, so he helped Amzi to perform that task with appropriate respect.

They closed them up as Lila looked on. She trembled at the meaningful scene she was being allowed to witness, and felt a sense of relief that at last these two ancient young women would rest in a proper place.

And where is that? What does Umayo know?

~*~*~*~*~*~*~

Chapter 3: Ships in the Mountains

The little party—Umayo, Amzi, and Lila, with the two llamas now loaded with the sarcophagi—slowly turned towards Atahuaqa, and moved to the tall, narrow gateway leading to the temple. *Like a religious procession*, Lila observed, as she walked in measured steps forward with them.

"Lead the way," said Amzi. *Will this be like before? Where are we going?*

"Yes," said Umayo softly. "Follow."

Guiding the two llamas, the two men, with Lila, walked solemnly through the edifice, huge bricks of stone fit neatly together, now clear of jungle overgrowth, that stretched toward the back of the ruins. *Is this a vision, or was the way actually cleared?* Lila had that feeling again, of going back in time. Monkeys and toucans looked down through the trees at them, and bright butterflies flitted in warm dappled sunshine, high overhead among bromeliads, hanging orchids and flowers, the air sultry, filled with mingled scents of flowers and decaying jungle vegetation, twitters of birds and monkeys. They walked on through ancient stone streets and buildings, and came out on a lower level where an expanse of broken foundations of small, round stone houses had once made up a substantial community.

As they continued on, Lila noticed they were heading toward a great wall on the far side. As they came nearer, she wondered if they would stop there, but then she saw an opening, hidden from view until they were right upon it.

"Watch your step," Amzi said, as he helped Lila down a moldering stairway that passed inside the wall, into darkness. She heard water dripping. Amzi held her elbow.

They came out onto a narrow ledge overlooking a deep valley with stupendous mountains on the other side. The breathtaking drop-off overlooked the alpine abyss from dizzying heights, clouds drifting below them. A condor passed closely above their heads, so near, they could hear the silkiness of its feathers in the breeze. Then it turned in a wide arc and slid down through the clouds.

Lila felt faint for a moment, as if she were falling, but Amzi caught her. He held her tightly against him and kissed her forehead as she found her breath.

"There," said Umayo. He pointed farther along the ledge, where the cliff face curved around, hollowed out—they could see a row of ancient sarcophagi. These looked out over the valley, almost like mirror images of the ones in the picture of Kuelap. The ledge was still wide enough, where the little party had stopped, so that Umayo and Amzi could unload the sarcophagi from the llamas. Lila stayed with the animals as Umayo and Amzi each took an end of the first coffin, and carried it carefully along the narrow ledge. Umayo seemed to know just where to place it, and how to secure it. Then they brought the second one.

Amzi remembered what he and Lila had read, that the Chachapoyas seemed to consider people equal in death, and Maupi, the assistant and special friend to Priestess Tica, was given the same privilege of entombment as the others. He was sure by now—yes, they were Chachapoyas. As he was musing on this, he looked at Lila. She was thinking the same thing—he could tell. He made his way back along the narrow ledge to her, and held her as her trembling diminished. She looked up at him, and smiled.

"Let's go," Amzi said quietly.

As they picked their way back along the precipice, they were startled to see ancient paintings on a protected wall that had been behind them when they came out onto the ledge. It showed people, and ships—old ships with square sails and long oars.

"Ships?" said Lila. "What... what kind are they?"

"Kane-an-im," said Umayo.

They turned to look at him. He had taken off his hat. His snow white hair fluttered slightly in the breeze.

Lila and Amzi stared at Umayo. The last time Amzi remembered seeing him with his hat off, his hair had been reddish brown. He hadn't thought much about his friend's age before. He felt startled, yet thought maybe it wasn't as sudden as he imagined. He Looked at Lila. She had tears in her eyes. *What's going on?*

"We will go back now," said Umayo quietly. "You have seen."

~*~*~*~*~*~*~

The trip back to Vilcatambo was unusually silent. Amzi and Lila were consumed with questions that they felt would be somehow disrespectful to ask, and Umayo didn't offer any more explanation. He seemed lost in thought as he walked, and Pacay, too, seemed very solemn, even at the campfire.

"Your hair, Father," Pacay whispered to Umayo when they were out of earshot. "Is the time getting near?"

Umayo glanced back toward Amzi and Lila, who were preparing their sleeping bag. "Yes. It will be, within the year, I think. I began to see the signs a few weeks ago. Tica knows."

~*~*~*~*~*~*~

At the hotel, Amzi and Lila found their four kids, eagerly waiting to tell of their adventures.

"We went to see Saqsaywaman the first day," said AJ. "It was really thought-provoking to walk around among those huge stones and see how precisely they were designed and fit together. I'd seen pictures, but I think you can't really imagine it until you see it in person. We watched a special ceremony and procession put on for the tourists. The colors

24

are so bright, and the music makes you want to move with it."

"Yes, I love the music," said Daisy. "Sometimes it's kind of haunting—with that quavering sound of the panpipes, mostly in a minor key, yet the accompaniment of the strumming charangos and other instruments sounds joyful. The upside-down stairway was amazing. Such a mystery! There must be a story behind that, but I guess we'll never know."

"There were llamas wandering free all over the place," said Danny. "We fed them a little sometimes. I'd like to get one when we go home, or maybe an alpaca—or two. Do you think we could?"

Amzi smiled, and nodded approval. "We can look into that."

"I like that idea," said Ben. "I think the alpacas are more friendly, but I like both kinds."

"What did you and Mom do? Where did you go?" asked Danny.

Amzi looked at Lila and raised one eyebrow slightly. "We went to Atahuaqa. Umayo had a special job to do there, and asked my help. It had to do with Priestess Tica." *Might as well tell them at least some of it. They'll question us until I do.*

"Oooh, that sounds exciting," said Daisy. "Did you take any pictures, Mom?"

"I don't think...well, it was such a sudden decision for me to go, I didn't take the camera." She looked at Amzi, and saw approval. A camera would have seemed disrespectful. *Best that no one in the outside world should see that place, even by accident.*

Amzi thought of a distraction: "I'm hungry! Let's go to dinner. We can continue the stories at the restaurant."

The kids were excited enough, telling of their own discoveries, that they didn't notice that Amzi and Lila didn't go into details about Atahuaqa. They all had a good night out at another restaurant, savoring the famous Peruvian tamales—corn dough wrapped around a filling of chicken, peppers, cheese, raisins and olives, with peanuts and red onion salsa; *huatia*, made with *huayro* potatoes, baked in an

25

earthen oven and served with *uchucuta* hot sauce, and fresh *capchi*, a dish made with wild *callampa* mushrooms that grow especially well, they say, where lightning has struck recently. Lila tried a new dessert this time, a special Peruvian chocolate dish, instead of her favorite alfajores. They returned to their suite.

"We can all go somewhere together tomorrow. What do you think of going to the Fortress of Kuelap?" said Amzi. He and Lila shared a look—*it should be really interesting now, in light of what we've just seen.*

"Hey, that's a 'yes!' from me," said Daisy.

The boys chimed in with approval. This would be a great adventure. "Let's read up on it again tonight, and refresh our memories about it," said AJ.

Amzi and Lila had brought along a big zippered binder, into which they'd crammed brochures and the latest news about places to visit in Peru. "We should look at the different tours and see which would fit our purposes best," said Lila as she sorted out the papers. "I think we could stay over one night in the town of Chachapoyas and see the Gocta Waterfall, too, and the Leymebamba Museum. It's near Kuelap, and they have a big display of mummies there that were rescued from being damaged by local farmers and looted by huaqueros."

"Yes," said Amzi. "I think it will be safer there, so far up north, farther away from the Sendero Luminoso gangs that know us here."

Lila wondered if they would ever quit looking over their shoulders in Peru. But maybe this excursion would be a relief to Amzi, so he could relax and enjoy the trip more.

"Yes, then, it's settled! I've been wanting to see this waterfall—it's really high. You have to trek through the cloud forest to get to it."

"We'd better get a good night's sleep," said Amzi. "Early rising tomorrow!"

As they lay in the darkness, Lila and Amzi stared at the ceiling. "This week was astonishing, don't you think?" said Lila. "After our talking about the similarities between Tica and her father, with what we read about the

26

Chachapoyas, I had been thinking more and more about it. Kind of a 'what if' idea—but I never saw such confirmation."

"Umayo was really quiet on the way back. I sensed that he didn't want to talk, so I didn't ask some of the questions I wanted to. I was amazed when he took off his hat—I'm still wondering if his hair turned white suddenly, or was I just not paying attention? Is he one of them, too? How else would he know all that stuff about them, and what to do, and how?"

"Did he ever say how old he was?"

"No, we never talked about that kind of thing. We've been good friends for years, working together, but I just assumed he might have some mixed blood—so many Peruvians do—because of his reddish hair, back then. Come to think of it, I did see a little blonde girl at their village one time. Only for a few seconds, and then she was taken inside."

That reminded Lila of her similar experience. "That article I read said there were still scattered Chachapoyan descendants of the survivors from the Spanish and Inca attacks. They made small villages in the more remote parts of the mountains and stayed to themselves... Vilcatambo is really secluded, and has a wall around it. Did you ever ask Umayo what tribe he belonged to?"

"I did, once, and he just said, 'We call ourselves the People.' I never thought any more about it, just supposed he meant mixed blood."

She was quiet for a while.

"I can't quit thinking about those ships," she said. "Did I hear right—did Umayo say 'Canaan-im'? Canaanite?"

"That's what it sounded like to me."

"Isn't that the same as Phoenician? That sounds like too much of a mystery to even contemplate. I can't get my mind around it. What do you think?"

"I think you think what I think," Amzi smiled in the dark, and kissed Lila. "That's what I've always loved about you."

"Go to sleep, Old Man, we've got a long day tomorrow." She turned her back and snuggled into him.

~*~*~*~*~*~*~

27

Chapter 4: The Sea of Atlantis

Spring, 146 BC -- Anat, eight years old, sat on the beach under a *Palmito* tree. The island of Majorca was rugged, with little sandy patches between the rocks, where Anat liked to sit on sunny mornings. Only recently had her young mind begun to understand that Majorca was not the whole world, but one of the Balearic Islands in the western Mare Hibericum, near Iberia. Her home, one of the stone houses in the village behind her, was near the beach, backed by rocky hills and low mountains at the center of the island. She gazed curiously at the horizon, wondering what was happening. Nothing looked unusual. She was too naive to realize she was several days' travel and upwind from the firestorm, too far away to see anything.

Many boats had been coming over the sea to the island for weeks now, from the direction of the great city of Karth-Hadash to the east. She watched from a respectful distance as the people from the boats talked with her parents and others of her village, pointing, waving their hands, and sounding scared.

Anat had now noticed a sudden increase in bustling activity, beginning before dawn and continuing all morning. Another wave of strangers, coming from the east in their boats last night, had gathered in little knots with the Phoenician villagers, Kena'anim, as they called themselves. They were Canaanites, but the Greeks had named them Phoenicians.

Some adults had crouched around the evening fires in their houses, talking in low voices. The men of the village had been preparing the ships since before dawn, loading them, while the women hurriedly cooked and served meals to their families, the men eating on the run. Some people were packing up everything. Others stood by, watching, confused.

Nobody talked to Anat.

The cool breeze coming off the sea riffled her dark hair as she dug her toes into the sand. She heard someone calling her.

Her mother, Tanith, came hurrying down the beach, grabbed her arm, and half-dragged her to their home in the village just a few yards away.

"What is happening?" Anat asked, as she ate her barley bread and hummus.

Her mother passed her a steaming bowl of *puls*, cooked cereal with figs cut into it. "Don't ask questions, just eat. We are going on a journey." She extinguished the cooking fire, and rinsed the pots and dishes with water and sand. She wiped her wet hands on her tunic, then stood with her fists pressing the small of her back, and gazed across the water while Anat finished eating. "We heard that the Romans are attacking Karth-Hadash again. People who escaped, in all those boats we've been seeing, have come and told us. This time it is much worse. They tell us the Romans are destroying the whole city. We are not going to sit here and wait for them to come for us. Father is loading our ship now, and we will join him and your brothers soon."

Anat's father, Akbar, was owner and captain of the family trading and fishing vessel. Her brothers, Kanmi and Danel, were 13 and 11. They had been learning seamanship from Akbar and the other men. Balearic sailors, they were renowned for their seafaring skills. They were traders, fishermen, and explorers. Many times the ships had gone out through the Pillars of Hercules to the great waters of the Sea of Atlantis, traveling south down the western shores of Mauharim, or north to explore the islands and coasts of Iberia, Gaul, and Britain. Rumors had it that they had discovered more distant lands, but they kept the locations secret. Most people of other lands were afraid to venture far from familiar shores, citing stories of sea monsters, and a few even worried about falling off the edge of the Earth. That was fine with the Phoenicians—it was all to their advantage, allowing them freedom to explore without interference from others.

Anat had often wished she were a boy, to grow up on the great ships like her brothers. Now, it seemed, she would be getting her chance to see what it was like. She ate hurriedly while her mother packed up the last of their belongings, along with the cooking utensils she had just used. She doused the fire and stirred it to ashes.

"Aren't we coming back?" Anat asked. She had noticed that Tanith seemed to be cleaning out the whole house of their possessions. This was not to be a short jaunt. The house looked strange with its bare rock walls, nothing hanging or stacked against them.

"Come," said her mother. "Let's head for the ship." She struggled to carry her belongings and cooking equipment. Fortunately, their few heavier household items had already been loaded.

Anat ran after Tanith, clutching her doll and dragging a bag of clothes, looking around at the village of mostly empty houses and more people hurrying along behind and ahead. A few of the people had elected to stay in their homes, though their round eyes betrayed fear.

They came to the landing, and followed along with the others to the edge of the dock, where the water lapped against the sides of the ships. That sound was nearly drowned by the shouts and murmurs of people loading their families and goods onto their designated vessels. Tanith handed their bundles up to her husband and turned to help Anat as she climbed the ladder with her doll.

Anat had never seen so many ships in their harbor before. Word had been sent out for all those who were near enough, to congregate for an orderly departure.

The trading ships of the Kena'anim, *carpássios*, were long and large, with cargo space and room for the crew, including the rowers, but now they were crowded with the families of some of them. It would not be a pleasure trip.

"Up with you!" said Akbar, as he lifted the girl over the side. "Find a spot where you will not be underfoot," he ordered her and her mother. "We will set sail soon."

Anat's chest felt tight with excitement, tinged with apprehension. She watched the flurry of activity onboard all the ships, as families and groups of people clambered in, stowing belongings below, setting up small areas on deck for occupation. They, too, seemed nervous and distressed. *Did this really have something to do with the news from across the water?* It seemed so far away.

"Where are we going?" Danel asked his father.

"Do not ask questions when we are busy," Akbar said gruffly. Then he turned, softened, and put a hand on Danel's shoulder. "We are going on a journey, son, and even I am not sure just where we will finally come to rest." He stroked his bushy black beard as he gazed across the water. "Our leaders know the way."

It had been a long-kept secret, the "big island" that had been discovered so long ago. The seafarers back then had been blown off course during a trading journey down the coast of Mauharim. The storm went on for days, and the southern ocean currents caught them and carried their ships far west, across the formidable Sea of Atlantis. The place they landed weeks later seemed to be a very large island, full of mountains and rivers, rich with fertile soil and all kinds of animals and fruits. "This is a place our people could go, if we are ever threatened by our enemies," they told each other. "We must keep this place a secret for our people, under penalty of death, if need be."

And now, after hundreds of years, it was time.

It was not long before the first of the ships began to move, sluggishly at first, as the sailors climbed masts and pulled ropes, unfurling the sails. The sides and masts creaked and the sails flapped and snapped as they caught the wind and filled out, high overhead. Anat felt, and smelled, the sea breeze, a thing so familiar every day of her life. Now it would carry her and all these people - - where?

Excited, she peeked over the side and saw her best friend, Elissa, on her own family's ship nearby.

As they got underway, the ships drifted farther apart. Elissa waved to Anat, and the two girls smiled nervously at each other just before Elissa was pushed down by her mother. Another, faster, ship slid between, moving forward, blocking Anat's view.

"Stay out of the men's way," Tanith reminded her gently. "We need to let them work unhindered."

Anat squeezed herself into a corner and watched as the men and older boys worked the sails, shouting to each other. She watched the oars, below, as the rowers pulled on them. She studied the carved horse-head on the front of the bow, then looked down at the foaming water below, and held her doll close. Tanith had made it for her, of rags stuffed with wool. It was soft and cuddly, and comforting. She had dressed it in a little tunic like her own. With a good vantage point, higher, near the back end of the boat, she could occasionally stand up and see over the sides.

"Here, eat some pomegranate," said her mother.

Anat loved pomegranates. She liked to pretend that their beautiful red seeds were rubies, all packed into the round, tough peel like a pouch of treasure. (One time, Akbar had let her and her brothers peek at some of his gemstone trade goods brought back from a far venture. The rubies were her favorite.) Her mother had saved the fruit for a special treat to comfort her in this stressful situation.

The people relaxed after they had been sailing a while. Anat lay back on her sleeping pallet and watched the starry sky as her mother sang soothingly to her, and soon she was asleep.

The ships plunged on through the sea, day after day, and through the nights, while Anat studied the shores of Iberia as they passed. She couldn't see anything that looked familiar. She was glad to have her doll, but sometimes she even grew tired of that. There were a few other children she knew on the ship—one was a girl, Babatha, a little older than Anat, another a boy, Fuano, about four years old. Several families traveled in each ship, the wives and children of the owners and some of the crew. But there was

32

no place for children to play without being underfoot of the sailors, unless they huddled together in a cramped corner and talked, or played with small toys or watched fish or sea birds together. Tanith sometimes taught Anat how to sew and mend small things, or talked of her own girlhood days. Anat longed to get out and just *run*.

One evening, after about a week of sailing, Anat settled on a soft bag of clothes and dropped off to sleep. Later, her mother poked her. She awoke looking out at a huge rocky bluff, pointy at the top, silhouetted black against the starry sky to the north. The ships were passing through the Pillars of Hercules.

The stars were brilliant in the black sky, but soon the dawn would begin. They broke out into the open ocean. Far to their left, and disappearing behind them as they turned north, was another shore her mother pointed out. She told Anat that it was the western edge of a land the Romans called Libya. "Farther east, they call it Afrika, the Arabs call part of it Alkebulan, the Indians call it Besacath, but your father says it is all one big land. Later we will go down the western side of Libya, which *we* call Mauharim. Our people have explored it for many years, and it is one big land, not an island, as some think."

Tanith, wife of Akbar, was a woman of unusual knowledge and wisdom in their village. She was the daughter of Zaracas, a Shaman, and was his only child. He had passed on to her all his expertise of healing and herbal medicine, as well as some of the magical arts of the Talayotic people from whom he had descended. His wife, Tanith's mother, was Yasha of the Balearics.

Since her marriage, Tanith had also learned from her husband much of the geography of the lands and ports he had visited. She knew about the land extending far south, past the Pillars of Hercules and down the coast of Mauharim, where her husband and many other Phoenician traders had explored. She had a hunger for learning, unusual for a woman in these times, but Akbar enjoyed telling her tales of his discoveries in far-off lands, delighting to see her eyes light up at the treasures he brought home to her.

Now he was taking his family to a new world—new adventures to share with them all.

~*~*~*~*~*~*~

As the migrants traveled north, they skirted the western shores of Iberia for many days, stopping now and then for water and trading for supplies. Anat felt a little confused, with the dawn coming up over the land, and the sun setting over the sea now, the opposite from when they were heading south from Majorca. She was not used to things changing like this, and it made her feel grouchy, but her mother explained it to her and she felt better. Finally one day, they saw a great gathering of ships in the distance.

"We are coming to Brigantia, a city in northern Iberia," said Tanith. She boosted Anat high against the side rail of the ship so she could see better.

Anat squinted to see the far-off ships as they drew closer. They were a little different than the ones she was used to seeing. They were huge, and had no oars. Some had tall dragon heads on arching necks rising from their bows, and others the head of a swan. Her father's, and many of the Phoenician ships, each had a horse head carved on the bow.

"The horse head honors Yamm, the god of the sea," Tanith had told Anat.

Anat wondered what the dragon heads represented.

Akbar and the other men seemed happy to see the strange ships. Akbar held Tanith and Anat close to him, as Danel and Kanmi stood near, watching the far-off scene become clearer as they closed the distance between. "Those are the Celts," he said to his family. "We sent word overland to northwest Iberia some time ago, and they are coming with us. They don't like the Romans any better than we do." The pre-arranged cue had been set up over the last few years to coordinate with the Kena'anim's escape if the war became a threat to them all, and now the Celts had

34

been waiting, watching for their allies to come through the Pillars and up the coast to rendezvous with them.

Soon Anat could make out several people on the nearest Celt ship. A big man with yellow hair and a dark, bushy beard stood up front, grinning and waving, and Akbar returned the wave.

"That's Fearghus the Strong," he said. "We have fought side by side in many battles."

The Celts of northwest Iberia, Celtiberians, had often gone to war alongside the Balearic and Carthaginian Kena'anim. All were known for their skills with the sling, training their boys since earliest childhood for accuracy and skill. The Balearic Islands got their name from the Greek word ballo, "to throw," and the islanders were the best of all. They and the Celts hired themselves out as mercenary soldiers, and the Balearic soldiers even wore an extra sling wrapped around their heads as a badge of honor, a sign for all to recognize that they were the famous slingers, proud warriors.

An alliance would be profitable to everyone in this venture. The Kena'anim were traders, not colonizers, and hadn't established many settlements in places they'd visited. They were not like the Celts, who raised cattle and sheep on their lands in Iberia and other countries where they had colonies. They could use each others' expertise in a new land.

As the ships gathered, leaders of clans and groups rowed over in small boats and congregated on the deck of Fearghus' ship to share barley bread and honey, with beer and wine, and some of the Celts' special mead, brought for the occasion. They settled themselves with Fearghus in the middle, to solidify their final plans. Fearghus had invited one of his elderly sailors, Dougal, and his son, Cullen. As a youth, Dougal had been on one of the later expeditions that had crossed the Sea of Darkness, and had witnessed the wonders of the mysterious land. Both the Celts and the Ken'an'im had traditions of this mysterious island, held secret for generations. "Our forefathers said it was a

35

paradise of plenty and peace," said Akbar, "something we are looking forward to, these days."

Fearghus gave him a hearty slap on the shoulder. "And we have had little of that, these many years. It is good that we may finally find it. I am weary of counting bodies and wondering when the next attack will come."

Old Dougal gave them information—memories that he had kept in his heart all those years, of the currents in the sea that flowed westward, as well as the winds, and landmarks on the shores of Mauharim at the turning place, and all he could recall of the ancient stories.

The next day, the large flotilla began the long journey south. In several weeks they again passed by the Pillars of Hercules and later sailed along the shore of Mauharim. "We'll be going along this way for a while," Tanith told Anat.

It had become a nervous habit that everyone looked back from time to time, but the Romans were concentrating on Karth-Hadash, so there was no sign of pursuers. The sailors struggled to put as much distance as possible between them and their ancient enemy. They paused at times to fish, but only enough to replenish food supplies and for trade. They bypassed islands where they had often stopped to trade, knowing it would take up extra time, and observers might tell the Romans of seeing them.

Every few days, the ships would come to a familiar village of Mauharim, where they had stopped before for trading, and felt safe to put in, refill their amphorae with water and wine, and renew their other food supplies. They knew the people of different settlements, and had a good bartering relationship with them.

Anat looked forward to these rest stops. It felt so good to get off the ship and stretch her legs, and she knew that Tanith would use her brazier and make good hot food for a change. Cooking on the heaving, windy deck of a ship was nearly impossible. Sometimes when there was a very calm day, they could set up a brazier on a bed of sand within an enclosed space, but it was seldom done.

The people of the coastal villages were eager to trade their salt, spices, dried fruit, gold, jewelry, and pottery for the fishermen's catch, so everyone enjoyed these times. There was plenty of chicken and goat meat, killed for a welcoming feast. The native fruits were interesting: dates, a variety of melons, tamarinds, Natal plums and watermelons. Anat tried some *marula*, a plum-sized fruit with thick yellow peel and white flesh. She liked them because they didn't have seeds and could be eaten whole. She felt refreshed and strengthened by the nutritious drink made from Baobab fruit that had been dried and pounded into a powder and mixed with water or goat's milk. Anat's favorites were melons and especially the dates, so sugary-sweet and plentiful. Much trading was done to stock up on good things to take along, and mothers saved seeds to take with them for gardening in their New World.

Anat had never seen so many black-skinned people in one place. She watched the natives, especially the children, as they danced to the drumbeats and other musical instruments. *I like their music. It makes me want to dance.* She wished she could overcome her shyness and try it herself. She and Elissa stood with the other boat children, clapping their hands and swaying to the music.

Anat and the other children were warned to stay near their parents. It was a little scary in this strange place anyway, so they didn't need to be told twice. She and Elissa had precious short time together to talk and compare their impressions of the trip. They began to notice some of the blonde and red-haired Celtic children, both groups shyly smiling and making friendly gestures, but not knowing each others' languages. Maybe some day, in the new land, they would be friends.

Akbar, Fearghus, and the other men congregated around crackling campfires, drinking beer and wine, telling stories, and laughing heartily, their deep voices wafting across the throngs. Some discussed the journey and its destination in low voices by the fire. "Yes, our people have whispered about it since the ages faded into the past. We, too, are tired of those stinking Romans and the other hordes that sweep over the land, murdering our families and taking all we have. It will be good to find this place." Fearghus chewed thoughtfully on a hunk of goat meat, light flickering on his face as he gazed into the fire.

The migrants felt a great relief from the boredom of the sea, yet harbored an underlying urge to get going again.

All too soon, the call to re-embark came, and everyone headed back to the boats. Anat and Elissa skipped along, glad for the chance to do even that, after so long on the confined decks.

It was easy to lose track of time, sleeping and waking, always sailing, the wind always blowing, salty spray flinging into their faces. Storms made everyone wet and miserable, shivering, trying to shelter under makeshift tents on deck, or crowding together below, where the air was thick with the stench of fish and unbathed bodies.

On good days, Anat lay on her back, looking at the clouds, making up pictures in them, or at night, watching the stars. She spent time with the other children in the ship, quietly playing games, talking, or watching things. Babatha had a doll that her father had carved of ivory, with jointed arms and legs. Anat thought it looked fun, but it wasn't soft and cuddly like hers. Her brothers sometimes had a little free time to play games with her, and taught her some of the things they were learning about knots and stars. Sometimes they watched for different kinds of fish and porpoises together. They saw flying fish, and once, a whale. She shivered and drew back when she saw its huge eye looking right at them.

Tanith cradled her. "Don't be afraid. They don't attack ships like some people say they do. People like to make up scary stories, but the ocean is our friend. It will keep us separated far from the Romans."

Anat hoped her mother was right. She watched the sea birds, too. Gulls, and a huge albatross followed the ships, hoping for food scraps. After a time, she noticed that the ships were all changing course. They had found the westward-flowing current in the ocean, and the winds that had carried seamen across so long ago, to the rich new land of ancestral tales. The shores of Mauharim were now disappearing behind them, and again the sun, moon, and stars seemed to shift their position in the sky as they sailed west. Anat watched the skies for much of the time, since there was not much else to hold her attention. At night, she watched as Akbar taught her brothers how to steer this new course by the stars. As the land receded behind them, she had noticed there were fewer and fewer birds. Morning came. Now they were really far out on the Sea of Darkness, the Sea of Atlantis. What lay ahead, and how far?

After a time, certain foods were becoming meager—Tanith explained, "We will have to make our stored food and water stretch over a long time while crossing the water. I've brought nuts, grains, and dried fruits, and if we're careful, they will last for quite a while. It was good that we could add more in trading in the villages along the coast of Mauharim, but that is now far behind us."

Fish would now be the most dependable food source. They cut thin slices of fish and laid the flesh out in the hot sun, preserving it, and ate it dried most of the time. Anat could hear other children complaining with whiny voices, and sympathized, as she, too, felt hunger. But they had fish. And more fish.

Anat was getting sick of fish, and dreamed of pomegranates.

They sailed for days, weeks. How long, Anat had no idea, just that it seemed endless. She hated to see dark clouds forming. These times, a storm would come up, wind tossed them, waves were gigantic and scary, thunder and lightning were terrifying, and those who stayed topside tried in vain to keep dry under the canopy stretched over the deck for shelter from driving rain. Below decks it was worse—the smells from too many people crowded into the small space made Anat gag. People told stories to try to pass the time, but after a while, they lost their imagination and tried to sleep. Some who were weak or elderly became ill and died, Old Dougal among them. But the migrants continued on, holding fast to their dream of the western lands, and freedom.

Then one morning, she awoke to sounds of excitement up at the front of the ship. She looked over the side and saw people on the other ships, pointing ahead and yelling. Scrambling to a better vantage point, she looked toward the horizon.

Land! She wondered if it were real, or a dream.

~*~*~*~*~*~*~

Chapter 5: Kuelap

The big day had arrived. Finally, Lila and the children would get to see the land of the Cloud People, Kuelap and the surrounding area, including the sights at Gocta Falls, Karajia, and the nearby Leymebamba Museum. Amzi had visited Kuelap years before, but since then it had been cleaned up, and new amenities added for tourists. They planned to take several days to see it all.

Amzi and Lila took the kids to breakfast at a favorite restaurant before leaving Cuzco. They had sweet humitas, *picarones* (donut-shaped, deep-fried sweet potatoes), scrambled eggs and salsa, with coffee and papaya juice, substantial choices for the long day ahead. Then they boarded a plane for the Chachapoyas region, landing about mid-morning, just in time to catch the four-hour bus ride to Gocta Natura, where they would spend their nights at the Gocta Natura Lodge. They were really hungry by the time they arrived, and found a quick lunch at a small restaurant there.

After a bumpy but scenic RV ride through the cloud forest of Chachapoyas Region, they came to a remote village, Shipata, where the trail to view the sarcophagi began. An Arawak Indian guide accompanied them as they walked along a trail through terraced farmlands. Lila was reminded of her first introduction to high-elevation farming in Peru, where she had learned how their nearness to the Equator made the sunlight's angle and temperatures more conducive to farming, even above 10,000 feet, and with longer growing seasons. True, the soil was thin on the steep mountainsides, but the farmers gathered it into terraces, adding compost, charcoal, and other enrichments, and were renowned for their growing many varieties of vegetables.

"Mom, didn't you bring your camera?" asked Ben.

"No, I can get really good postcard pictures of these things, and I didn't feel like carrying anything extra today," she said.

"I wonder how many of those 4,000 varieties of potatoes they're growing here," said Danny. "I see the fat ears of that choclo corn on the stalks over there. Interesting to see it growing."

As they descended a hill on the winding trail, they saw beautiful panoramic views of the valley below, sometimes through filmy clouds. Most of that part of the hike was downhill, ending at the bottom of a cliff. As they looked up, the guide pointed to a high niche that had been carved out of the rock.

There they were, the famous sarcophagi of Karajia, standing watch, gazing out over the valley. "The height of the cliff has protected them from looters for over 500 years," said the guide. "You can clearly see the designs that were painted on each one, though they're faded with age. They were colored with yellow ochre and red-brown and black pigments on the white background. The tallest ones are about seven or eight feet tall. There were eight of them for a long time," he continued, "but in 1928 an earthquake caused one to fall. It was broken open in the fall, and people were astounded to find a mummy inside."

Amzi and Lila were awestruck at the resemblance of these sarcophagi to the ones at Atahuaqa. They stood silently, thinking, for a time before their musings were interrupted.

"That is really eerie, isn't it?" whispered Daisy, "how they have stood way up there for hundreds of years, like they're standing guard over their people." She moved closer to her mother, and seemed to feel—something—for these ancient artifacts. The boys, too, were transfixed.

"The brochure says we can read more about them at the Leymebamba Museum when we go back," said Lila. "Their construction is quite interesting, I understand."

Amzi squeezed her hand.

They returned along the same path, more slowly, as it was uphill this time, and stopped at a little rest area to eat a packed lunch they had purchased to bring along—barley bread and hummus, with boiled quail eggs and salsa, and papaya juice. Back at the village, their car and driver were waiting for them, to take them back to the Gocta Natura Lodge. They were all tired, and decided to relax a while, and visit Gocta Falls the next day.

"It's an amazing feeling to actually be here, where all this has been built and history played out for hundreds of years," said Lila when she and Amzi were alone. "I know I'm going to feel even more of that 'connection' when we visit Kuelap. I wonder if the archaeologists will ever unravel the history that happened here—before the time of the Incas."

"Yes, that would be really fascinating to know, in light of what we've seen so far, I wonder if they'll uncover any ancient paintings or writings. They've only studied certain areas, so far."

Everyone slept well, exhausted from their long hike that day. But they were up and ready the next morning after a quick breakfast. They had a pleasant trek through the rain forest, after walking through farmland in a high valley where sugarcane and other crops were being grown. Soon, the flora changed to the lush jungle of cloud forest, watered more constantly by the mist. Sometimes they had to scramble up steep inclines, and twice they were passed by tourists on horseback, another option for excursions on lower trails. As they progressed farther, they crossed small streams and gorges on primitive-style rope bridges, all scenic and beautiful. Lila was getting tired, but didn't want to say anything, thinking more about Amzi's prosthetic leg than her own fatigue. But he seemed unfazed, actually relaxing and enjoying the trip.

After a time, they began to hear a far-off roar, increasing in pitch as they neared the falls. With about a third of the way yet to go, they came to a viewpoint where

43

the vegetation parted, and they could see the full extent of the falls, plunging in two colossal leaps down the mountain. The sheer volume of water was stunning. They stood for a while to rest and enjoy the sight. Then they continued along the path, discovering five more viewpoints, each closer, until they arrived at the base, where they had to crane their necks to see up the bottom half of the falls above them. Here the top was hidden from view. The sound was like overwhelming thunder, and they were getting damp from the clouds of mist thrown up where all that water pounded into the pool.

"This is so thrilling," said Lila, straining her voice to be heard above the roar as they stood watching the water. "I knew it would be, but the brochures can't give the full feeling of it."

Reluctantly, they retraced their steps. Several other falls were visible along the way, but none as tall as Gocta. They arrived at the lodge in time for a good lunch and a much-needed rest in their rooms. After dinner, Amzi and the kids turned in early so they could be rested for the long hike to Kuelap the next day.

"I have so many sights and ideas running around in my head," said Lila. "I feel boggled by it all, but we haven't even seen Kuelap or Leymebamba yet." Lila had decided a few days before to start a journal of this trip. She knew it would be something she would always remember, but she was also aware that memory fades, and small but important details drop out with time. She spent the evenings writing.

After a very early breakfast, the family took a bus to Tingo Nuevo, a small village where the trailhead to Kuelap was located. It would be a grueling hike, 5-1/2 miles uphill, but they were used to doing these things together. Once at the village, they found the sign marking the trailhead, and started off. They had purchased lunches and water, and Amzi hired another guide to go with them, since they were advised that it would take at least four hours to get there.

Lila was getting fatigued by the time they were nearly there, but the mountain scenery, hillside farmlands and interesting people were stimulating enough to keep her going.

Here are some of Lila's journal notes with her comments on the trip and about Kuelap itself:

The trek begins by walking or on horseback from El Tingo, a town on the banks of the Tingo River at about 5900 feet elevation. The area is covered with cloud forest, orchids, bromeliads, and quite a variety of tropical trees, with beautiful birds and butterflies. Small farms cling to the hillsides, using terracing, and friendly dogs come out from the farms to trot along with us.

Kuelap is located about 10,000 feet above sea level on a limestone ridge in the Andes of northern Peru, where the rainforest meets the mountains. One brochure said, "The Chachapoyas, like the Inca, wanted to get as close to the sky as possible—for both strategic and religious reasons." Archaeologists believe that the residents had a custom of trying to "hit the clouds" with stones from catapults, to cause rain to fall. Is that true?

Kuelap is one of the largest ancient stone monuments in the New World. Some of its massive stone blocks are bigger than those used in the Egyptian pyramids, and it's about 1,000 years older than Machu Picchu.

Human occupation at the site has been dated by some to the 5th century AD or even several centuries before, but most of the structures were built between then and 1100 AD. (Where did they come from, before that? I wonder, did the Pahuacas split off from here, to found Atahuaqa? – when? and why?) Foundations of over 400 small round buildings have been found here. (Like those we saw at Atahuaqa!)

The city held possibly as many as 3,500 inhabitants, but was abandoned after the Spanish conquest. It was accidentally rediscovered in 1843 by Juan Crisóstomo Nieto, a judge from the city of Chachapoyas. In 1870, a survey, the first of many, was conducted by Antonio Raimondi.

A lot of restorative work has been put into Kuelap, making it safe and easy for tourists—things like boardwalks spanning over delicate and mostly still-unstudied sites, and signs telling visitors about what's known of the "Cloud People."

One thing they mentioned: The Chachapoyas had three ways of interring their dead, one of which was under the floor of their little circular houses! Another was inside the walls—they liked to keep their dead with them. The famous sarcophagi of Karajia are another method, probably to honor the more important leaders, priests and priestesses. They stand upright, some as tall as eight feet, each with a large, oval disc-shaped face attached at the top. The base color is creamy-white, with decorative details painted on, to look like necklaces and feathered tunics, in yellow, black, brown and red. (Just like Umayo did!)

The massive stone walls of Kuelap, up to about 65 feet high and some up to 8 feet thick, overlook the deep Utcubamba Valley, and make it seem like a fortress, at least for defense, if not warfare. The three entrances, two to the east and one to the west, each form very narrow corridors between high walls, growing ever more constricted until only one person at a time can pass through.

(That's really interesting, since most entry gates of cities are massive and grandiose, showing off their power and prestige. These seem to be for defense only. I wonder what gave them this particular mindset?)

They say the Chachapoyas had "a drive to build, born of an ancient threat." (Was that threat from the Wari tribe, or something, someone, more ancient yet?) They were always secluded, rarely venturing from their mountainous land, and cordoned off by three rivers. This is why they held out so long against the Incas, only to lose it all, as trusting victims of the conniving Spanish who allied themselves with them until later betrayals, and who then brought in new diseases, like smallpox, that nearly wiped them out. A few scattered survivors fled to inaccessible mountain reaches, established small settlements and stayed to themselves, a cultural pattern that had continued for hundreds of years. (I wonder if Vilcatambo is one?)

The outward surfaces of many stones in the walls of Kuelap have reliefs of people, animals and geometric designs carved on them. Stone canals supplied the

46

settlement with spring water from the top of the mountain, even to individual homes, with hygienic drainage systems. On the southwest part of the settlement, there is an 18-foot-high structure called El Tintero (Spanish for Inkwell) or Templo Mayor (Spanish for Main Temple) built somewhat in the shape of an inverted cone, which contained ceremonial artifacts – it is speculated to have been used as a solar observatory. (I'm not surprised, considering I've heard of so many ancient civilizations that paid special note to the heavens.)

In the northwest part is a sector with a wall almost 38 feet high, known as Pueblo Alto (Spanish for High Town). It is accessed by two narrow entrances. Just north of there is a tower-like structure named Torreon (Spanish for Tower) nearly 33 feet high, where stone weapons were found, and round stones, that look like the kind you would use in sling warfare, so they think it may have been used for defense.

The inhabitants were not only warriors, but merchants, shamans, and farmers. Much of the city has yet to be excavated, so there are surely more mysteries to solve, like the meaning of the cat's eye and zigzag patterns in the stone work. Some say the zigzag represents a snake, and the cat's eyes represent a jaguar's eyes. These show up everywhere, on walls and houses in Kuelap itself, and in nearby villages all over the area. (Are there still some hidden chambers or niches where there might be paintings or writing?)

The Darrows spent most of the day exploring among the buildings and walls at Kuelap, more interested in details than most of the other tourists. They tried to get a sense of what it was like hundreds of years ago. Seeing the house foundations with some of the doorways, steps and fireplaces that remained, gave them a feeling of what it must have been like to walk the streets and trails, and to come home to one of the houses, even though it had been ages since the place was occupied—or even had walls. They had no problem with crowds—there were not many people there anyway. Most of them were Peruvian people, looking into their own history. Kuelap just isn't as well-known as Machu Picchu, and is harder to get to.

The trek down the mountain was a little faster and easier, though it began to rain before they arrived at Tingo, and it was hard not to slip in the mud. Some of the time they held onto each other to stay upright, and laughing about it in the wetness would become a fond memory. They took a bus back to the Gocta Natura Lodge and collapsed in their rooms after taking good hot showers. They devoured their hot corn soup (lawa), tamales, choclo and juanes with good appetites, finishing with delicious hot chocolate drinks.

Tomorrow they would see the Leymebamba Museum.

~*~*~*~*~*~*~

Chapter 6: Kidnapped

After another good night's sleep, and scrambled eggs and humitas at a nearby restaurant, the family was ready to see the Leymebamba Museum. The building was surrounded by exotic gardens of native plants, with a replica of a round Chachapoyan house next to it. Amzi and Lila were particularly interested in its construction, comparing it to the foundations they had seen at Atahuaqa and Kuelap. This one was complete with a conical thatched roof, based on what the archaeologists believed they had been like, though there was some conjecture over the proper slope.

"It's a little eerie, isn't it?" said Daisy, "You can almost feel as if you're going back in time."

Amzi and Lila looked at her. *Is she getting that feeling for the Chachapoyas?*

AJ was very quiet, seeming lost in thought. "Yes," he said slowly, "They seem so real. Well, of course they were real, but I mean, more than just historical."

They entered the main building. At the doorway was a replica of a Karajia sarcophagus, looking like new, and beautifully painted. Several more sarcophagi were lined up on a mound outside the museum, displaying a variety of symbolic paintings of necklaces and dress. Lila and Amzi looked at each other. *These must be the ones that Umayo made. They are beautifully done, very artistic.*

Inside, the museum was divided into four rooms. The first two displayed weapons, ceramics, textiles, quipus,

49

carved wooden figures, and other decorative artifacts of the Chachapoya region, and some from the Incas, as well. The next rooms held over 200 mummies—adults, babies, all ages, set on shelves behind protective glass, some wrapped, some in bags with a face embroidered on them, some starkly exposed. They lined the walls. Some were deteriorated or damaged, and others mere skeletons, but another kind looked as if they had been preserved by more recent methods, probably influenced by the Incas.

Most of them were sitting in a somewhat fetal position, knees drawn up, arms crossed in front and the hands covering the faces. The lower jaws tended to drop down, causing them to look as if they were frozen in a silent scream. Lila was suddenly reminded of a famous painting, *The Scream*, by Edvard Munch, that seemed similar. It gave them both a frightened and a frightening look, though the guide explained that it was just a way of keeping the body in a compact position so it would be easier to wrap and move.

"Eeeyech!" said Daisy. "I don't like this. Some of them look like they're looking at us. I feel as if I'm encroaching on their privacy." She turned away, folded her arms, and shivered.

"Daisy, I feel the same way," said Lila. "I think I'd rather see another part of the museum now." They moved away, through another doorway.

Amzi, standing nearby, watched as the boys stood, silently studying a certain mummy. They were unusually quiet. He moved closer. "What are you thinking?"

"I feel as if... these are... you know, real people, maybe that we could have known," said Danny, "and I don't know if I like seeing them on display like this."

AJ and Ben nodded agreement.

"I know," said Amzi. "It feels that way to me, too, but in another way, they are being protected. These were found up above Laguna de los Cóndores, Lake of the Condors, being looted and vandalized by local farmers and huaqueros. They hacked open the bundles with machetes and rummaged through them, digging around for souvenirs or treasure. The farmers even let their cattle trample over them. But here,

50

they are being preserved. I don't really like the way they are displayed under bright lights like this, but their history is being shown to the world, and in that way, they live on. That's something they desired, but I doubt they would have pictured it like this." *I would hate to see Tica displayed this way.*

They joined Lila and Daisy in a small gift shop where the two were perusing the historical brochures and books.

"Here," Lila moved toward a display. "Here is the description of the sarcophagus construction." She and Amzi and AJ picked up copies of the brochure. It had photos of the different stages, and some showed Umayo working on them.

"Look, his hair is dark—reddish, not white. Did he tell you how long ago this was?"

"No, but the museum was opened in the year 2000, so I assume it was around that time." He fingered the pages of the brochure. "Here it tells more about the construction of the sarcophagi. They were not all alike. Some were not as tall or as detailed, or even painted at all."

AJ had been listening, looking a little perplexed. "Why are you talking about Umayo's hair? What has that got to do with all this?"

"It was just interesting to us, to see him with white hair. I hadn't realized he might be getting elderly—not everyone has my premature graying, but he still tramps the mountains with vigor, so age hasn't slowed him down." *Maybe some day we can tell you the rest, son, when we figure it out ourselves.* Indeed, Amzi's hair, silver when Lila met him, had now turned snow white.

Outside, they strolled through the surrounding tropical gardens, and admired the red hummingbirds, a kind native to the region. They petted the friendly llamas and alpacas that wandered the pathways with them. AJ and Ben encouraged their affectionate nuzzles.

"Do you think they've been trained not to spit?" Danny asked. "Or maybe they're just used to a lot of people coming around."

51

"We've got to get a couple of these, don't you think, Dad?" Ben ruffled the deep fluffy coat of a dark brown alpaca.

Amzi smiled. "I think that could be arranged."

They flew back to Cuzco and enjoyed dinner together at a newer restaurant they hadn't noticed before, *The Fallen Angel*. It was somewhat hidden in the corner of a plaza, but advertised as "funky and outlandish," and the kids wanted to see it. They were rewarded with an unforgettable experience. The decor was wild and artsy, flying pigs and cherubs everywhere, and most of the walls were bright red. Some of the tables were made of thick sheets of glass covering bathtubs in which tropical fish swam. One of the main foods featured was excellent spicy steak with garlic salsa. The family conversation was animated, with so many adventures and ideas to process.

Lila spent several hours writing in her journal that night.

The next day, they paid a visit to the town square, watching festive dancers in colorful costumes put on a show for the tourists. With so many nortéamericanos on summer vacation, there were people everywhere, all kinds of noises, and lively music.

Amzi, uneasy again, was scanning the crowd as Lila and the boys watched the dancers. Daisy saw some intriguing jewelry at a nearby vendor booth, and wandered aside to look. A friendly-looking woman beckoned for her to come and look at some special pieces.

Amzi was looking at something across the street, a flash of light that had attracted his attention. Someone over there was directing sunlight from a mirror toward Amzi and Danny, and then at the other boys and Lila. The flashes were irritating, causing them to shade their eyes and automatically look toward the source.

Daisy leaned forward to look more closely at the jewelry. *I should get back, but these necklaces are so beautiful... Oh, blue opal, like Aunt Elfie's... Just a quick look....*

Hands suddenly pounced from behind a curtain and seized Daisy, yanking her into the darkened market booth. Another hand clapped quickly over her mouth—she was pulled roughly through the darkness into an alley, then shoved into a waiting van parked in back. She struggled and tried to bite them, but expert hands held her with a well-practiced grip.

"Daisy! Dad! Where did Daisy go?" shouted Danny. "She was right here. Now I can't see her! --- Dad!"

Amzi pushed through the crowd, tearing frantically into nearby shops and booths, causing no end of consternation as vendors tried to hold their constructions and wares together.

A young boy with frightened eyes came up, pointing. "Men took her—there!" he said. Then he ducked away and melted into the crowd.

Amzi crashed through the jewelry booth and into the darkened alley behind it, just in time to see the van disappear down the back street. No license plate. Sendero Luminoso. Shining Path.

A bag was yanked hurriedly over Daisy's head. It smelled musty, like rotten vegetables. She gagged, and tried to hold her breath. She wasn't tied, but she was wedged on the seat between two people who were holding her arms. Soon the road became bumpy, and the van swerved from side to side, uphill and downhill. She wanted to ask, *where, why, what?* but she knew that was ridiculous. What would they tell her, anyway?

Then she sensed that the van had stopped, and the side door opened. The people on each side of her pushed and pulled her out onto the ground. They supported her while she found her footing, then led her up some steps. She could tell, from the sounds and air currents, that they were taking her into a house, and then the bag was removed. She looked around, but it was dark inside, several people loitering in the shadows. Mostly she just saw the whites of their eyes, looking her up and down. Then they brought her through another doorway, and stood her before a swarthy man, with curly black hair and broken teeth--*El Jefe*, the Commandant. He fingered a fat cigar in one hand.

"We will not harm you...if your father comes to us himself." He smiled, like a crocodile.

Nothing doing. That could be his death sentence. Hold out, hold on.... Dad will know what to do. Hurry, Dad.... She refused to say anything. Her stomach rolled and shuddered.

El Jefe was not surprised. He muttered to one of his men in Spanish, "She will come around, with time, and maybe we'll put her on the phone to Señor Darrow. She will be convincing, by then."

They put her in a stifling hot, tiny room, where a small, grimy window with bars on it let in little light, and an old bucket was set in a corner. She felt as if her insides had turned to quivering jelly.

No way out! Oh, if only this were just a nightmare, just imagination! But I can't wake up from it. This is real. What is going to happen to me? Will they kill Dad, just because I made a stupid mistake?

As her eyes became used to the dim light, she noticed a dirty pallet on the floor under the window. *That must be to sleep on. Ugh, it looks filthy. Will I be here so long I'll have to sleep on that? Will I get a disease from it, or will I even live that long?* She felt nausea, but steeled herself against it. *Oh, Dad, I'm so sorry!*

Amzi called the police, some of whom remembered him from 20 years ago. They immediately began a search, and a detective came to help Amzi, but they knew this was going to be complicated.

"They had someone distract us with flashing light," said Amzi. Inwardly, he kicked himself for falling for such a trick. "We all fell for it—we were all looking the other way when Daisy disappeared." He gritted his teeth, cursing under his breath. *We walked right into it....*

Lila and the boys returned quickly to their hotel room to wait—and worry.

*Ohhh, nooooo...*thought Lila. *I was afraid this would happen. I didn't want to think it, but I know Amzi was*

54

concerned, too, and he was trying so hard to watch us all. Daisy was just too good a target. Hold on, Daisy. She doubled over, sobbing, hugging herself, aching with painful regret and fear.

The boys paced back and forth, feeling as if they should help—should have helped. But how? *Keep Mom safe*, they agreed. *That's one thing we can do.*

At home in Maryland, it was a normal, quiet day at Spurwink, and the three dogs, Qhawa, Bartleby and Lionel, were sleeping in the yard. Qhawa had been sleeping most of the time, day and night, in his advanced age, sometimes willing to play, but generally slowing down.

Suddenly his head jerked up—*danger! His family was in danger!* He jumped up, howled and ran yelping, back and forth, setting off a cacophony as the other dogs, startled, began to bark.

Aunt Melanie and Elfie ran out to see what was going on. Qhawa howled again, raced down the driveway and disappeared. The other two dogs looked back at Melanie, wagging their tails uncertainly and whimpering. The two women looked at each other. *This is not good. Something has happened, but what?*

Lila and the boys alternately sat or paced, waiting. Lila was reminded of waiting in fear, when Amzi had fallen into that hole back in the Ravenwood warehouse, no one able to find him. So frustrating, not knowing... *Daisy, where are you?* All concerns and thoughts about Atahuaqa were forgotten in light of this frightening development.

After a few hours, Amzi came back to the hotel, and the family clustered around him, their eyes pleading the obvious: *Is there any news of Daisy?*

"I just wanted to fill you in on the progress—or lack of it," Amzi's face was colorless, grim. "We have nothing yet, but that's not surprising. We should hear from the Shining Path soon, and they probably will want to... trade Daisy... for... me." He dreaded the effect those words would have.

Lila gasped. *How horrible is this going to get?* Her love for her children and Amzi was tearing her apart. *Why did I ever insist on coming down here? But Amzi would have come alone, and at least he has us here to help him—or are we a hindrance?* At that thought, she buried her face in his shoulder and cried.

He held her until she relaxed a little. "I'm going back out," he said. "We have every available police officer and detective working on it, and watching over you here. Try not to worry," he said—instantly realizing that was ridiculous. "Well, just stay together, out of sight. I'll be back when I can."

~*~*~*~*~*~*~

Chapter 7: Daisy and the Shining Path

Daisy stood in the hot, grimy room, trying to calm down and figure out what had happened to her. First of all, *where am I? And who are these people?—Are they those Shining Path terrorists that Mom and Dad always talked about? I never thought about them much—never thought we'd really be in any danger from them, as long as we were careful. Dad didn't want to scare us! I saw him watching the crowds all the time, but I thought—what did I think? Why didn't I think? Why did I wander off, away from the family? I didn't take it seriously. I'm so dumb!*

She continued to berate herself, while trying to think what to do. She put her ear against the door, and could hear muffled voices, but couldn't make out words. *Oh, they're probably speaking Spanish! I took Spanish—maybe I can tell what they say, if they don't speak too fast, when they are near—Oh! I don't want to be near them! What are they going to do with me? To me?*

The one small window in the room was set into the thick adobe walls. On the inside opening of the window, three hefty iron bars were embedded in the frame. She wiped off the bars, in case they were dirty, pressed her face against them, and looked out the grimy window. She could see part of the house she was in, plastered adobe walls, tile roof. They were on a hill above a dirt road, grass and weeds growing tall in the bumpy yard, a few bromeliads and palms here and there, but no real thought to landscaping. She could make out a path going by the front of the house, and more tile roofs down the slope below. She noticed familiar adobe walls topped with tiles to keep the rain off, between houses and the street. Some old car tires were set into the ground, forming a kind of makeshift fence to separate two properties. *They have strange ideas of yards here.* She tried to see farther down the hill. *They must have brought me up that way.* She tested the bars on the window, but they held firm. *Of course. No way out that easy. Dad, please hurry! But be careful—don't let them get you.* She was determined not to cry, but her limbs felt numb, and she desperately wanted all this to not be real—*I just want to wake up from this bad dream. Why can't it be just a bad dream?*

Amzi paced back and forth, unable to sit still, his mind thrashing about for an answer. *My little Daisy—my daughter! How could I let them get my one and only daughter? I'm an idiot. Why didn't I hang onto her, keep her between us?*

The police and detectives had sent out special searchers with dogs. Amzi had found Daisy's tote bag lying in the alley where the van had taken her away. It was a good object for the animals to sniff before being taken out for the search. But this was like looking for a particular stone in the walls of Kuelap—the van had probably taken her miles away before they had taken her out—and in which direction?

Amzi remembered that Yachay, his head gardener and handyman at the old hacienda, had a friend, Tamya, who listened to the street talk, and had warned them about the Sendero Luminoso's plans back in 1993. Would he still be around?

Amzi could hear the stress in Yachay's voice over the phone. "Yes, I heard. I still have my network here—the news spread quickly. I'm so sorry. I haven't heard anything yet about where they took her. My people are on high alert, though, you can be sure."

"I wish I hadn't had to call you about something like this, Yachay. I was hoping to visit—well, we *will*—after Daisy is back safe with us."

"We will find her, Señor Darrow. With all of us working together, they can't keep her hidden for long."

"You have my number. Let me know of any clues—anything!"

It encouraged Amzi, that he had more help than the terrorists knew about, but he still agonized for every second that his beloved daughter had to be with them. It was no consolation knowing that Lila and Daisy's brothers were sharing his same torment.

Lila and the boys sequestered themselves in their hotel, sending out for dinner, and surreptitiously watching even those who delivered the food or anything else, for any hint of suspicious actions, and checking for listening devices on anything brought in. The worst thing, of course, was the waiting, the not knowing anything, and trying not to imagine what was happening to Daisy. Lila felt ill, and couldn't eat anything. They didn't even try to go to bed that night, knowing they wouldn't sleep. Amzi called Lila every few hours, but there was no news before morning.

Daisy paced the floor of the little room, trying to think of something she could do, wondering what her captors were planning. *Will they just keep me? Try to get me to persuade Dad to come? Would they torture me, or ....?* She shut down her mind. *No! I can't borrow trouble. Listen and wait. I wish they hadn't taken my phone, but I know that's the first thing they looked for. Oh, Dad, where are you? Can you find me? Will they kill you just because I made a stupid mistake?*

Daylight was fading. With no lights in the room, she would be totally in the dark. *I'm not afraid of the dark, but I'm afraid of what's IN the dark.* A tear slid down her cheek, and another. She wiped them away angrily. *No! I won't let them make me cry.*

Yachay's friend, Tamya, was still making himself useful as an informant. Long ago, he had perfected an inconspicuous way of moving, in disguise, from place to place, always with some other purpose evident, moving near people who were talking, just passing by. He had a very good ear for whispers and low talk.

He had acquaintances who saved special news bits for him as he made his rounds. One was an older lady, Carmella, who lived near one of the houses where prisoners were occasionally held by the Shining Path. She exaggerated her age and feigned simple-mindedness, bringing vegetables around from her garden and fruit from the trees behind her home, to sell to the occupants of the house.

One of the younger terrorists, Micos, was fascinated with Daisy, and his intent was all too clear to her. She tried to stay away from him when he brought her food, but in the small room, it was impossible. He edged up to her and pressed her against the wall, groping her, grinning. She could smell Chica beer on his breath. He held her hands down, kissing her with his slobbery mouth. They were both sweating from the heat of the day. She wondered desperately if the older men would control this young scoundrel. *Should I hit him with my knee, the way they say – or will he kill me if I hurt him?*

"NO! Stay away from me! Go AWAY!" she cried, as loudly as she could. *Did they hear me?*

An older man came in and slapped Micos behind the ear, then roughly sent him out. He turned to Daisy with a yellow-toothed grin. "Ah, señorita." He looked her up and down. "Pretty girl, you would do well to cooperate and get yourself out of here. The boy would like to keep you." He grinned and pulled at his gray mustache. "Eat, now." He said, and left, locking the door behind him.

At least one of them speaks good English. I shouldn't let them know I might understand what they say. She looked at the food in the fading light. *Is it safe to eat?* It seemed to be beans and tortillas or something, and smelled okay. She tried a little, but found she had no appetite. *I don't want to eat in the dark. Who knows what's in this stuff? Bugs? Maggots?*

She sat down on the pallet. *Bugs. I wonder if they have cockroaches or spiders in here.* Quickly, she got up again, squinting down at the pallet. *I guess they won't let me have a candle or lantern. Oh, I hate the dark.*

She went to the window again, and rubbed a clear spot in the grime, trying to see if there were lights or people, or anything outside that could be useful to know. Not much. She could hear music and some talk, like a distant radio playing. A 3-wheeled vehicle buzzed by on the road. A dog barked, and farther away, another dog answered.

After a while, the older man returned with a flashlight to take her plate away. "What's the matter, you don't like our food?" He looked at her, and she thought she saw a hint of compassion in his expression.

"Please, do you have a bathroom?"

He shrugged, and pointed at the bucket. "Sorry, but that's all we can give you right now."

"Oh. I was afraid of that," said Daisy. "Can you give me any kind of a light...please?"

"You can have this flashlight, but don't keep it on all the time. The battery will run down."

"Oh, thank you so much! I'll only use it when I have to. I'll be careful."

He looked as if he regretted mellowing, but turned and left, locking the door again.

Daisy used the light to examine all around the pallet, poking and prodding it with her foot, to see if any roaches or spiders jumped out. None did, so she went over all the corners and cracks in the room, making sure nothing crawly was around, killing one spider, in case it was poisonous. The pallet was dirty, but she decided she would have to lie down on it. *You can't stand up all night*, she told herself. *Just get over it, and do what you have to do.* She used the bucket, and then lying down gingerly, she tried to make herself comfortable. *I'll never complain about anything again*, she thought.

~*~*~*~*~*~*~

61

Chapter 8: Old Carmella

Daisy awoke early, after a miserable night on the thin pallet. She stood and stretched her aching muscles and looked around as the dawn light increased. She checked for any crawling bugs, and shivered. The night had been long, cold and damp, and even when she did doze off, some strange sound would wake her, and she'd wonder what it might be, especially if it might be someone like Micos, sneaking in. She was glad to get up off the dirty bed, but trembled again when she thought of the men on the other side of the door. She pushed down a wave of nausea.

The house was still quiet, so she used the bucket and readied herself the best she could, physically and mentally, for whatever was going to happen this day. Soon, she heard someone stirring, and low murmurs of conversation.

"Old" Carmella trudged slowly down the path with her basket of vegetables and fruit. She knew the occupants of the small house were probably ready to buy something to eat, as it had been a few days since her last visit. She walked with bent posture, so as to look even more elderly and slow. As she passed the house, she glanced at the small barred window in back. She had seen people in there before, looking out with fear or sadness in their eyes. She hoped to see the young señorita, so she could relay information to her associate, Tamya. He had told her to watch for a young red-haired girl.

Today as she came down the path, she didn't see anyone at the window, but she thought she detected some movement inside. She didn't dare stop to wait for the occupant to notice her—it might arouse the men's suspicions—so she continued on up to the small verandah in front.

Micos was lounging on a bench outside, keeping watch. He got up and moved to block her way. "Let me pick something out," he said in Spanish, selecting a ripe mango. He grinned at her, his youthful beard competing with the grime on his face.

"What if El Jefe wants that mango?" Carmella eyed him sharply. "You will be in trouble." It was a familiar banter each time.

"Not if I eat it before he sees it." He chuckled, cut into it with his knife, and finished it off before he allowed her to go farther. He threw the peel into the yard. "Now you can tell them I took a little piece." He smirked as he opened the door, announced Carmella, and she was allowed in.

She disposed of her food without mentioning Micos. Her main mission was information. She took note of how many were there—four men in the front room, besides Micos—and accepted the small payment they offered. There wasn't any visible sign of a captive. She dawdled, counting her money, making mistakes and starting over, as long as she could. It was her usual routine.

Leaving the house, she passed slowly by the window again, watching for any sign of a prisoner. This time, Daisy noticed the movement outside and came to the window. Carmella noted her red hair, so she raised one eyebrow and put her finger briefly to her lips as she turned away and shuffled along the path back to her home.

Tamya was encouraged by Carmella's news. He quickly notified Yachay, who relayed the location to Amzi and the police, with the information on the number of men in the house. At least now they knew Daisy was alive.

When Lila called Amzi, he told her they were making some progress, but it wouldn't be a quick and easy rescue. Even though they now knew where Daisy had been seen, they couldn't just go charging in—they needed to plan and coordinate operations.

"I know. Just... just be careful." She couldn't think what else to say. Her heart felt caught in her throat. *What will they do now?* She paced back and forth, wringing her hands.

It wasn't long before the older man came in with some beans and bread for Daisy's breakfast, and a metal cup of water. "Eat. Soon we are taking you to another place." He picked up the flashlight and left.

She inspected the food, in good light this time, and it looked all right. *I'd better eat it, and keep up my strength*, she thought, tasting a small bit. *Hmm, not too bad. Okay. I wonder if that man would help me. I suppose not. He probably took a chance, just giving me the light.*

She had almost finished eating when the men came for her. They took her out to the van, but she noticed that El Jefe was not with them. *Of course. He would be more important. That must have been his own car, going on up the road ahead of us.* Micos was along, though, and sat pressed up next to her in the van. They didn't put a bag over her head, for which she was thankful. *Maybe I'll see some landmarks or tell which direction we're going. I might need them if I escape.*

One thing she noticed was a little house they passed, with a familiar old woman sitting on the front step. She gave Daisy a fleeting, significant look as they passed, no more than a raised eyebrow, so that Daisy was the only one that noticed it.

That lady is going to help me.... somehow.

The van bumped and swayed around curves and over holes and rocks in the road. They dodged people walking, riding bikes, or driving 3-wheeled tuk-tuk vehicles, people busy going to work or the market. On and on they went, off into the hills away from Cuzco.

Carmella immediately contacted Tamya, to tell him Daisy was being moved. But she couldn't tell where they were going. It was too late for the police and Amzi to catch them at the little house.

Sometimes Micos would surreptitiously sneak his hand over to Daisy's leg or arm, but she flinched and slapped at him loudly. The older men laughed, but scolded Micos and made him stop—Daisy could understand their tone, but couldn't interpret their Peruvian accent very well. *So much for high school Spanish.*

Oh, no, thought Daisy. *How far away are they taking me? How will Dad ever find me? Have they contacted him yet?* The smell of sweat and Chica beer was thick in the closed-in car.

Finally the road improved. They were in one of the canyons between some high mountains, approaching a beautiful hacienda of gleaming white stucco, with arched windows and doors, and a deep red tile roof. Flowers bloomed everywhere; parrots and toucans flitted among palms and tree ferns.

Armed guards patrolled the grounds.

Daisy was taken out of the van, and Micos took the opportunity to put his hands on her as much as he dared, as they brought her into the house. Reluctantly, he left with the crew as soon as she was delivered indoors. It was cool and clean, and she noticed a servant removing a silver tray with an empty glass. In a spacious room, El Jefe sat enthroned in an ornate chair with a fat cigar between his fingers. A ceiling fan rotated silently above, and a beautiful red parrot preened on a perch nearby. El jefe was like a king in his own dominion, each gang of the Shining Path having a particular turf where their will was law, and illicit riches flowed like water.

"Well, little señorita, did you have a good night?" He flicked ashes into an elaborate crystal ash tray.

Daisy didn't say anything, but pursed her lips and stood straight. It was deceptive—inside, she felt like quivering jelly. She looked him in the eye, wondering what was coming next.

"We haven't talked to your father yet. But soon we will see about our little bargain, Eh?" El Jefe grinned, an evil twinkle in his eye. "He will be glad to see his little girl is unharmed. For now, we will put you in a room." He nodded to one of the men, who guided Daisy down a hallway. The man opened a door, ushered her in, and then left, closing and locking the door behind him.

Daisy looked around, and shivered. At least this is much better than the first place. *Oh, look! There's a real bed!* She checked the windows, all barred. A door at the side opened into a nice bathroom. *Oh! A bathroom! I never thought I'd be so glad to see one!* Right away, she washed her hands and splashed cool water on her face. Almost happily, she saw that a hairbrush, mirror, toothbrush and all the necessities were provided, just nothing that could be an effective weapon. She brushed her messed-up hair quickly. *Now I feel a little better. I hope I never see Micos again. What a creep. But the others are probably just as bad. I have to believe this won't last forever and that Dad will be okay in the end, too.* She trembled again.

She continued to explore her new prison. Looking out a window furnished with ornate cast iron bars, she could see a fountain and extensive tropical gardens, lush and well-tended—with guards patrolling to and fro. *I guess there's no use dreaming about getting out. But how will Dad and the police get in?* She lay down on the bed to think.

She was tired from her difficult night, and drifted off to sleep for a little while. A noise awakened her. It was the lock. The door opened, and a woman came in, with lunch.

Lila was overjoyed to hear that Daisy had been observed, relatively safe, even though they didn't have her back yet. She wondered, though, how they would rescue her without Amzi being endangered. *It's so hard to just sit and wait. Amzi will have to be careful, and they could still hurt Daisy. Oh, I hope this is over soon, and both of them safe. I cannot let myself think of any other outcome.*

The phone rang. It was Umayo. "Señora Darrow, I want you to know, we have heard what happened, and we will help in any way we can. We just wanted you to know, you have friends in more places than may meet the eye."

I wonder what he meant by that? Lila thought. *Well, it's comforting, anyway....*

Outside El Jefe's hacienda, one of the guards set a bowl of water on the ground.

"What is that for?" Another guard asked. "Are you getting soft-hearted again?"

"There's no harm. It's just an old dog, and he's thirsty. See how he pants?"

The old Peruvian hairless dog looked gaunt and tired. He lapped up the water and smiled a big doggy smile at the guards.

Chapter 9: The New World

146 BC – Northeast coast of Brasil: The flotilla of ships, Kena'anim and Celtiberians together, traveled north along the coast of the new wild country, looking for a way inland. They had successfully traversed the great Sea of Atlantis. Their initial thought was to get out of sight in case a Roman war fleet might come looking for them. When the Kena'anim had first escaped their home islands, there was a very real possibility of being chased and overtaken by their old enemies, who had destroyed Karth-Hadash. A month or two after they left, the Romans *did* actually send out search parties in ships to look for them, going south down the western shores of Mauharim, ('Libya' to them) but finding no sign of the escapees, they gave up and returned to Rome. It would be some time before their quarry, in revisiting non-Roman ports much later, heard of their enemies' unsuccessful pursuit.

The migrants' attention was now drawn to what they could see as they skirted the strange new shore. This land looked like the kind of place they had heard whispered about all their lives. The tropical breeze brought tantalizing whiffs of new discoveries waiting. They could see lush, steamy forests and rivers as they made their way north along the coast. Was it an island? It seemed endless. They occasionally stopped to send out small parties from each ship, going ashore for water and to see what food might be available. These men found the country teeming with animals, birds, and fruit trees. The people on the ships, famished for fresh food, waited impatiently, and the boats returned heavy laden with a wild bounty.

Anat was thrilled to learn they had finally found a land where fruit was abundant. She tried bites of everything, eating as much as she could, until her mother warned her not to make herself sick. The samples that the scouting parties first brought back were considered safe for food because the men had seen monkeys or birds eating them, and because some of the old sailors remembered them, from their own or their fathers' secret travels to this land, long ago.

Anat watched some of the old sailors as they scanned the shores, gazing with a vague recognition of the lay of the land, noting the way the taller trees towered over the main jungle canopy. It seemed as if they were seeing a Promised Land that had been hidden for a lifetime, remembered as in a dream.

They found masses of delicious fruits hanging from the trees—every shape and color and taste they could imagine seemed to grow in this wondrous land. The older sailors had remembered names of some of them, learned from natives encountered on earlier trips. One weird kind they noticed immediately was jabuticaba—they looked like plum-sized, juicy, dark purple grapes that grew all over the trunks and large branches of the huge jabuticaba trees—no stems—the flowers and fruit were attached right at the bark surface. Peculiar, but delicious. Exploring further, they found that some of the other fruits (cacao, mango, jocote, papaya) grew in much the same way, and came in more strange forms and flavors than they ever could have believed.

Anat decided, somewhat grudgingly, not to think about pomegranates any more.

They were looking for a way inland that would lead them away from the coast. They soon found the mouth of a large river, and sailed about 15 leagues upstream, only to find it became too shallow for their ships to continue. This was not far enough for their purpose. They stopped for a while to send out an exploration party, looking for a good place to set up a camp. Women and children stayed on the ships, unsure of dangers.

While they waited, some of the men examined the nearby area, finding many large boulders, and bedrock right in the shallow stream. On one long, smooth rock, they found a series of dots, lines, and simple pictures carved into the stone. Who had been here? How long ago? Was it a message? A couple of the older Celts, Bran and Murtagh, studied the dots, markings and spirals, feeling a strange recognition.

"I don't know what it is, but these things give me a funny feeling." Bran ran his finger along a spiral, carved deeply into the rock. "Do you remember something like this?"

"Those coiled-up things look like something I used to see when we went up north to Britain," said Murtagh. "And this—this row of dots and lines, doesn't it seem familiar?" Then he fingered the depressions of a tree-like shape on the stone. "I never learned to read anything. It's hard to imagine the meanings."

When the exploration party returned, they brought with them several natives who were eager to trade for beads and cooking utensils. They all sat around the fire and made halting gestures, trying out words, gaining a little understanding. Something of a guarded friendship arose. Some of these coastal natives had traded with others from ships long ago, and remembered a few words that the sailors understood. They indicated by motions and words that the river was called "Paraíba," which meant "bad for boats."

At one point, Bran stood up, and pointing to the big rock, which the natives called "Inga," gestured in sign language of his own invention, hoping to learn who had made the carvings.

One of the older natives, Todo, stood also, and rubbing his chin, pointed at Murtagh, who was a big man with blonde hair and a red beard. "Ing-gah," he said, and pointed at the rock.

"I think he's saying the stone-carvers looked like you." Bran grinned at Murtagh. "I wonder when that happened? It looks old. Did some of our people come through here in the past?"

Murtagh rubbed his beard. "Remember the handed-down stories old Dougal used to tell, about finding a far-off land and leaving signs on rocks, so if any of our people came after, they would know?"

"Someone had to stay here for quite a time to do all this." Bran sighted down the length of the stone. "Did they have a camp, or settle a village? The natives seem to remember *something*, but so long ago...."

"Even *they* have forgotten now. I guess we'll never know."

Then Todo looked at the ships anchored nearby, and pointed to one with a Celtic dragon head at the bow. He began waving his hands excitedly, then gesturing in a way that seemed to show boats turning and going back to the sea.

Bran nodded understanding. "I can see that. This river is not big enough. Too shallow, and too many rocks. We'll have to keep looking—maybe like our earlier wandering kin, whoever they were." He stood gazing out past the ships, trying to imagine his own ancestors coming here, camping, carving their messages, then going on. *Where did they go from here?*

They began the return trip to the ocean the next day, then continued north and northwest, skirting the coast....

The Great River

After many more weeks' travel, and trying out several other streams, they came to the mouth of a mighty river. It was so wide that at first they didn't realize it was a river, thinking it might be only a bay or gulf along the coast. But they soon realized it was brown, fresh water. It poured with a powerful current for miles out into the sea, and as they entered the mouth of it, sailing upstream to the west, there were islands, but they could not see the other shore. They surmised that the water would be deep enough for their ships to travel for many leagues, and they felt more and more hopeful, concealed from the open waters of the ocean.

Unsure of the lay of the land and this new waterway, they stayed within sight of the south shore, the only one they could see. Now they were thinking of finding a place to land. Would it be safe? On and on they sailed, with some of the adventurous Celts fanning out to see if they could locate the northern banks.

The burning sun beat down, and the migrants began to put up shades to keep cool. The flat vastness of brown water reflected the blue sky and white, puffy clouds. Brightly colored butterflies fluttered along the steamy banks, and multi-hued birds appeared in the branches of the trees. Some were blue, some red, or green and yellow; one kind was mostly black, but had a huge, colorful beak. Another kind, a fish-eater along the river, was black, with a long and snake-like body and long, thin beak. One of the sailors said it was called "anhinga."

Anat, watching the passing scenery from the ship, detected a brown face peering out through the leaves. "Mother! Look there, a man—oh, several men—in the edge of the forest."

Tanith looked, then glanced over at her husband and other sailors. "Yes, I see them. Our men are watching them, too." The ships skimmed on up the river, with another sighting now and then of the inhabitants of this new land, whenever they neared the shore. The migrants' ancestors had, in those secret times past, already done some trading with tribes along the coast. But would these inland natives be open to trading and friendship? Or would they attack encampments? It would be natural for them to fear such a large mass of intruders. Older sailors, some of whom had actually been on former trips to this place, advised caution, but to be ready to offer friendship. Their advice was to always keep a supply of beads, cooking pots, tools and cloth, to trade for whatever the natives had to offer—a good way to earn trust on such encounters.

What would they call this new land? The Celts had a legend from their ancient culture about an island called *Hy-*

Brasil, a fantastical place known only in old seafarers' stories. Since this new land seemed to fit the description of a mysterious 'island' remembered by both the Celts and the Kena'anim, it came to be called Brasil.

Continuing inland, they began to stop more often to look for food and water, and to set up camp in the evenings for cooking meals. Still unsure of dangers, they slept on board their ships. Hunting parties were able to bring back "bush meat,"—monkeys, birds, and peccaries, to roast over campfires or in the braziers. A great variety of fish was available, too.

Many more miles upriver, they found a spot of flat, open land, where they camped for a longer time, appraising it for a permanent settlement. They sent exploration parties farther inland, and caught glimpses of natives staring at them from the jungle. Were they friendly? Dangerous? Who would make the first move?

On one such excursion, two of the men were making their way through the jungle, when one, Hanno, said quietly to his friend, Cambus, "Don't move suddenly. See those people, there? Hand me a string of beads, and a cooking pot." He held up the beads, then the pot, gesturing with exaggerated smiling facial expressions and motions of his hands. The natives held back at first, but then a bold one stepped out from the jungle.

There is always a bold one, thought Hanno.

The young man, his face painted with several red stripes, was of shorter stature, mostly naked, except for a loincloth, a bone necklace, and something in his hair. Wary, he advanced slowly, stopping every few steps. Would he want to trade? What would he offer?

Slowly, the aboriginal pulled a bone knife from his waistband, and held it up, the blade pointing at the ground. He pointed with his other hand at the cooking pot.

Ah! He knows the better value! thought Hanno. Cambus grinned.

Trade made, Hanno patted his chest, and said, "Hanno," pointed at his friend and said "Kam-bus," then gestured toward the young man, "You?"

The native looked at him suspiciously for a minute, then said, "Tawa." He patted his chest, repeated "Tawa," and grinned. Then he turned and ran back to his friends, waving the pot. They gathered around excitedly to see the prize, then melted into the jungle.

"I think it was a success," said Hanno. Cambus raised his eyebrows, smiled, and nodded agreement.

One immediate danger was obvious—crocodiles! At least they looked very similar to the crocodiles some of the sailors remembered seeing, back in the old country which the Romans called "Libya."

One elderly sailor liked to tell a tale of his death-defying escape from a croc along the Nile in Egypt: "We had waded along the shore of the river," he said, "looking for some fruit growing on the banks. I thought I saw a log floating nearby, but I didn't look close enough. The 'log' suddenly came alive and lunged at me with big snapping jaws full of teeth. I was barely able to jump out of the way, and nearly drowned, trying to get away. Some natives who were with us speared it." He waved his hands and gestured wildly as he talked, enjoying the wide-eyed attention of his audience. "These beasts here must be the same thing, and we'd better keep a good distance from them."

They quickly learned to avoid wading or swimming alone, and were very careful while beaching, loading and unloading boats. Even leaning out from the side of a boat was taking a big chance, as Tauratis, a young Celt, found out. He was in a smaller boat, looking over the side at some interesting fish near the surface. As the fish swam under the boat, he leaned out, trying to see. The water exploded below him, and great jaws snatched at his face, its teeth snapping in empty air. He nearly fell into the water, but one of the men had seen what was about to happen and yanked him back, just a hair ahead of the croc's snout.

The migrants assigned a group of men with weapons, ready and watching, at all times. These terrible beasts were petrifying! Some of them were 15 or 20 feet long. Anat shivered to think of them. Usually the men could find fresh water sources at inland streams or lakes, but even there they found crocs, huge snakes, jaguars, giant hairy spiders and other dangers.

One young boy was snatched as he sat on a branch overhanging the river's edge. He'd thought he was high enough to be safe, but a crocodile leaped up from below him. Terrified, the boy lost his balance, and fell into the river. Anat had nightmares about it, unable to forget his screams and thrashing in the water.

Some things about this fantastic new country were as horrible as others were wonderful.

~*~*~*~*~*~*~

Chapter 10: Kanmi's Axe

143 BC – In the last several years, the People, as they now called themselves collectively, had finally found just the right place, far up a tributary of the Great River, where they could build docks, after they had learned how to deal with the crocodiles, snakes, and other dangers. At last they had a small, hidden harbor for their ships. They continued to make trading runs out to the main river, sending small boats ahead down to the ocean, carefully watching for enemy ships to make sure they were not observed.

From the mouth of the river, they established trade with natives along the coast as before, and also made occasional trips back across the Sea of Atlantis. To do this, first they sailed north from the mouth of the Great River, then caught the eastward-flowing currents back toward the Old Countries. But once they drew near the Romanized ports, they headed south, out of sight of land. Mauharim was the only safe trading area now. It was too dangerous to try to trade where the Romans had taken over—Iberia, Gaul, and Britain, as well as the countries bordering all of the Mare Hibericum.

They were extremely careful not to let any ships follow them home. They never did see any Roman warships on the west side of the ocean, but the notion to be watchful had become deeply ingrained.

They now created a settlement with a mixture of styles of buildings, as they evolved in their growing interaction with the natives from this new world. The Kena'anim continued building their rectangular huts and the Celts the circular, but all were made of jungle materials—bamboo and palm fronds. Some of the men had taken Brasilian wives, as they had not had families to bring with them on the migration.

Anat had mixed feelings. She felt safer on the ship, but the smells from overcrowding and a long time of no privacy or freedom of movement encouraged her and her family to try out the new huts. At night she lay listening to jungle sounds—monkeys, birds, jungle cats, and strange noises she could not identify. She thought of the slithering anaconda snakes she had seen, the crocodiles, and the terrifying, huge, furry spiders. Could they get into the huts at night? It was hard to sleep.

She tried to remember what it was like to sit on a sandy beach, digging her toes into the warm sand, the cool, refreshing sea breeze riffling her hair on her home island far away. Something she had taken for granted, it had been just *there*, in the background, those friendly, sunny islands, now harder and harder to recall. ...Dreams came, then nightmares of scary, leggy, slithery things... Anat would end up whimpering in her mother's bed.

The local natives had settled into a peaceful relationship with the migrants, and trade with them continued. Hanno and Cambus made more forays into the jungle and made lots of friends by trading with the river people. The first and boldest of the natives they had met, Tawa, had gone back to his village to show off the wonderful cooking pot he'd acquired from the new people of the ships. Others began rummaging in their huts for something they could offer. Tawa brought his friends, with more things to swap. Eventually the People were able to barter for instruction in building, food preparation and fishing methods. The natives invited them to their villages, and the newcomers discovered with amazement that an extensive network of towns was connected by primitive roads reaching far into the jungle, away from the river.

Life was never dull in the rain forest. There were new discoveries all the time. One of Anat's favorite new staple foods was cocona, a yellow fruit with an acidic flavor, not sweet. It was abundant and gave good flavor to many dishes. Another plentiful food was a whiskered fish with tender white flesh. Tanith wrapped the meat in large leaves with several other jungle foods and spices, and cooked them on her brazier. A beautiful little fish called *jaraqui* was abundant and tasty. It was silvery with a bold orange and black striped tail.

As the children of the various tribal groups began to get acquainted, a young Brasilian boy, Ollo, came to the migrant camp with a little green bird riding on his shoulder. It had a rounded beak and made sounds like people talking. Anat was transfixed. The boy showed her how to handle it and feed it fruit and insects. Then he made the "trade" sign. Anat, thrilled, ran back into her hut to find something to swap. She found a necklace of carved bone beads that Akbar had brought back from Mauharim. They were nice, but Anat had other jewelry she liked better, and had never worn those beads. She snatched them up and ran back out to see Ollo. She held up the string of beads, smiling with delight. Ollo grinned, handed her the bird, and took the beads.

She named her new pet Chitee, and taught him to fly to her hand and ride on her shoulder. It was easy to find food for him, and she felt joyful every time she was awakened by his chirps in the mornings.

Kanmi and Danel, Anat's brothers, continued with seamanship instruction under their father, and joined him on occasional trading trips to replenish their supplies and trade goods to barter with the Brasilian natives. Careful trips back to the shores of Mauharim yielded cargoes of goods that seemed wonderful to the Brasilians up the river. Salt and spices, ivory beads and carvings, pottery, metal dishes and utensils, all kept the locals enthusiastic, watching to see what was next.

The People, as well, looked forward to the arrival of cargo from the latest excursions. They saved the most valuable and useful items for themselves, as new goods became available. One such was a beautiful bronze-headed axe, acquired in a difficult trade. It had a symbolic deer head with antlers carved on it, a reminder of the Old Countries and the Celtic shamans' antler headdresses. It had made its way to Brasil through numerous trades. The competition was stiff, but Kanmi finally won out, offering a gold pendant he'd been holding back for just such an occasion, an edge over others' hand-crafted objects of nearly equal value. He wore the prized tool attached to his belt as he worked. Kanmi was beginning to lean more toward farming, as well as construction. He spent more time with the Celts, and liked to help Tanith and Anat with new family plots of jungle fruits and a few vegetables. All the men hunted to supply bush meat for the migrants.

Akbar approved. "It is good to learn more than one way of life, in case circumstances force you to change, as you can see, even here." He held Tanith close as they surveyed their village, enjoying the harmony of many different people working side by side.

The people of the growing community were learning, from the natives, how to make things from home-grown or foraged materials. The immigrants were fascinated, watching their nimble fingers, skillfully manufacturing useful products. They experienced a precarious relationship for a while, with frequent misunderstandings because the different tribes spoke so many languages, but they gradually became more fluent in each others' speech.

Game abounded in the jungle, and so many kinds of fish it was hard to keep in mind which were good for eating, and which ones would eat *them*, given a chance. One fish, the *pira-na*, would attack in numbers, with razor-like teeth in double rows, able to tear through flesh rapidly—terrifying!

Another was the *arapaima*, a gigantic, armor-scaled, carnivorous fish. Sometimes growing to a length of nine feet, it could weigh as much as a large man. A dreadful sight, with a gaping mouth full of teeth—even on its tongue—it devoured other fish and occasionally a careless bird. With its hard armored skin, it was impervious to the pira-nas.

The men hunted for *capi-bara*, (strange rodents, like giant guinea pigs), monkeys, birds, peccaries, deer, and snakes for meat. They learned to make wide clearings around the camps and trails so that nothing could ambush unsuspecting people or livestock.

The people still dwelt somewhat separately, the Celts making their round huts in one area and the Kena'anim still building their houses mostly in the old rectangular manner nearby, but they were all beginning to intermingle and try more of each others' ways, incorporating use of Brasilian building materials, like palms and bamboo.

Gardens appeared—small plots next to the huts. The women tried out different kinds of seeds they had brought along, to see what would grow in this new place, along with native plants, like manioc roots, squashes, maize, ynchic, caja, papaya, and peppers. The indigenous people taught them how to cook the curled new shoots of ferns, tender young stems of bamboo, and to flavor their *kakawi* drinks with *vainilla* and sweet fruit juices. Trading expeditions brought extra flavorings, like salt, *pippali, cinnamomum, singabera,* and other precious spices from faraway caravans of the Old Countries' spice trades.

As the men worked to extend the docks for their ships, they each kept a wary eye on the waters even though they employed guards to watch for crocodiles and snakes. One day a large anaconda slithered like liquid onto a tree limb that grew directly over a new dock being constructed. The branch, sagging under the accumulating weight of the big reptile, slowly sank lower and lower over Kanmi's head as he chopped at a supporting post.

The limb sprang upward as the serpent dropped.

"Look out!" yelled his friend, Finnbar.

Kanmi leaped aside, while slashing at the serpent with his axe. It lunged, clamping its mouth onto his leg, looping its body, intent on wrapping itself around him, and it took the mutual struggle of both men to finally kill it and pry it loose. Still shaking, Kanmi leaned against the dock, inspecting himself for injuries—then suddenly realized that his wonderful axe was gone! He felt all over in the gooey mud of the river bottom with his feet, and probed with a long pole, but it was nowhere to be found. Saddened, but glad to be alive, he slumped, and sat staring into the fire that evening. Even weeks later, he was often observed poking around in the area, but it was never found.

On a sunny afternoon in the jungle clearing, Anat, now 11, sat with Chitee on her shoulder and a bowl of peki fruit pits in her lap, cracking open the hulls and preparing the kernels for her mother to roast in the brazier. Getting to the kernels was a laborious effort. The spiny inner pits were set aside to dry after eating the juicy fruit. The spines had to be scraped off the pits; then they were cracked open to get the kernels. Crunchy and tasty when roasted with a little salt, these were only one of many wonderful treats from the jungle. Once in a while Anat gave Chitee a kernel to eat.

She was getting used to camp life now, where the People had found a good place to live for a while. The huge variety of foods provided fun for Anat, learning to cook at her mother's side, even as Tanith learned new possibilities herself. They grew a few vegetables near their hut, but it was difficult, with the dangers from the tangled forest so near. Tanith dreamed of living in a place where they could have safe spaces to garden, or just walk and play freely.

It seemed to Anat that the jungle wanted to eat them alive. *I wish we could have stayed home on our peaceful island,* she thought wistfully, *but it's probably been overrun by Romans now.* It seemed they had jumped from the brazier into the cooking fire. Would they ever find peace?

She mused on these thoughts as she sat, shucking the dried peki kernels into her bowl. Chitee twittered a low warning as someone came up behind her.

"Hello," said the Celtic boy. Anat and her friends were becoming fluent in the Celtic language, and the young Celts were learning to converse with the Kena'anim children.

"Hello." She looked up with questioning eyes. *What does he want?*

He took her hand, turned her flattened palm up, then bent forward and opened his mouth. A tiny green frog hopped out. She caught it, and smiled.

"Look," he said. He showed her that the little frog's legs were almost transparent, and when he turned it over on its back, they could see its heart, lungs, everything, working. "A see-through frog!"

Anat smiled. *One way to make friends*, she thought. They sat together for a while, and began a halting conversation.

In succeeding days Anat, and Ewan, who was three years older than her, became good friends, exploring the surrounding jungle and enjoying their discoveries together. He was tall and blonde, the son of Druce the Wise. Anat felt safe with him nearby to protect her. They helped each other gather tropical fruits and other materials that their parents used. Ewan taught Chitee to say a few Celtic words. Anat had noticed the bird seemed to mimic her, but she hadn't thought of teaching it real words. She was impressed.

Tanith noticed the friendship first, and nudged Akbar, who smiled knowingly with approval. *This could be a good thing.*

Druce noticed a subtle change in his son. He was happier and more enthusiastic in his work. *Ewan is learning well, and will become a good member of the community some day. In a few years, he will be ready to move into his own home, and serve as a holy man for the community.*

141 BC – Early on a steamy morning in the Amazon jungle, birds and monkeys called and chattered as butterflies and hummingbirds flitted from flower to flower in mottled sunlight. Anat, 13, walked cautiously down to the river's edge to fill a jug. The men had cleared wide swathes of ground around the camp and pathways, but Anat knew to watch for other signs of danger—drag marks on the shore or ripples in the water—made by a crocodile. She stayed away from dense plant growth where jaguars or snakes could hide in ambush, and peered at the water, straining her eyes to see if there were any shadows under the surface.

Suddenly the water seemed to explode in her face! A big croc came flying at her with a roaring hiss, its huge mouth gaping, full of teeth.

She screamed and fell backward.

The beast was almost upon her when it was hit in the eye by a bullet-like missile. It fled, bleeding and hissing, back into the water. Strong hands grabbed Anat's arms and dragged her quickly away from the river's edge. She was still screaming and gasping when Ewan put his arms around her, helping her up, and calming her.

Trembling, she looked up as he put away his sling. "Ohhh...." she groaned. "Oh, Ewan, I thought I was dead, for sure." She gazed into his handsome, smiling face, framed by a mop of sunlit blonde hair. He kept one arm around her, helping her up the bank.

"You must be more careful, little one," he comforted her in his teasing way. "I can't be around all day to rescue you." Ewan was sixteen now, well-schooled in medicine and mysticism by his father, the well-respected Druid wise man in the Celtic part of the village.

As he was about to take his arm away, Anat caught it, and held herself closer, looking up into his eyes. They stood, lightly pressed together for a long moment, not wanting to part.

Finally, Ewan said, "I think we should talk to our parents."

140 BC -- Anat's and Ewan's wedding was a combination of the cultures of both the Celtiberians and the Kena'anim, adapted to their new tropical home. Anat was a dark-eyed beauty, wearing a crown of orchids and a new tunic made by her mother, of precious linen from her father's trading journeys. Members of both families joined hands in a circle in the center of the village, surrounding the bride and groom, who were barefoot, symbolizing closeness to Mother Earth. Akbar squeezed Tanith's hand and Tanith smiled with brimming eyes, as Kanmi and Danel and their native wives called friendly taunts to the happy couple.

Several musicians joined in playing traditional melodies on their panpipes, and then a Celtic musician added to the beauty of the ritual, playing a lyre. Anat's and Ewan's hands were clasped together and a ceremonial piece of linen was wound around their hands, while Druce the holy man presided. They held a great feast, with the whole village contributing and partaking of the bounty. Many partook a little too much of the wine, made from jungle fruits, but it was amiably overlooked on this occasion of great celebration.

Later, Anat and Ewan stole away from the crowd, and stood gazing into each other's eyes, smiling. Then a funny thought came to Anat.

"Your eyes are laughing," said Ewan. "What are you thinking?"

"I was thinking of the little frog. When we first met. It was the beginning." She snuggled her face into the hollow of his neck.

"I almost forgot about that." Ewan held her close. "Yes, that was the beginning, but I had been watching you from a distance. I didn't know what I would say to you, but I could see that you liked to study the animals and things—then I found the little frog to help me."

Anat smiled. "Little frogs are good. Let's go see our new home."

The bride and groom's new house was a traditional hut, made of bamboo trunks in the native way, thatched with palm fronds, yet reflecting the Celtic affinity for circular houses with conical roofs. It was a little larger than some, more like two circles joined, made to accommodate Ewan's inherited occupation as a holy man. He had finished his training, a kind of apprenticeship with Druce. He had a large collection of herbs and potions, a spare bed for patients, and other equipment for doctoring.

Anat was thrilled to be presiding over her own house now: her own cooking fire, pots and utensils. She brushed her hand over her new brazier with a little thrill of pleasure and pride. Her father had acquired it on trading trips in the carpássios between Mauharim and Brasil. The future was bright for Anat and Ewan on their day of new beginnings.

84

One day a few months later, after Ewan and Anat had settled into their life together, Druce came by to visit. Anat was pleased to show off her wifely talents in serving fruit juice and treats she had made.

They sat around the fire for a short while, talking. Then Druce spoke: "Ewan, my son, I think you are ready to begin taking over some of my work. One of my patients is a boy in the village, Jabnit, who is suffering from a fever, and it would be good practice for you to take care of him." He smiled as Ewan and Anat perked up and looked at each other.

Ewan felt his heart jump. A real healing! This was like a final test. He thought about the herbs and medicines that he had gathered and prepared for his own collection. He put together some containers of herbs and went with his father to the boy's home.

The mother, Hanna, was a little reticent when Druce told her that his son would be helping Jabnit, but he assured her that he was fully confident in Ewan's abilities.

Ewan came into the hut where the boy was lying on a woven, stuffed pallet. "Hello, Jabnit, how are you doing? Your mother tells me you've been feeling achy and hot." He felt the boy's forehead. He was burning up with fever.

Ewan asked Hanna to heat some water to make tea, so she busied herself with the task. Ewan dipped a cloth in cool water, squeezed it out, and swabbed it over the boy's face, neck, and body, helping to cool him. Then he took out the mortar and pestle he had brought, and mashed up a special concoction of leaves.

Hanna brought Ewan the water she had heated, poured it into his container of leaves, and stood looking down over Jabnit, twisting her hands together.

"This is *guanabana*. It will take away your fever," he told the boy. He strained juice from the steeped pulp into a cup, and held him up so he could drink.

Jabnit sipped a little of the brew and made a face, but then smiled weakly. Ewan sat with him for a while, until he began to feel better and managed a weak sigh of thanks.

Ewan felt his forehead. "You don't feel as hot now. Drink some more." He sat with the child for another hour as the fever cooled and Jabnit relaxed into a deep sleep.

Ewan packed up his supplies. "Cool him with the wet cloth if he begins to feel hot again," he told Hanna. "I'll come again tonight before sleep time, and see how he's doing."

Hanna was smiling as she handed Ewan a bag of pitanga fruits. It was not demanded to pay for healing, but often done in gratitude.

Anat greeted her husband at the door of their hut with smiles. "I'm so proud to be the wife of a holy man! I have made a special meal for you. Oh! Pitangas! Those are so good, like pomegranates."

~*~*~*~*~*~*~

Chapter 11: Amzi Comes for Daisy

Daisy, awaking after dozing off, looked up to see a handsome woman bringing lunch on a tray. Carrying it over to a corner where a small table and chair were set by a barred window, the woman laid out utensils and poured water into a glass.

"Please don't think about keeping the fork as a weapon," she said matter-of-factly. "We want you to be comfortable, and we keep track of the utensils." She left, locking the door.

They want me to be comfortable? Why don't they let me go home? Daisy thought sarcastically. She sat at the table. Tamales and beans, and a salad. *Could be worse.* She tried not to think too much while eating. Thinking made her stomach wrench into a knot.

The day went on and on. Nothing seemed to happen, no word of her father, no communication from her captors. Nothing.

They know they have the upper hand. The longer they wait, the more anxious my parents, probably. Is that how this game is played? She alternated between trembling with fear and then seething with anger, but, in her helplessness, fear dominated.

The same woman brought dinner. She smiled slightly this time, but said little. A young man came in to collect the dishes. *Glad it wasn't Micos. Hope he's gone for good! What a jerk!* She tried not to think of his grinning face, his beer-breath. Her skin crawled at the memory of his filthy, searching hands. *Ugh! I feel sick.*

Night came. *At least they have electric lights here. Nice, but bare. No TV or magazines, or anything to do. Not that I could concentrate on anything like that anyway. Just wait. It's just one more psychological ploy. Wish I had someone to talk to, or at least a dog or cat.* She thought wistfully of old Qhawa, with his big doggy smile, at home in Maryland. *Why won't they tell me anything? Well, why would they? It's my dad they want to see. Ugh. How is that going to go? Will they torture him? No! I can't think of that.*

She had too much time to think. Finally she decided they weren't going to do anything that night, so she went to bed with most of her clothes on. *I wish I could lock the door from the inside,* she thought. *I feel so creepy.*

She drifted off to sleep, and after a while, a dream came to her. A pink mist seemed to gather at the foot of the bed. In it, she saw a tall young woman, light-skinned, with dark reddish hair, and clad in a robe of iridescent bird feathers. A glittering necklace of emeralds and deep blue lapis graced her neck, with a softly glowing pink stone in the center.

"Daisy, young lady Daisy?" she said, "Be calm and have patience. Your father will come, and others will help." Then she faded away.

Daisy sat up in bed. *What was that? Was that the priestess Tica that Mom and Dad talked about?* Somehow she felt better. She relaxed, and slept until morning.

Amzi and the police had been searching or talking to people, non-stop, trying to find witnesses who might have seen something. So far, Tamya and Carmella had come up with the best tip, but Daisy had been moved before Amzi and the police could get to the little house in the foothills. In his mind, Amzi railed against the slowness of organized policing, but he didn't say it aloud—they were trying to help him the best they knew how. Still, he was boiling, raging inside.

"I'm afraid she's been taken to one of the big haciendas of the Sendero Luminoso," said Captain Cortez. "They hid her quickly at first, in one of the little halfway houses they use, and then they probably moved her to a stronghold where they are more confident."

"What do we do now?" asked Amzi, rubbing his temples. He was so tired he couldn't think clearly. His head throbbed, and he wanted to slam his fist through the wall.

"First, we have to find out which hacienda she was taken to. There are several gangs in the area. That's what we're working on now. We have a network of informants, and it shouldn't take long. Or, they may just call us with their demands. At this point, Señor Darrow, I think you should get some rest, and something substantial to eat. Then you will be strengthened, and ready to do more when things break loose."

Amzi couldn't argue with that. He felt totally drained. He went back to the hotel to see the rest of the family.

Lila and the boys didn't look good. They were almost as exhausted as Amzi, dark circles under their eyes. Numb, they hugged each other for a long time, without much to say. Amzi held Lila as she sobbed, just needing to let it out. They sent out for some food, but hardly noticed what they were eating. Finally, they went to bed and tried to sleep, but they all just lay there, staring at the ceiling, listening to each other breathe. How could they relax, while Daisy was in such danger and needing them? They had to wait now for the terrorists to make the next move.

Early in the morning, the telephone rang in the Darrow suite. Lila sat up, her eyes wide. The boys came to the doorway.

Amzi answered it.

"Good morning, Señor Darrow," said a man's voice, sugar-sweetly. "We wanted to tell you that your little daughter is just fine. We would like to talk with you today, if you can find the time. I understand you have been quite busy, with the police."

"Damn you!" Amzi snarled. "Where are you holding her? What do you want?"

Lila and the boys gasped, but held onto each other, trying to stay quiet.

"We do not want to trouble the police, now, do we? Come alone to the north part of the city square at noon, and a car will bring you to visit us. We can have a nice talk."

As Amzi hung up, Lila clung to him. "Amzi, don't let them get you, too! Find another way! I can't lose both of you."

"Lila, it's *me* they *want*. I think they will let Daisy go, once they have me. If we tell the police, there are spies— someone will know, but we have other friends they don't know about. Please don't worry. Oh, what am I saying? Of course you'll worry! Just hold tight, and we'll get through this."

Lila dropped her hands. "Ohh," she moaned, "I hate this so much! I wish you didn't have to go. There's no other way?" She looked up into his dark blue eyes. They seemed to boil like storm clouds.

"Right now, I don't think there is, but... well, we'll see...."

Amzi sneaked out to a phone in the lobby, in case the one in their room was bugged, making sure no one saw him. He called Yachay and Umayo, and talked briefly with each, then went back to the rooms.

At noon, Amzi was waiting at the square. A black van came up, and a man opened the side door. Amzi got in; noticed several other men inside. The back windows were darkened, but he could see out. They took off, driving over the back roads, bumpy at first, then smoothing out as they neared El Jefe's hacienda.

Some distance behind, a small motorbike just happened to be going in the same direction as the van.

As they came up the drive, Amzi noticed an old Peruvian hairless dog standing beside the road. *That dog looks so much like old Qhawa,* Amzi thought absently. *No, that's really reaching—couldn't be. Focus, now! Don't get distracted.*

Then the dog made eye contact with him and gave him a big doggy smile as they passed, showing one canine tooth missing. *Just like Qhawa –*

No! Couldn't be.... Could it?

The car stopped at the front of the gleaming white hacienda, and the men escorted Amzi to the entrance. *How is this going to go?* wondered Amzi. *I suppose they're planning tortures for their entertainment.* He tried not to visualize what they might do to him. *Focus! At least I'll see my little Daisy. I've got to get her out of their clutches, no matter what happens to me. Umayo knows, so he may have some way.....*

The man with the motorbike parked it and followed through the trees at the side of the road, out of sight. He spoke into a small radio....

Amzi was taken down a hallway and out to a terrace shaded by palms, brilliant blooms of bougainvillea and other bright tropical flowers, overlooking a fountain where black swans and other exotic water birds fluttered in the pool.

El Jefe sat in a magnificent throne-like chair. Several brawny men stood nearby, watching. He motioned for Amzi to sit facing him, and flicked his cigar ashes into a large marble ashtray. "Well, well, well, as your people say. Now we have the Big Man himself. Would you like to see your beautiful little daughter?"

"What do you think? Of course I want to see her. She had better be in good shape." Amzi's anger concentrated into a blue glare at his enemy.

"You are not in a position to say what shape she is in. Just be glad we did not harm her." He flicked his ashes again, and nodded to a man, who went to Daisy's room.

Daisy was feeling numb, wondering what was going on. Sounds were different today. She looked out the window as she heard a car approaching, and saw her father getting out with El Jefe's men. *Oh, no! Dad, don't come here! No!*

After a few minutes, a man came for her, holding her arm tightly, walking her out of the room.

Amzi heard them coming down the hall.

"Dad! Don't do it! Don't let them have you!" She wept, knowing those words were too late. She wanted to run to him, but the man gripped her arm. She struggled, gasped, and sobbed.

91

"Daisy, honey! Are you all right? Did they hurt you?" said Amzi. He glowered at El Jefe, who smiled his crocodile smile, clenching the fat cigar in his teeth.

"I'm fine, Dad. Why did you come here? Isn't there another way?" She gritted her teeth, knowing there probably wasn't. *Is it too late? What will happen to Dad, now that they've captured him?*

"Okay, you have me," Amzi growled to El Jefe. "Take her back. Let her go to her mother." He glared at his enemy, knowing it might not go that way. *You'll dance in Hell for this...*

"Oh, soon enough, Señor Darrow." El Jefe grinned. "But we must have assurances. We know you probably have other people involved." His glare hardened. "Make them back off, or your pretty little girl might go home ...not so pretty."

"Damn you!" Amzi spat. He looked around at the men standing guard. An ornate clock ticked on the marble tabletop, but it seemed as if time were folding in on itself. There seemed to be no way out, but there could be a possible chance to save Daisy.

"Okay, give me the phone." He called Umayo, explained to him the situation, and not to try to rescue him because it would endanger Daisy. But he used code words that also gave Umayo additional information, pre-determined, depending on the scenario, especially if there was a spy in Umayo's village.

Amzi didn't call Yachay. He hoped the terrorists didn't know about him, but Umayo would contact him, as agreed.

El Jefe eyed Amzi suspiciously. "That was too easy." He leaned forward. "Do you have another idea up your sleeve? Don't try anything heroic."

"I love my daughter, Señor. I have lived a good life, long enough..."

Daisy gasped, hearing this --

"...I want my beloved daughter to have hers. Now, let her go."

The guard loosened his grip for a second. Daisy yanked free and ran to her father.

92

"Nooooo, Daddy," sobbed Daisy, clinging tightly to Amzi as the man pulled at her and dragged her off. The man let go of Daisy again, grinning, teasing, as she ran back to her father and slammed into his arms, sobbing. "Oh Daddy, I wandered off. It's all my fault. Don't let them hurt you."

Amzi held his daughter in a tight grip, kissing her forehead, comforting her, glad to have her in his arms even for a fleeting moment. "Don't worry, sweetie. We'll get through this. It wasn't your fault. They're professionals at snatching people. They would have found another way, no matter what."

The man yanked her away again, and took her back to her room. He shoved her in as she struggled vainly.

Amzi gritted his teeth as he heard her screams shut off by the closing door.

El Jefe grinned in amusement, his eyes glinting with evil.

~*~*~*~*~*~*~

Chapter 12: Qhawa: Intrepid to the Last

Umayo had discovered the true identity of the Shining Path spy in his village of Vilcatambo. This was a man, Juan Carza, who had come to them for help the year before, saying he had been burned out of his home, and had nowhere to go. That was his story.

But now that Umayo knew the truth, he was able to set up false messages for Carza to overhear, throwing off the Sendero Luminoso so that certain people could escape their clutches. So now, too, he was able to give them false security, without their realizing that the people of Vilcatambo had any way to help Amzi and Daisy.

El Jefe didn't let Daisy go—not yet. He wanted to keep her for a little extra entertainment he had in mind. He had Amzi taken to a room down the hall from Daisy's, but not next to it—so there would be no chance they'd find a way to communicate.

"You will be close to your little girl," said Diego, the guard. "But you won't be able to talk. If you want to try anything, just remember I'll be here in this room between you." He grinned at Amzi, showing several crooked teeth and a scar on his chin. He looked forward to the usual 'entertainment' their boss let them have with the hostages. The pretty girl looked promising, and her father could watch. Then they would let her observe as they took out their revenge on Amzi. A quick death would be too good for this enemy. Diego took his dinner in the middle room, and settled down for the night.

Time seemed to stand still at the hacienda. The hostages were fed, and most lights went out. What would happen next? What were Umayo and Yachay doing?

As the occupants of the compound slept or stood guard, the night became strangely dark, no matter how many lights were on. In the guard's room, between Amzi's and Daisy's, Diego sat, listening uneasily, straining to hear as a sinister silence soaked into the darkness. A few curls of a black fog began to flow under the door....

Early in the morning, before dawn, Daisy heard something scratching at her door. She arose quietly and slipped into her shoes, then tried the handle and opened it, amazed that it wasn't locked. It was Qhawa. He ran out his tongue in a big doggy smile. She fell to her knees, hugging him silently, stifling sobs. *But what about Dad?* Qhawa seemed to read her mind. He padded quietly down to another door and scratched at it, then it opened. *Why were they unlocked? Did someone else help?* No time for questions now. Amzi, looking only slightly surprised, stepped into the hallway, took Daisy's hand, and they quietly followed the dog.

As they passed an open door to another room, they saw a man lying on the floor with horrible, seeping pustules covering his face and arms. A black fog was receding. *Tica's work,* thought Amzi.

Daisy's eyes grew wide at the sight of the dead man. She had never seen such a thing, but had heard the incredible stories from her parents when she was growing up.

Amzi pulled on her hand. "Come on, don't look at that. We don't have time." They sneaked down the hall, past other doorways giving glimpses of writhing, gasping men, to the back way out, and followed Qhawa into the jungle.

Amzi remembered the black fog that had engulfed the grave robbers in the sacred tombs back in 1992. They had died, if not treated immediately, covered with seeping inky-purple blisters on their exposed skin. Then again, a menacing dark plague-cloud at Atahuaqa had frightened away the Shining Path men who were chasing them from their family hacienda in 1993. It brought a shiver to Amzi's spine to see it again.

After about a half mile walk, they came to a clearing, and found Umayo and two men—Pacay, his son, and Auqui, a trusted friend from Vilcatambo, waiting for them.

"How - - what - - ?" Daisy began,

"Later!" said Amzi. "Let's get out of here."

The party started off into the jungle, and soon were climbing higher into the mountains. They passed by spectacular overviews unknown to outsiders, and around cliffs on narrow paths cut into the rock, then into the rampant foliage again, higher yet, permeated by clouds and mist.

At one point, Umayo paused, and said, "Stop." Then he pointed up. Above the trail, draped on a long, horizontal tree limb, a huge anaconda looked down with a hungry, cat-like eye. "He would like to give you a little squeeze," Umayo chuckled.

They skirted around, not under, the snake. Daisy trembled. *We're not out of this yet.*

They trekked on all day through misty vines, trees, and ferns, and spent a night camping in the jungle, with Umayo and his men standing watch. They had brought cold camp food, not wanting to risk a fire, and a couple of sleeping bags for Amzi and Daisy.

Daisy slept fitfully, listening to strange sounds and wondering if any tarantulas or snakes would crawl into bed with her. Sometimes Amzi reached over and patted her arm, calming her.

In the morning, they had a breakfast of barley cakes and hummus, with dried fruit and bananas. They collected water from a small stream, as howler monkeys serenaded them with raucous screeching. A flock of brightly-colored wild parrots wheeled overhead, disappearing into the mist. The little party took off into the mountains again, crossing chasms on quivering rope bridges and scrambling ever higher, along several dizzying ridges above uninhabited valleys. They began to hear a far-off roaring sound. Qhawa was leading them toward it.

After about an hour, they came to the edge of a cliff next to a thundering waterfall. Amzi wondered if this one was a known cataract, or was it deep in the unexplored Andes? Where would they go from here?

Qhawa and Umayo led the way along a faint path that passed under the falls. The party was sprayed with cold mist, but they didn't mind. In the semidarkness behind the cascading water, they came to a narrow tunnel in the rock, and Umayo said, "Come."

It was inky dark, but Umayo found a torch hidden in a dry niche in the rock. He lit it, and led them on. Water dribbled down the walls and the ground was slippery, but Daisy and Amzi held onto each other. Dreamlike, they plodded on. Daisy lost track of how long they were in the tunnel, but she was so happy to have her dad and herself safe and on their way home, she didn't care.

They began to see light ahead, and came to the back opening of the tunnel. As they emerged, Umayo cautioned them to watch their step. Daisy gasped as they came out onto a narrow ledge overlooking an abyss that seemed to have no bottom. A few clouds floated below, and condors circled at different heights. Amzi looked across to the other side. Barely visible in the misty distance, a row of Chachapoya sarcophagi stood facing their ledge, standing guard over the great wall that rose up behind them. Two of the sarcophagi were new.

"Where are we?" asked Daisy.

"Look across the way, there," said Amzi, pointing. But he held her firmly, as she was wobbling a bit.

"Kuelap?" she said, confused. "No...those are different." Then she looked to the right. "What...?" She could barely make out, on the wall off to the side, the representation of a fleet of ships, ancient ships, with square sails and many oars. "What place is this?"

"Daisy, remember this as long as you live, but don't tell anyone outside our family. This is the back side of Atahuaqa."

97

Daisy nearly fainted, and Amzi held her up. Umayo and the others nodded their approval of Amzi's cautionary words.

As they stood, looking across the chasm, they heard sounds echoing in the tunnel behind them. The Shining Path? As Amzi had expected, El Jefe, insane with fury, had sent men to follow them after discovering they'd escaped— and the men were closing the distance.

Qhawa growled. Before they could catch him, he raced back into the tunnel.

"Qhawa! No!" cried Daisy.

"We have to go. NOW!" said Umayo.

They hurried after him. From far back in the tunnel, they could hear echoes of Qhawa's desperate barking, and crying out—then silence.

"Hurry!" said Umayo. They followed the ledge down, down into the entrance of another tunnel, this one descending gradually and coming out into another high valley.

They never saw Qhawa again. He had given his life to slow the Sendero Luminoso, allowing his human friends the time they needed to escape. Slowed, but...were they still coming? Daisy could hardly see through the tears flowing down her face as she stumbled on.

The small party traveled quickly across the valley and found five horses tied along a fence near a hill, where the path came to a fork.

"Here is where we say goodbye," said Umayo, "Beloved friend, Señor Amzi." The two men embraced with a brief back slap, and Umayo turned to Daisy and smiled, taking her hand. "Take good care of your father," he said simply. The others in the party also embraced Amzi, and, smiling, inclined their heads toward Daisy, who was blinded by tears.

"Follow the path on the right for the rest of the day, and you will know where you are," said Umayo. "The way to Vilcatambo is just over that other ridge by the path on the left." Then they mounted three of the horses, and rode toward their village.

Daisy and Amzi stood looking after them, and then at each other. They embraced for a minute, Daisy shedding more tears, and kissing her dad's cheeks.

"Oh, Dad, I'm so sorry all this happened. If only – "

"No 'if-onlies.'" he hugged her again, not wanting to let go. "But we've got to get out of here. I don't know if those men are still coming." They mounted the two remaining horses and took off at a gallop, putting as much distance as they could between themselves and any pursuers.

When the exhausted terrorists came to the fork in the paths, and saw horse tracks going at a fast pace both ways, they gave up—they would never be able to catch Amzi and Daisy. Now they had to find their way back, to face their boss. Or did they? It was later rumored that some of El Jefe's men had disappeared.

Amzi and Daisy found that the path they followed eventually led them to a mountain overlooking Cuzco, with a way down to the edge of the suburbs, where they were met by Yachay and his friends, Tamya and Carmella.

Daisy and Carmella hugged. "Thank you so much," said Daisy to Carmella. "I knew you would help me somehow."

Finally they arrived at the hotel in Cuzco, and had an ecstatic reunion with Lila and the boys. They didn't want to stop hugging each other. It seemed as if they were waking from a nightmare, and had to keep reassuring themselves it was real.

Lila, too, thought she must be dreaming. "How --?" Amzi gave her that look of "tell you later," rolling his blue eyes, then smiling and grabbing her in his arms, devouring her with kisses all over her face and neck as she sobbed.

The boys and Daisy hugged each other and laughed, dancing around, and hugged some more. Daisy screamed with pure joy.

That evening, the family held a big dinner party at the restaurant where Qhispi, Amzi's cook from the old hacienda, now worked. Yachay and Tamya were there, and "old" Carmella, who didn't look so old anymore. Captain Cortez of the Cuzco police, and many of the detectives and others were there, too, as well as some of Amzi's friends from the Antiquities Department. They nearly overflowed the restaurant, and partied far into the night.

"We need to get out of here," said Amzi after the celebration wound down and broke up. Lila and the kids heartily agreed. They had enjoyed the first part of their trip to Peru, but they had seen more than enough of it now. They packed their things that night and took the first available flight back to the States the next morning.

~*~*~*~*~*~*~

Chapter 13: Fly Away to Spurwink

Amzi and Lila sat with Daisy snuggled between them on the flight home. It seemed they couldn't get enough of being near each other, and feeling safe.

"I don't want to think about Peru at all for a good long time," Daisy said, "I can't shake the feeling that I might wake up and still be at that nasty place." And Lila agreed—the reality of waiting to hear if her child and her husband were dead or alive was still fresh in her mind. Amzi knew he would probably be overprotective for a while, and hoped Daisy would understand. Exhausted, they all slept most of the way on the plane back to the States.

Daisy tried not to think about Qhawa. She told herself that he had grown old for a dog, and had had a long and eventful life. It was his own doing to end his life the way he did, protecting his family. "He went out in a blaze of glory," Daisy had said, smiling through tears. Her mother warned her not to mention him being in Peru when they got home. Aunt Melanie would be telling them he had run away, which would be something she could understand and believe. Lila had never explained to her in detail how Qhawa and Missy, her cat, had come back from Peru in 1993.

Lila had often mused on the whole scenario. *Tica has a thing for beloved animals. That must be part of their Earth Mother beliefs.*

It was so good to be home at Spurwink! Melanie, Elfie, and the rest of the family were full of questions. Lila had been afraid to phone home during the kidnapping, and Melanie had become increasingly worried when she didn't check in. Lila had given her a quick call the morning they left Cuzco. It was difficult knowing how much—or how little—to say. Cousin Elfie and her family were so curious, as well as relieved. They wanted to hear the story of Daisy's kidnapping by the Shining Path. To them, being so far away, it was exciting, but didn't seem as real, almost an adventure, to hear about. Some day it would be a good episode to discuss in detail for their conversations up in the cupola, but right now, it was too fresh, too raw.

"I'm sorry to have to tell you," said Melanie, "that Qhawa is gone. It was just last week, he was asleep outside, and suddenly jumped up and started howling. Then he ran off down the driveway and never came back. I don't know what happened to him."

Lila and Daisy looked at each other, and at Amzi. Lila spoke up quickly. "That's really strange, isn't it? What day was it? What time?" They confirmed that it happened at the very time Daisy was snatched in Cuzco. "Yes, that's really weird, but I've heard stories of dogs sensing things from long distances like that. It's as if they have ESP or something."

"But where did he go?" said Melanie. "Shouldn't we look for him? I put up some posters around Ravenwood, but haven't gotten any calls, and the Humane Society hasn't seen him."

Amzi and Lila looked perplexed. No use doing that—but how to tell Melanie what really happened—it's unbelievable! She had always been skeptical of the pink emerald's supposed powers. She went along with it because it was a real ring and had actually been stolen.

"We'll just have to wait, I guess," said Lila, squeezing Daisy's hand. She could see the tears welling in Daisy's eyes, and knew what she was remembering.

"There, there, darling," Aunt Mel patted Daisy's hand. "I know you felt closer to Qhawa than the rest of us. I'm so sorry. You know, he might still come back."

Daisy hugged Aunt Mel and looked at her parents over Mel's shoulder: *It's okay, I know she doesn't understand.*

Amzi and Lila went to visit his parents, Courtland and Lorna Darrow, at Oakland Manor, the Darrow family home, as soon as possible. They hadn't heard about the incident until it was over.

"I didn't think it necessary to give you more worry, when I could just tell you the whole story once I got here," Amzi told them. "I was, well...a little busy during the actual experience."

Lorna looked relieved, trying not to be upset. "I guess I'd rather learn of it this way, now that I know you're all safe."

Amzi's father just shook his head. "Amzi, you get into the most amazing escapades. So what do you plan to do next? It would be hard to top that one!"

They wanted, of course, to hear more details about the kidnapping of their only granddaughter, and Amzi and Lila did their best to give the most believable version. It was exciting enough without anything being said about Tica's magic.

"But how did Umayo and his friends get you out of the terrorists' hacienda?" asked Lorna. "I still don't understand how you just walked out."

"There was a special trained dog there, helping the rescuers," said Lila. "It's hard to explain what he did, but he was part of the plan, along with Umayo and Yachay's help. He distracted the guards outside El Jefe's hacienda, while they brought in help to incapacitate the other guards. It wasn't hard, since they were drunk after celebrating Amzi's capture. El Jefe himself was not there that night, so they were being careless. Several others of our friends helped, too. The commandant had told Amzi to call his friends and tell them to back off. He did call Umayo, with a coded message, but the abductors didn't know ALL our friends. It worked wonderfully well."

"Some of them did pursue us as we escaped," said Amzi, "but the dog held them off long enough for us to get away. Unfortunately, the dog was killed. He was a great

103

dog." A quick glance at Lila showed him her eyes brimming, but she turned away for a moment.

"And how is our little Daisy doing?" asked Courtland.

"Oh, she'll be fine, I think," said Amzi. "She just doesn't want to think about Peru."

Indeed, Daisy busied herself with anything she could think of, to keep from attacks of hysteria and shivering. Counselling and therapy sessions helped. She cleaned her room from top to bottom, and went on long horseback rides, accompanied by at least one of her brothers at all times. They didn't really fear that the Shining Path would come to Maryland, but it would take a while to get rid of those jitters. She didn't talk much at all about her kidnapping experience. She began to think harder about planning her future, wondering how college life would be. She had been putting it off after high school, just tired of the academic routine. She had sent for several college catalogs in the spring, still trying to make up her mind, then applied to the Maryland Institute of Art, the same school her aunt Elfie had attended.

In the interim, she and her mother enjoyed time together, playing with the two new kittens that Amzi had brought home. One was a long-haired tortoiseshell, named Foxy, and the other a short-haired ginger named Elmer. They were comforting and entertaining, their warmth and affection helping Daisy and Lila regain a sense of normalcy.

But fall would be coming all too soon, and Daisy had been accepted at the Maryland Institute of Art. She began to feel excited about it, pumping Elfie for information about her experiences there. Her parents were relieved to see her confident attitude growing.

"Do you have any qualms about being on your own, away from home?" Lila asked her. "You know, you could take a year off first, and no one would blame you."

"I thought about that. I'm still pretty jumpy, but I think by the time school starts, I'll be okay. I'll be in a dorm with a roommate. Hopefully I'll be able to cultivate a good relationship with some girls who are sensible and don't take chances. Maybe I'm paranoid, but the memories of those hands reaching out of the dark and grabbing me, and that *jerk*, Micos – Oh! They haunt me still!" She shivered.

Lila put her arms around her daughter, looking over at Amzi. "I'll try not to worry, but I hope you'll keep in touch with us pretty often."

"Oh, don't worry about that," Daisy said with a sigh. "This is going to stay with me for a long time, and I'll need to talk."

She went off to her first year at art school in the fall, feeling pretty good by then. She found that throwing herself into creative activities helped tremendously. She roomed in a quiet dorm, and soon had some good friends there—Julia, who was interested in interior decorating, and Kate, who majored in painting and sculpture. Daisy had a knack for sewing and took classes in upholstery and drapery design.

Danny and Ben were able to procure two alpacas, named Olga and Igor.

"Why not Peruvian names?" asked Amzi.

"They were already named when we got them," said Danny. "And they come when called by name. Anyway, they're cute and fun, and that's all that matters. We're learning their language a little—never knew they communicated with hums and clicks and screeches."

Ben especially liked Igor, the larger, reddish-brown one. Olga was mostly white with some brown spots, and seemed to make comical faces, which was fun for Danny, who enjoyed taking pictures of them. Both the animals liked to play and snuggle with the boys, chasing them around the pasture. They had a pen in the barn, with a few goats to play with, near the horses' stalls. The brothers spent long days taking care of the animals, but enjoyed music lessons as well, Danny taking flute, and Ben on the piano.

The young Darrows liked to ride, as did their cousins, Elfie's kids, and they took turns on the three family horses. With seven young people living at Spurwink, it would be too many if each had their own, but they didn't usually all want to ride at once, anyway. If they did sometimes, they borrowed a few from Oakland Manor.

AJ liked animals, but was more interested in his studies, spending long hours on his computer at home. He returned to Yale that fall, to continue his studies of Pre-Columbian History and Languages. He was still interested in finding out more about the Chachapoyas and their origin. "The Shining Path may be important in Peru," he said, "but with so much more there that is fascinating, they pale in comparison."

Christmas of 2013 was a big family affair, at both Spurwink and Oakland Manors. All the family members came home for the holidays and went back and forth between the two homes for get-togethers and parties, sleigh rides and gift-giving.

Melanie was full of joy, having the family grown so large again. "Oh, Lila, I wish your mom could be here, and see all this. Our family nearly dwindled down to nothing for a time."

"Yes." Lila gazed wistfully out the window. "Mom would have loved it, and never would have dreamed that I'd marry Amzi."

AJ, home from college for the holidays, had exciting news. "I've been reading some intriguing things on the Internet about Peru, especially the Chachapoyas...."

~*~*~*~*~*~*~

Chapter 14: AJ Returns to Cuzco

Winter, spring of 2014 – AJ, majoring in History and related courses at Yale, had been making more discoveries on his own about Andean tribes in Peru. He had first taken the usual introductory courses having to do with world history and ancient classical history, and courses in Latin, Spanish, and archaeology. Allowed to design his own major, he found a professor who specialized in early Latin American history to be his advisor. On his own, he started reading everything he could find about the Incas, their rise and fall in history, how they subjugated other tribes under a system of serfdom, and about some of the other important tribes of Peru—Quechua, Moche, Wari. He studied early Spanish history, and more history of Pre-Columbian Peru.

One day he came to Amzi with a question. "Dad, could I see Donna Gerard's llama-skin again? I'd like to make a copy of it to take back with me for next semester. I won't show it to anyone else."

"I'm glad to see your interest in it. We really need to understand it."

AJ carefully copied the ancient symbols, the writing that Donna Gerard had so painstakingly studied back in the 1850's.

~*~*~*~*~*~*~

At home in Maryland, Dan and Ben were becoming more serious about farming. They loved the alpacas, had bought several more—and now there were babies. They began right away to realize how communicative the animals were. They hummed and clicked and chattered all day, sometimes "orgling," or "screaming" an alarm. They found that alpacas are very vigilant, and sometimes sounded an alarm when surprised by their own shadow! The boys were glad they didn't have neighbors near enough to complain.

Dan had been thinking. "We need to sell some, or pretty soon we'll be overwhelmed."

"I know," Ben pushed two animals apart to walk between. "but which ones? I'm getting too attached to them. Oh, I know, we have to do it. I just want to make sure they have good homes." He cuddled one of his favorites, a fluffy white female he'd named Pookie. She snuggled her soft nose under his ear and hummed.

"That's a consideration," said Dan. "Let's put an ad in the paper and try selling them that way first. We can talk to people who are interested, to make sure they're a good fit."

And so was born the Spurwink Alpaca Ranch of Ravenwood.

Elfie and her husband, Jason, were busy with their interior decorating business, and their niece, Daisy, was excited to see their progress each time she came home from art school, bursting with her own ideas. At other times, she and her mom spent hours in the sewing room, working on projects together.

Lila laid a bundle of fabrics on a table. "I never knew our family had such a creative streak. These last 20-odd years have been such fun, I hardly have time for reading books anymore, like I used to do." *And so many of this family wouldn't even exist if I hadn't found the ring.* Tears came to her eyes, and she hastily wiped them away and turned to her daughter.

Daisy unfolded the latest project she'd been working on at school. It was a quilt with an adorable appliquéd llama in the middle, with tassels and colorful designs around the edges that had a distinct Peruvian look. "This is for you, Mom. I don't want all our memories of Peru to be negative."

"Oh, honey, it's wonderful. Such good depictions of Peruvian designs, and the llama is precious. I love it!" Daisy smiled. "I do like llamas and alpacas. But I can enjoy being around Ben's and Danny's, and let them keep the duties of their care and feeding." She winked, and picked up one of the kittens. "I still miss Qhawa. He was such a companion when I needed him."

"I know, sweetie, but he had a long life for a dog. Hey, you know, I think instead of putting this on the bed, I'll have your dad hang it on the wall." She folded it over her arm. "Where is he?"

"I think he and AJ are still going over AJ's notes and pictures up in his room. Want me to get him?"

"No, that's okay. I'll put this on our bed until they're done. They won't want to be interrupted."

AJ and Amzi were, indeed, deep in concentration over the ancient puzzles. "I think, next, I'm going to have to just *go* there," said AJ.

~*~*~*~*~*~*~

July, 2014 -- At the museum in Cuzco, an elderly archaeologist looked up from his desk at the visitor who had just come in. Something about the young man was so familiar. What was it? He had dark brown hair, with a dark mustache, and partially-shaded glasses, which he took off. Startled by the deep blue—and suddenly recognized—eyes of his young guest, he was speechless.

"Dr. Holcomb? I think you know my father, Amzi Darrow." AJ waited for the man to recover—he looked as if he'd seen a ghost—and held out his hand. "I came in disguise, in case the Shining Path is still watching for our family. My name, for my time here, is Gene McGuire, but my real name is Amzi Darrow, Jr."

Dr. Holcomb was momentarily tongue-tied. He'd thought he'd never see Amzi Sr. again, or any of the family, after the kidnapping of Daisy Darrow. Still a bit dazed, he rose and shook hands exuberantly with 'Gene,' and motioned for him to sit down.

"You can imagine my surprise," he began. "I must ask, how are your father and the family? I was so glad to hear they—you—all returned home safely after that unpleasant incident."

'Gene' grimaced slightly. "We have all recovered well, but I think we have Peru in our very blood. I've been studying Peruvian history—ancient history—at Yale."

Dr. Holcomb smiled as he settled back in his chair. "I've missed seeing your father around here." Then he leaned forward. "What brings you here, Mr. McGuire?"

AJ grinned. *I'll have to get used to that name.* "I believe I have a good background knowledge, academically, of Peruvian history, and the people, but after studying the many tribes of the Andes—especially the Chachapoyas—I have so many questions."

Ah, yes, the Chachapoyas, thought Dr. Holcomb. "Yes, they are one of the more enigmatic of the Andean tribes. We haven't made a great deal of progress in figuring them out."

"I know. I'm hoping I might be of some help. Maybe I could acquire a small job around the museum? Perhaps I could be allowed to look at some of your records and artifacts. I'd just like to get the feel, the atmosphere, of the place, the people. As you know, my family lived here, but it was before I was born."

"I think we can accommodate your request," said Dr. Holcomb. "I assume you have a place to stay for now? I'll talk to some of the others today, and let you know—Mr. McGuire."

"Thank you. I know the Shining Path has spies everywhere, so for now, at least, I hope that only you will know my real name. Here's my number at the hotel." He stood up to go.

"I'll be in touch soon." Dr. Holcomb rose and shook his hand again. "It's good to meet you."

Back at his hotel room, AJ stretched out on his bed, needing a rest after the trip and his visit to the museum to see Dr. Holcomb. *I'll have to get used to wearing these glasses. They're only shaded at the top, enough to hide the color of my eyes, so I should be able to read, I guess.* He needed to think. He recalled the conversation he'd had with his dad before he left:

"Dad, could you tell me again about the murals you saw back in 1993, at that last dig, just before the terrorists came? I may get a chance to see them soon. I'm still working on theories about the writing, and hope to make some progress on what all this might be about."

"Well, I couldn't get a detailed study of them, as I was trying not to be conspicuous, but the first one I saw showed the fall of Atahuaqa, and the second had two light-haired people in it, who seemed to be giving a small bright object, like a gem, to a priestess in a feathered robe."

"And you think this was you and Mom taking the pink emerald to Tica?"

"I couldn't think of any other explanation," Amzi had said. "It seems that Tica and her father, and others of their tribe, can time-travel, or have visions. I don't know how else they could know the future."

"Okay, and the other mural, farther into the tomb?"

"That was the one with the six-winged bird! It seemed absurd at first, but I came to understand that it was how an ancient person would interpret a helicopter. It was an accurate prediction of our escape. That's why I couldn't tell anyone." He shrugged. "They wouldn't have believed it anyway."

"Ha! I can understand that. But was there some writing on the murals?"

"Yes, there was writing of some kind in several places in that tomb, but it's done in a way that could be mistaken for decorative trim. That first mural was so exciting because it actually showed, according to *our* understanding, the story of Tica and her father, and the fall of Atahuaqa, though the archaeologists didn't recognize what city it was. We can thank Donna Gerard for figuring out the story. I think she had real intuition—or 'help'—you know? Then farther in, well, both of those two murals with the 'pale ones' in them—I couldn't get close enough in that dark, crowded tomb to see all the writing. After all these years, it should be cleared out so you can get a much better look at it."

"That's what I'm hoping to do, and maybe put something together from that, with the symbols on the llama skin."

"So you are going to Cuzco? Be careful down there, son. I'd like to talk with you some more before you go."

"I was hoping you'd say that."

They did have several deep conversations before AJ left, everything Amzi could think of, to encourage his son to find out more, but also to warn him again to keep his interest in Atahuaqa to himself. He could probably be a help to the researchers down there, anyway, with general interest in the digs and all the different tribes. They'd also discussed the need for AJ to travel incognito, to avoid discovery by the Sendero Luminoso, if possible. Amzi was a little worried, but told himself his son was now a grown man, though still gaining experience with such things.

"Please don't go into any dark alleys," Lila attempted to make a joke of it, but she grimaced involuntarily. She hugged AJ. "Is there anything I can help with?"

"Mom, I know you have reason to be apprehensive," said AJ. "Really, I will be careful. They probably won't expect any of us to come back, after what happened with Daisy. Still, I hope I can avoid waving any red flags."

Now, here he was, by himself, in Cuzco. He lay on the bed in his hotel room, trying to visualize his next moves.

Drifting off to sleep, he had a dream: A pink mist materialized at the foot of his bed, and a tall young woman with light skin and dark reddish hair stood, smiling, cloaked in a beautiful robe of iridescent bird feathers.

Chapter 15: 1 BC in the Amazon

1 BC – The People, as they called themselves collectively, were a tribe of striking appearance, tall, light in complexion, with dark brown eyes, and a range of hair colors from blonde to black, and a few with red hair and freckles. Some of them were descendants of Anat and Ewan's family.

They had adapted well to their new home, in everything from diet to house construction; hunting methods to music. They went to their holy men for advice and leadership, and saw no need for a local ruler. Owing to their experiences with the warlike peoples of the Old World, they knew the trouble a power-hungry leader could incite—or inflict. At first the Kena'anim had traditionally revered the ancient, almost legendary, Hiram, great king of Tyre, but the old kingdom was a world away and his reign long past. They might never hear of Canaan again, except in the storytellers' tales.

Anat and Ewan were held dear as beloved ancestors. Ewan had gone on to become a wise shaman, and developed a great gift of healing, while Anat matured in her close bonding with animals, passing it on to their offspring. As she grew old, she became a beloved grandmother. Respectful groups of young people gathered around to hear her stories of the Old Country, the wonderful islands and the dangerous journey across the Sea of Darkness. It became tradition to tell the stories, and certain descendants became special memorizers for the tribe, passing their history on down through the generations. The tribal historians memorized the genealogies of all the families, spiced with tales of their adventures and contributions to the tribe.

One thing painfully missed from their old home origins was the high, rocky country where they were able to entomb their dead honorably in caves in the cliffs. The Kena'anim continued some of their traditions, burying the bodies in a fetal position, wrapped lovingly in soft fabrics, sometimes with a favorite object from their lives. The Celts of Iberia had a tradition of cremation, interring the ashes in urns. Both dreamed of finding high, dry bluffs, where they could follow their traditions—some day. For now, they had no choice but to create cemeteries in the jungle.

A place of their own, to live in peace and trade—that's all they dreamed of in life. But they were ferocious fighters in response to outside threats. Though they used more traditional weapons like bow and arrow and spears in the jungles, they continued to train their men, starting as very young boys, to use the sling with deadly accuracy. It had served them well for thousands of years. Here, it was more difficult, in the thickly forested terrain, to have clear space to use the slings, and a challenge to find ammunition. The muddy river banks and soft humus of the jungle floor offered few if any rocks, so they used hard fruits and nuts as substitutes.

They still had that old apprehension of enemies stalking them. It had caused them to keep moving their temporary villages west, up the Great River, to new hidden places. Sometimes, too, they moved on because of clashes with the local natives. Why did it seem that civilizations always degenerated into distrust and war? Would they ever find a permanent, peaceful home?

32 AD – The People's new village had sprung up on another tributary of the Great River, many days' travel farther west. They were building a new dock and shipyard, where it was well-hidden from any boats that might be traveling up and down the main stream. The men who had the inclination and ability for sailing and trade still continued

the familiar routes of their forebears back to the shores of Mauharim, passing near, but out of sight, of Roman-held ports. They had sworn to run their ships onto the rocks rather than to allow foreigners to follow them and discover their adopted homeland. Returning sailors passed on information they had gathered concerning the foreign ports of Britain, Gaul, and Iberia. They had been surprised, in the early years, to learn that Rome had continued its interest in plundering and controlling only the countries of Europe and the Mediterranean. After its initial search party had no success in finding the escapees, that was the end of it. Rome was not a concern in this raw young world anymore, but there were plenty of new enemies to worry about.

Some of the People became farmers and builders, a good balance with the seafarers. They had learned to clear areas for gardens and orchards, enriching the poor jungle soil with an ingenious method learned from the Brasilian natives, adding such materials as charcoal, bones of fish and turtles, manure, and broken pottery. It produced a rich, dark earth. The natives traded seedlings of the wonderful indigenous fruit trees—*kakawi, guava, caja, pitanga*—from their own plots.. They taught the newcomers how to grow the tasty ground-nuts, called *ynchic*, a hearty and filling food that had many uses, and a wonderful juicy fruit called *ananas*. In turn, they began to grow newly-introduced vegetable crops from seeds brought over by the traders, like *lentes, faseloi, pisa, kickere, unio*, and *keras*. They learned crafts and skills from the People, too. New pottery began to appear in native villages, decorated with the favorite spiral and snake patterns of the Celts, sometimes with pictures recording important events of the times.
Sometimes the natives traded small animals, especially birds, which they had tamed as pets, and a kind of small jungle cat was sometimes raised from kittens that had been found orphaned.
Some years before, a small fleet of carpássios had returned from Mauharim, bringing a few precious young goats and lambs, highly prized. Several families were able to trade for them, and so a new farming endeavor began,

limited only by their ability to protect the pastures. The introduction of dogs, brought in from other excursions, helped keep predators away.

55 AD – Ysabel, a descendant of Anat and Ewan, was being groomed to become a priestess of the People. There were always several priests and priestesses in every generation, the descendancy usually kept within a family line, unless an offspring from a different family displayed unusual talent.

Ten years old, Ysabel and several other girls around her age were living in the temple that had recently been built of timbers and bamboo from the surrounding forest, plastered with mud, and the roof thatched with palm fronds. In this temple, large stores of medicinal herbs and potions were kept, and the priestesses and priests were well-versed in their use for healing sicknesses. They were trained to deal with other afflictions, too—splinting broken bones, childbirth problems, or treating injuries caused by wild animals. Over the years, the People had incorporated some of the South American religion of the Earth Mother, finding it fit their forest habitat and developing way of life.

Ysabel and the other girls were being educated by Brigid, another descendant of the line of Druids from the family of Druce. Tall and blonde, with a slight sprinkle of freckles across her nose, she was seventeen, well-trained in the shamans' skills of the People.

"Our forest is known for its useful herbs and medicines," Brigid said one day. "We have studied the basic ones, but tomorrow we will take a walk into the jungle and I'll show you how to find more of them." The girls, sitting on woven mats, listened eagerly and organized their collections of dried herbs in special pouches they had learned to make from animal skins.

Ysabel had a keen interest in medicine, and had already learned many of the plants, minerals and other sources from which remedies were made. Even when she was little, she had been found studying plants, their parts, and observing how they were picked and preserved. She had practiced on her pets, helping them heal when injured

116

or sick. As she grew older, she had helped neighbors with their animals. She was gifted, a natural healer.

She kept a pet ocelot, named Chichi. Ysabel had found the orphaned kitten a few years before, when it was injured by a ferocious mother peccary, protecting its own young. She'd saved Chichi's life, and he had formed an intense bond with her.

Brigid had taken a liking to Ysabel early on, and sensed the child's talent. They became close friends, sharing long conversations at Brigid's fire in the evenings.

"Teacher, will you tell me about the *wapotok* herb, please?" Ysabel asked one night. They were roasting some jaraqui fish over the fire. Chichi leaned against Ysabel, eyeing the fish and sniffing towards it, but he shrank from the fire.

"The wapotok is a plant like cocona, about as tall as your knee, that grows along the river bank where the sun breaks through. It has a little yellowish flower and small yellow-orange fruits that you can eat. They aren't sweet, but it's a good, savory flavor. When you rub the leaves or stems, they have a nice smell."

"What things will it cure?"

"Oh, it's good for a lot of things. It's used for cuts and wounds, fevers, ear-hurting, and all kinds of skin diseases. And it's good for getting rid of worms, too."

"How do you prepare it?"

"First," said Brigid, "you collect the leaves, and fruit if it has some, and mash them up in a bowl until you have a gooey mess. Then you smear it right onto a cut or wound, For fever or worms, mix it with water to make a drink."

"Could we look for some tomorrow? Can we dry it for later, or does it have to be used fresh?" She broke off a piece of fish for Chichi, blew on it to cool it, and set it down. He approached cautiously, sniffed it, then ate daintily.

"You can use it fresh, but it's good to have a supply of it dried, in storage. Then you can freshen it with hot water. We can find you some tomorrow. I'll show you how to dry it. Do you know someone who needs it?"

117

"Today I was watching the Shaman, Gabrius, helping Tabnit's mother. She had fever and shaking, and I heard him say 'wapotok' was what he was using."

"Someone has big ears," Brigid teased. "But that's good. You're collecting useful knowledge." After they ate, she braided Ysabel's dark red-brown hair as they talked.

Ysabel did have 'big ears.' She was a very curious girl, always watching and listening.

One day, a few years later, she was collecting leaves from some *tuyuya* vines in the forest, to be used for relieving pain and as a tonic tea for cleansing the blood. The warm air was thick with the scent of forest humus and decaying leaves. Dappled sunlight sprinkled the soft ground, which was layered with dead leaves and tangled roots. She was reaching out toward the vine, when a bee stung her arm.

"Aieee!" she yelled, jumping back and trying frantically to scrape the insect off. Startled, a screeching swarm of tiny monkeys scrambled away through the trees. Finally the bee fell away, and then she noticed more of them zooming around her. *Oh, no, I've disturbed a nest—got to get out of here!* She stumbled over a root and fell down.

Someone was running toward her. It was a boy who had danced with her at the festival of the full moon. "Here, I'll help you," he said. He picked her up and ran toward the village with her.

"I'm not hurt that bad," she said. "Put me down!"

He stopped and let her down, then grinned. "Yes, I see you are well. Remember me? I am Eppo, son of Samio. I was looking for mushrooms and heard you scream. Is the sting bad?"

"It will *get* bad if I don't find something to put on it."

"I know what plant you want. I'll look too," he said. They began searching the nearby forest, and found a small patch of cordoncillo plants. He helped her crush the leaves and apply it to the sting, which had started to swell. The smear of leaves brought instant numbness.

"That will make the pain go away," said Ysabel. "I have more herbs for a poultice, back at my chamber in the temple, to draw the poison out. Thank you for helping me."

The two became good friends, both interested in the healing arts. Eppo had no plan to become a shaman, but he used herbs and potions for family ailments and his three young goats. He was from a farmer family, taking over some of his father's plot of land. He loved animals and growing things, and had planted his own small orchard and an herb garden. He came often to visit Ysabel, and they would sit outside the temple in the moonlight, listening to the night sounds.

"I love the song of the *jurutai* bird," said Ysabel, "even though it sounds unhappy. My teacher told me that the natives have a legend about it: The jurutai fell in love with the moon, and tried and tried to fly up to it. When it failed, it was so sad that it sang to the moon at night, with its tears flowing down to become the Great River."

"Yes, I've heard that story, too." said Eppo. "I heard that some of the natives light fires when the moon is big and round, and they sing and dance, trying to get the jurutai to sing."

"It's a strange-looking bird," said Ysabel. "I saw one in the daytime, sitting in a young mahogany tree. Its feathers were mottled brown like the bark of the tree, and it looked at me with big yellow eyes like an owl. I think it needs big eyes because it's awake at night."

After a few more years, Ysabel completed her training, and she and Eppo married, setting up housekeeping on his farm. Neighbors among the People came to them with health problems, usually giving them young fruit trees or a goat or two in gratitude, and their farm prospered.

More clearings were made, farther into the jungle, as the population grew. Neighboring natives learned the People's language and began to incorporate new words and ways of living into their own communities.

When their children were asleep, Ysabel and Eppo still liked to sit outside their hut in the moonlight, listening to the horned frogs that made a mooing sound, and watching swarms of fireflies twinkling their soft greenish lights.

Now and then a flash of far-off lightning lit the sky above distant trees, followed by faint rumbling. Other nights were stormy, when thunder shook the ground and lightning made them cringe, the rain slashing down like knives outside their hut. On these nights, the children and dogs all piled together with them, seeking warmth and reassurance.

~*~*~*~*~*~*~

Chapter 16: Exploring the West:
Dannius Climbs a Tree

78 AD – The People sent out more scouts to the West to explore the surrounding country, bringing back discoveries of new foods and people, in new territories. They had explored many branches of the Great River, but these rushing streams were all diminishing, growing too shallow, fast, and narrow to travel much farther by ship, so the explorers began to use the Brasilian-style canoes.

They had seen low hills in the distance at times, offering hope that they might find land that wasn't swampy. One day an exploration party, on a far-western excursion up a larger tributary, began to catch glimpses of higher mountains. After weeks of traveling, the men began to find the river becoming even more swift and narrow, coming through low mountains. What lay ahead? They came to a bend in the river where there was some open land, and brought in their boats for the night. The ground was definitely becoming more rugged.

Dannius, one of the more adventurous members of the party, took two men with him to explore past the edges of the clearing, on up to the top of a hill. He had noticed an exceptionally tall tree with liana vines wrapping the trunk, something he could easily climb, and possibly offering a better view of distant land features. He hacked a path a short way through the brush and vines to the bottom of the tree, and began to climb. Up and up he went, grasping the twining, woody tendrils, up to high, branching limbs. Monkeys screeched, and a few jungle ants stung his hands, but it didn't hinder him. A flock of blue macaws fluttered away as he shook the upper branches, emerging high enough to see above the surrounding rain forest that seemed to stretch forever in all directions.

"What do you see?" called his friends.

He looked to the east, wondering if he could see the ocean he'd heard about, but could only see the flat expanse of green, stretching to the darkening horizon. To the south and north, some low, jungle-covered hills, and here and there another tall tree that emerged above the vast canopy. He climbed higher and looked west through an opening in the branches. In the far distance, on the other side of higher hill country, a range of tall mountains came into view, with peaks so high they were obscured in places by clouds piling up against their sides, the sun setting behind them. He had never seen nor even imagined such steep, craggy peaks.

After a loud whoop of excitement, he stared for a few minutes, amazed, trying to judge how far away they were. Then he reluctantly descended to tell his comrades, who each climbed up to take a look for himself. The mountains were barely visible beyond the boundless blanket of forest, but the sighting generated enthusiastic talk around the campfire that night. Might not those highlands provide a better place for the People to put down more permanent roots?

For generations, living on the Great River, the People had dreamed of a land where they could have more well-drained, open plots for crops – and no crocodiles! Could it be?

Dannius and the others hurried back to the settlement with the news, and soon mounted a long-distance expedition, traveling by canoe as far up the river tributaries as possible, then trekking overland toward the distant peaks. They camped in temporary shelters, enduring crashing thunderstorms that beat down with spear-like rain, drenching them even in their lean-to hovels.

On they went.

Weeks later, as they trekked the foothills, they found the land still covered with humid rainforest. But as they ascended, they discovered plants and animals different from the ones native to the watery river banks, and the trees were not as tall.

While hunting peccaries in the forest, they found strange animals with flexible snouts that looked like a cross between deer and pigs. These animals lived in the rising jungle slopes and wallowed in pools of water. Meeting more natives as they traveled, they learned that these were called "*tapi-ira*" and were good to eat. The men caught glimpses of jaguars and pumas watching them from trees and rocky bluffs, and foxes, hunting for small rodents like cuy, chinchillas, and viscacha, a similar animal.

They marveled at the condors swooping overhead— they had never seen such huge birds. These were even bigger than the eagles and sea birds they had occasionally seen, and didn't fly from limb to limb among the trees like most of the smaller birds in the rain forest, but circled high into the clouds.

The rugged slopes were festooned with all shapes and sizes of succulents and mosses, along with strange spiky *chaguar* plants that grew in the dry spaces opening among thick forests.

The scenery was spectacular from the heights. They found open land and a more temperate climate, and enjoyed the sunshine and freshness of the breeze. It reminded them of their ancestors' stories of the old homelands, the Balearic islands and northwest lands of Iberia, steep mountains with bluffs and ravines.

Above them, among the highest ridges, clouds seemed to bump up against the crests, enveloping crags and releasing rain on the damp slopes. The farmers in the group recognized conditions in which domestic crops could thrive. They envisioned terraced pastures for their small farms. Their traders could bring seeds to begin growing more of the vegetables they'd heard about from the old country.

Another thing they found was an abundance of *rocks* for building walls and houses. No more jungle huts. They

123

dreamed of freedom to inhabit the land the way their forefathers had enjoyed.

116 AD – A small part of the People who were committed to seafaring had continued in that way of life, separating peacefully from the tribe, making their own way, yet continuing valuable cooperation and trade connections. They sailed the seas along the shores of Brasil and islands of the New World in the sea north of the main body of land. Then they caught an eastward-flowing current across the Sea of Atlantis, and made cautious trading trips back to Mauharim and any countries not ruled by Rome. They kept up the shipyards built at the last settlement on the tributary of the Great River, making commerce their occupation, and continued associations with their people in the mountains, periodically meeting with them for trade at midway locations in the highlands.

In the new village of Ayatambo, colonists settled into a comfortable routine. The greater number of the People had found a new life here on the eastern flanks of the Andes. Memories and instructions were passed on by tribal historians, keeping alive the skills they were once again going to need. Gone were the jungle huts and crocodiles of the Great River. They were re-learning to build traditional circular houses with sturdy rock walls and thatched conical roofs instead of palm fronds and mud. It felt right.

Small farms terraced in the old way produced vegetables and fruit on hillsides along with narrow mountain pastures for a few sheep and goats. They brought with them some of the fruit trees that would grow on the slopes, including the one called kakawi, from which the natives along the big river had shown them how to make a special drink, sweetened with juice of other fruits, esteemed as a food of the gods.

The new settlers located springs, and channeled water to the ribbons of fields and gardens and their houses. Several of the farms belonged to descendants of Ysabel and Eppo, now expanding their own holdings.

It might seem that farming, especially growing vegetables, at that altitude, would be impossible due to colder temperatures. But they found that they had a much longer growing season coupled with a comfortable climate even at high elevations. For the most part, farming was successful. The soil was thin on the rocky slopes, but they knew how to gather it into terraces as their ancestors had done, enriching it as the Amazonians had taught them.

As they began to trade with the highland natives, they were introduced to a new vegetable: *batatas*, or *papas*. Hearty and filling, these tubers could be used in a variety of ways, and became an important crop, along with *mahiz*, amaranth, and tasty ground nuts, ynchic, useful staples grown by the indigenous people. Manioc, papaya and *kinwa* were important foods, as well as several types of squash, and their pisas, faselois and keras. Their traders began to bring seeds of the vegetables more suited to temperate climate—grains, root vegetables and squashes.

One discovery made a big difference—the *llama*. Andean peoples had domesticated the docile beasts, sure-footed, gentle, and able to carry large packs. They were already accustomed to travel on precarious trails, being native to the high mountains.

Another related kind, the smaller *alpaca*, produced an abundance of warm, soft wool. Both provided meat, and the natives taught the People to make *ch'arki*—dried, salted meat, useful on journeys and to store for winter. The people needed warm clothing, a comforting shield against the dampness and chilly nights, now that they lived in the uplands. Though they had sheep, they especially prized the alpacas' luxuriant wool. They began to spin and weave it, using a special kind of drop-spindle brought from the Old Country. They learned to make bright dyes to create beautiful textiles, precious for trade with neighboring tribes.

They still had to be vigilant for animals like jaguars and pumas, but it was worth it to inhabit this better locale. Better, if only the two-legged type of varmints would leave them alone....

125

The People still used the sling in warfare when necessary, ever ready in case of attack. Rumors of invasions of other tribes' settlements from both the eastern and western flanks of these mountains brought unease to the People. The more powerful enemy tribes lived far away, but, how long before the People suffered one of these frightening attacks? They had continued to train their young boys as they grew. They had been using hard jungle fruits in the slings. It had been a long time since they had been able to keep a good supply of ammunition, but this new territory of rugged ground provided plenty of small rocks.

Now, too, they had an abundance of large rocks for building—not only houses, but high perimeter walls for protection. They eventually moved their settlements to the loftiest ridges, overlooking surrounding valleys and rivers, anywhere from which attackers might be seen approaching. They had secretly sent word back to the Old Country for expert builders more recently experienced in the ancient skills passed down through generations, to cut and move large, squared stone blocks to build high protective ramparts around their villages.

It was a risky endeavor, these descendants having lived far away from the old homeland, to disguise themselves as simple merchants or farmers, to slip into the country and make the right contacts without arousing suspicion. One of the sailors, who had had repeated contact with people in the old land, went along to help them in and out of the country, and to help find a few young men in the highlands who were expert in stonework (and looking for adventure), along with an older master builder willing to come along to advise.

132 AD – Huarwar, son of Mungo, a Celtiberian from northern Iberia, arrived at the foot of the Andes, bone-weary from his long journey. He was a tall, well-muscled man, stonecutter, an expert builder of walls and large stone buildings. He had traveled with a group of younger stonecutters, eager to experience this new land they'd heard about. After a few days' rest, they began the last leg of the trip, marveling at the scenery and wonders of the great

peaks. Welcomed at Ayatambo, they were soon put to work, and gathered a larger group of men who were interested in honing skills that hadn't been practiced for generations. It wasn't long before the sound of hammers and chisels rang through the canyons, training more new artisans who spread to some of the People's other settlements.

As years passed, impressive walls and temples began to rise on the mountain ridges. They made the entrances to their cities narrow and the walls thick and high, impossible to break through, mirroring a style found in the mountains in the north of Iberia. Natural springs were channeled to bring water inside the walls, even to individual homes, and lookouts were stationed on constant alert to any movement below.

157 AD – The community known as Ayatambo had grown from one of the groups of settlers sent out to establish new colonies. They and others of their communities continued to build the now-familiar walls high on advantageous ridges and edges of steep cliffs, where they could look down through the clouds into surrounding valleys. Small herds of llamas and alpacas joined, and soon outnumbered, the sheep and goats of the Peoples' farms. Lines of pack trains were common between settlements on a network of narrow roads, paved with worked stone. The llamas were able to carry good-sized loads of fruits, vegetables, woven woolen fabrics, pottery, or whatever else the small farms produced. The population grew as trade increased.

Another commodity was precious stones—blue opals, lapis lazuli, and especially emeralds. The indigenous tribes had been digging them out for thousands of years, and the People soon learned to mine and cut the precious gems.

As yet they had not encountered any really powerful warring tribes. The People were still the greater influence over neighboring cultures, teaching them agricultural practices, pottery, and other new skills they had learned, so that those tribes prospered as well.

The People began to enjoy life, spending more time in games, ritual dances, and playing music. The indigenous people showed them how to make new kinds of flutes and stringed instruments. They already had panpipes, but now they learned to make them out of deer bones and condor quills, decorated with colorful yarns and beads. Andean melodies melded with those of the Kena'anim and Celts.

Tanitay, a young priestess-in-training of Pachamama, reclined on a massive stone, studying the flight of the condors and the path of the river below, a gentle breeze playing with her long, blonde hair. She was a descendant of Eppo and Ysabel, and farther back, of Anat and Ewan, their memory kept alive by the village historians.

She could hear echoes of stonecutters, calls of condors through the canyons, and nearby household sounds coming from the round stone houses of the village behind her. Someone was playing a haunting song on the panpipes. A cloud, coming off the jagged pinnacle above her, was dragging out shreds like alpaca wool being pulled apart.

Tanitay loved her lofty home. She treasured the history of her people, and often sat at the feet of the oldest village historian, Andoti. She reveled in his stories about the vast forest and Great River below on the sunrise side of their homeland, and how their ancestors had crossed a great, dark sea, coming from lands of rocky mountains and beautiful sunny islands—to escape armies of brutal soldiers. Such exciting stories!

One day, when Tanitay was twelve, Andoti continued his story. "Always we have avoided the loss of our freedom in any way we can, by moving away from troubled lands, establishing peaceful settlements, and keeping to ourselves. But when attackers come, we are ready."

Stirring his fire with a stick, he paused, raised an eyebrow, and looked at Tanitay. "I am thinking you have come to me for advice, young Tanitay. Is that true?"

"Great Wise One, I have a decision to make."

"Say on."

"I have been thinking of becoming a priestess, but in addition, I feel a strong need to learn the ancient memories," she said. "Is it allowed for a woman to do so?"

"You have already been doing so," said Andoti. "Have I objected?"

"I mean, I've never seen a woman *historian*. I want to become a real tribal historian, not just a listener."

"That can be arranged. You must go to the temple and present yourself to the Chief Shaman, and I will speak for you also."

Tanitay was surprised that it was so easy. "Thank you, Wise One. I am most grateful." Her heart fluttered as she rose, bowed slightly, and left the fireside, barely resisting the urge to skip as she walked away.

Andoti smiled to himself as he watched the young girl depart with a purposeful step. *She took a long time coming to herself about her calling. Perhaps she was afraid I would be angry or refuse her. But I see in her a talent for The Memories. She will do well.*

Chapter 17: AJ meets Umayo

Startled, AJ stared at the vision of Tica, realizing that now he, too, seemed to have won the confidence of the Ancients. What message did she have for him?

"Greetings, young Amzi." Her necklace glittered among the shining feathers. "You are much favored for your loyalty and care for our people. It is good that you will work with the men here. You must also visit Umayo." She faded into the mist, which curled in upon itself and disappeared.

AJ awoke with a jolt. *See Umayo. I've never really met him. How do I find him? I need to call Dad.* Still groggy, he tumbled off the bed and called home.

Amzi answered. "Yes, you may remember my mentioning that Umayo lives in a small, remote village called Vilcatambo." He told AJ where to find Rafa, the trustworthy driver that he had hired before, and Umayo's number, to inform him he was coming. Amzi chuckled to himself as he hung up. *Somehow, though, I think he already knows.*

AJ, as "Gene McGuire," quickly left the hotel, excited at the chance to actually go to see this mysterious place he'd heard about, and the equally mysterious Umayo.

Umayo had seemed to be expecting his call, and said he'd be most welcome. Trying to keep calm, AJ held onto the arm rest and glanced at the rugged landscape as the old car trundled precariously along a steep hillside road. After a couple of hours, they arrived at the village, AJ massaging his white knuckles after the hair-raising ride.

Umayo was waiting in front of the narrow entrance that seemed but a slit in the village walls. AJ had briefly met Yachay and the others who had helped Amzi, at the dinner party they'd held after Daisy's rescue. But he had never seen Umayo, who preferred to keep to himself. AJ studied his face as he approached the car, and wondered how old this man was. He had white hair, but was not wrinkled nor stooped with age, and looked quite vigorous. He smiled as AJ exited the car.

"Welcome, Mr. McGuire." He offered his hand, then said quietly, "Yes, for safety's sake you are called by another name, and I will use that, young AJ. You are welcome here, as were your parents. Please walk with me."

They started up the road together, away from the village, so they could talk privately.

"Umayo, I am so happy to get to see you," AJ said, trying not to gush. "I look forward to working with you. I have knowledge from formal schooling at my university, but I need to comprehend, on a deeper level, about the history here, and the people. Soon after I arrived in Cuzco I had a dream, or a vision, of Tica. She told me to come here to talk with you."

"Yes, I had the same. I don't say much over the phone, but I perceive that you have come to do research about the ancient tribes. It may be that I can help."

"I have only just arrived, but I've been studying everything I can find at the university in the States. I wasn't born here, but I've heard the stories all my life. I understand that it's very important that Atahuaqa be protected and kept secret as long as possible. Precious memories and traditions can be trampled, as well as actual personal remains, when the outside world gets involved. I have learned that the Cloud People, especially, treasured their freedom and privacy."

Umayo nodded, and smiled in approval. "I am most grateful. I appreciate that you and your family want to help preserve the artifacts and history of all our tribes here in Peru, and your father has been so helpful in rescuing our heritage. It has been difficult at times."

"The government and archaeologists from here and other countries are anxious to learn more and more, and maybe some of this brings them too close to discoveries you are not comfortable with. I was thinking that in helping them, maybe I could steer them away from Atahuaqa."

Umayo nodded slightly. "Yes, there are many lost cities and other things in the Andes that will not be dangerous for them to discover and study."

"Dangerous?"

"To Tica and her people. We realize that some day their history and private remains may all be exposed to the intruding eyes of the world, but we want them to rest peacefully in their sanctuary as long as possible."

"Umayo, may I ask, what is your connection with Tica? Are her people ... are you ... Chachapoyan?"

Umayo stopped walking and looked at him, his deep brown eyes seeming to smolder. "I think your parents have felt that, in their subconscious, for some time. We keep to ourselves, away from all others who poke and pry and bring trouble. You and your family have not."

Was that a warning?

"I assure you," said AJ, quickly, "I would never expose this to the public eye. I only ask to make sure I understand. I can work better if I know what I'm doing."

"Of course." Umayo smiled. "You are most welcome to ask what you need." *Inquisitive youngster, but he means no harm.*

They had returned to the village, and Rafa was waiting by the car. Umayo had suggested things to look for when AJ studied the specimens in the museum at Cuzco. He also told him what he'd need to see at the dig site with the murals. The paintings on the walls couldn't be moved, so after the transportable articles were taken to the museum, the site itself had been kept open only for supervised access by researchers.

AJ returned to Cuzco in time for a late supper at one of his parents' favorite restaurants. He savored the familiar tamales and juanes, but he didn't feel the same, eating alone. He had the sensation that eyes were watching him, and kept his shaded glasses on at all times. *I feel like a buffalo in a llama herd. I wonder if this is enough disguise....*

Dr. Holcomb called him the next day, with the job information. "Would you like to work in the museum's records department? That way you will have access to the details of the digs, and you will be welcome to look at artifacts and talk with the archaeologists. I'll explain that you're a visiting researcher from the States."

"That sounds perfect. I really appreciate your help. I hope I can learn enough that we can help each other."

"You can start Monday. "I'll introduce you to the staff and everyone you'll be working with. It will be light work, flexible, about four days a week, so you can have more free time to go to other locations."

AJ took the weekend to study maps of the area and get a good understanding of the sites he might want to visit. Dr. Holcomb had suggested a few to start with—the museum, of course, and several interesting new digs, some of which had been discovered recently, well after Amzi had worked at Cuzco. AJ wondered where, on the map, Atahuaqa might be. *Maybe I'll get to see it.* He felt his tensions rising. *I'll have to be circumspect with Umayo if I want to do that.*

He visited the site where the three murals had been found, and took pictures of them, with close-ups of the writing. He noted that it actually looked like decoration, around the edges of the pictorial designs, even mixing in small depictions of animals and flowers. *Ha! Good camouflage!*

I wonder if anyone here is getting close to deciphering this writing? Are they curious that it might reveal something important? I'll have to see if I can find any documents where they've been working on it and keep my ears open.
Evidently no one has discovered Atahuaqa. Maybe, with the new discoveries since Dad worked here, they've moved on to other interests.

Back at the hotel, he used his own equipment to make blow-ups of sections of the murals and writing, and printed them out, using tracing paper to highlight certain areas for study. He remembered seeing Arab calligraphy, how it could be highly stylized to look like decoration, yet could still be read—if you knew how. The muralists had to be careful back then, so the Incas didn't catch on to their scheme. Some things had to be hidden in plain sight. He remembered reading that, after it had been banned, one scholar had rediscovered the quellqa, but when the Incas realized it, he had been burned alive for daring to revive the forbidden writing. *It was an effective deterrent.*

AJ began his work at the museum, taking time to get a good working knowledge of the notes and photos available in the archaeologists' records. *This is fascinating stuff, but I've got to focus and not get distracted by some other interest. I wish I could employ some expert help here, but they might catch on to what I'm really looking for.*

At night, back at his hotel, he studied his photos of the murals. They seemed to be a linear timeline, not unlike the Bayeux Tapestry, the many-yards-long strip of embroidered cloth made after the battle of Hastings in 1066, telling the story of William the Conqueror. The murals from the tombs here showed figures that he knew must be Tica and her father, and other people—maybe priests? AJ's previous knowledge of the general story helped. The paintings were done in a style that seemed to portray the facial expressions of the 'others' with a decidedly evil look, and suggested activities that looked surreptitious. He thought it looked as if the death of Huaca brought a smile to the evil ones' faces. Tica, shown as smaller, was shut off with another girl in simpler garb—Maupi? Amzi had mentioned Maupi, Tica's maiden assistant. She had been buried beside Tica at Atahuaqa, in the ancient earthquake. *How much involvement have Mom and Dad had with Atahuaqa, that they haven't told me yet?* He had grown up knowing Amzi's love of secrets, a coyote teacher, one who preferred to let a person find their own answers, while he only gave an occasional word or two of guidance.

The second mural showed the two 'pale ones' bringing a small bright item to Tica. As symbolic art, they didn't look exactly like Amzi and Lila, but AJ, being accustomed to studying the stylized drawings, and with what he already knew of the story, could tell who they must be, by little differences in the portrayal of their hair and clothing.

Then AJ caught his breath a little, as he followed further along the mural, and came upon a stylized picture of a cat, lying on a pillow on top of a box or chest. He hadn't noticed it before, as it was camouflaged in the decorative art. *Missy? Is that old Missy there?* AJ felt a shiver. *Yes, they said something about her being 'transported.' Wow. But what does the writing say?* Frustrated, AJ went to bed late that night, thrashing in his dreams, where he saw his mother's cat, Missy, prancing with her fluffy tail held high, looking at him with yellow eyes.

I know secrets, she seemed to say, taunting him.

How could you know? You're a cat. You died years ago. But you were transported. Is that part of the secret? Is it time travel? And some kind of mystical molecular conveyance, like the transporter in Star Trek? Half awake, he struggled to open his eyes. *What was that all about? Just a crazy dream, from too much thinking....*

After about two weeks, he took a short trip to an ancient-looking hacienda tucked into the shoulder of a mountain a few miles from Vilcatambo. Umayo had mentioned a hillside there, where he would find several small caves. He was able to stay with a local family at their stair-stepped farm, people who were Umayo's relatives. They were welcoming and hospitable.

When he arrived, he noted that they were tall, and actually resembled Umayo quite a bit. Most of them had dark hair, but they had several children, two of whom were blonde, and one red-haired, with freckles. *Hmmm, that's very interesting....* but he didn't say anything. *I almost moved too fast with Umayo. Asking too direct a question about the Chachapoyas doesn't work.*

He enjoyed meals with them, and brought them some special chocolate treats from the café at the Choco Museo in Cuzco, something that they didn't often have.

He spent the first two days searching along the hillside near their terraced farm. He found several small cave openings, and finally chose one that looked most promising. He had with him a few archaeology tools, including a small shovel and flashlight, and his pocket-size digital camera.

Ducking under vegetation, he squeezed into the cave, and noted that it widened a bit once he got inside. It looked as if it extended fairly deep into the hillside. Nothing much at the front. *Hello, what's this?* It was some kind of pottery. He took several pictures, turning the shard carefully so as not to break it. Decorated with spirals and dots, it had a symbolic representation of snakes around the top. Excited, he shined the light around, and could see a glint of something farther in. Several pieces of broken pottery lay near some rocks, and one, nearly intact, was set on a little alcove shelf dug into the wall. They were decorated with spirals and cat's-eye designs, and some symbols or characters that looked very much like those on Donna Gerard's llama skin. With shaking hands, he managed to take pictures of them.

He looked around at the widened space. He could see that the rocks encircled a blackened place that looked as if it had been a campfire, long ago. Stirring it, he found a few small, scorched bones, remains of someone's meal—*how many years since that person had eaten here? Decades? Hundreds?* Nearby, he found pieces of black feathers that he imagined were the tips of condor quills, probably trimmed to make panpipes like those discovered in one of the digs. More photos.....

He slipped the camera into a deep pocket of his jacket, and picked up one small shard of decorated pottery to put in another pocket, then headed back toward the entrance of the cave, where he'd left the shovel. Somewhere a bit of dirt rattled down to the floor of the cave. He shined his light in that direction, but saw nothing. He turned back toward the entrance, and just then heard a faint rumbling sound, *like a truck going over a bridge* somewhere. *There are no bridges around here—or trucks.*

~*~*~*~*~*~*~

136

Chapter 18: The Cave and the Earthquake

AJ stopped to listen and caught his breath, suddenly feeling claustrophobic from being in such a small space, deep underground. More dirt and rocks dropped from the ceiling.

I don't like this. What's going on? Better get out of here. Suddenly a louder rumble began, and the whole place started to move like ocean swells. Earthquake! His heart thudding, AJ fell to his knees, and grabbed for his flashlight. *Got to get to the entrance!* Just then, a cascade of dirt and rocks fell over the opening of the cave, and closed it completely. Wobbly but unhurt, he sat on the ground, and turned off his light to save the battery. He had to think. It was darker than he'd ever seen dark. All was quiet.

He flicked his light on, and looked around. *Where's the shovel? Ah, there.* He could see the end of the blade, and dug it out of the loose dirt, grasping the grimy handle and getting his bearings. *I think the entrance was right here—got to dig in the right direction.* He began to scoop the dirt. *Oops. Better save my battery.* He put the flashlight in his pocket, so he wouldn't inadvertently cover it up. He dug in the dark, stopping now and then to shine his light on the area and see his progress. Several boulders had fallen into the entrance area. He shuddered, but was determined to continue. *It's going to take a while, but I can do it.* After a time he found the ends of some of the branches that had covered the opening, an encouragement just as his will was flagging.

Back at the farmhouse, the native family felt the vibrations. They were alarmed to see the surface of the hillside slipping—the hillside where their new friend had been exploring. A slide of fresh dirt cascaded from above. They tried to call for help, but the phone was out because of the quake. The lines were pretty primitive in that area, and they didn't have cell phones. They sent the eldest son out to get a message to Umayo and the police, but it took an hour to get word to them, then more time for Umayo to call Rescue, Amzi, and then the museum.

Night came, too soon.

Amzi and Lila arrived the next day after a grueling trip, Lila beside herself with grief and concern. No one had heard from AJ since the quake. It had been a small one, but enough to cause landslips in several places. Local people had been going over the hillside, but didn't know the exact location where AJ had been at the time, as none of them had been watching him just before the quake. Lila wanted desperately to go looking, herself, but Amzi persuaded her to let him go, telling her she could be more of a help by staying at the farmhouse, keeping up communications with the outside.

It began to rain.

After nearly two miserable rainy days, no one could find a trace of any of the cave openings that were said to be on the hillside, let alone a sign of any person, dead or alive. Lila hadn't slept or eaten at all. She felt dizzy, and had dark circles under her eyes. The farm family tried to make her comfortable. The sight of food gave her nausea.

Amzi sat with Lila, coaxing her to drink some coffee, but she couldn't stomach it. She sat huddled, staring, trying not to cry. They heard a knock at the door, and Amzi, since he was closest, went to see who it was.

A tall lump of human-shaped mud stood looking at them, blinking startlingly blue eyes. "What does it take to get a bath around here?" asked AJ.

Lila screamed. "AJ! You made it! How did you get out?" She ran and wrapped her arms around him, sobbing.

"Aw, Mom!" He hugged her. "Now YOU need a bath, too! I'm starving—got anything to eat?"

He had been digging for nearly two days. It took a lot of scrubbing to get all the mud off of him and out of his clothes. "This dinky little shovel saved my life," he said. "I think I'll have it gold-plated. I'm sure glad the entrance wasn't covered too deeply—boy, I nearly bought it that time." Then he grimaced. *Can't let on how scary that was. Mom looks really bad.*

Later, after a good meal, he told Amzi more details about his escape: "I nearly lost track of my shovel at first. I had left it near the entrance of the cave, and the slide partially covered it. Man, it was so dark! But I turned on the flashlight for a few seconds at a time, just to locate things and see where to dig. Had to dig in the dark, and around big rocks, hoping I was still going in the right direction. I wasn't sure how much dirt I'd have to get through before breaking out... but, heh! I didn't have anything else to do!"

AJ and his parents thanked the farm family and neighbors who had searched, and brought them special gifts in appreciation for their help. Then they went to AJ's room at the hotel and collapsed together. After another hearty meal in the room, they had time to talk. AJ told them about the pottery in the cave, and showed them the pictures he'd taken. The piece he'd put in his pocket had broken a bit, but he was still able to fit it together and show them the decorations on it. Some of them already looked familiar. They bent over the pictures and pieces on the table, moving them around, comparing one to another.

"I'll make drawings from these photos and this one piece," said AJ, "and compare them with the photos that I took of the murals. So many of them look somewhat similar to each other. I'm not showing everything to the archaeologists, though. We don't want them to see everything we find."

Later, AJ peeked out the window. "I wonder if it's safe to go out yet—I may have blown my cover. I lost my dark glasses and attracted too much attention with that little stunt."

"I'll contact Yachay and his friends," said Amzi, "and see if there's any talk going around. It might still be all right, but I wonder if any of the terrorists' informants saw your mother and me. We should all lie low for a couple of days."

AJ and his parents took some time to relax in their hotel room to regroup and plan what to do next. Lila pulled her hair back into a bun and wore her sunglasses to go out to a nearby store and buy two pairs of partially shaded glasses for AJ. "I don't want to hear of you losing them again," she pretended to scold him.

"Guess I still need my mom after all." AJ, laughing, gave her a hug and a kiss, and she rubbed his back.

These guys! Lila sighed with relief.

Yachay called to tell Amzi that no one in his network had heard anything specific about the Darrows being in Cuzco. "You may have caught them napping this time, but it still might be good to wait another day or two before going out. The aftermath of the earthquake has been a good distraction."

"We can use that time to plan and discuss things," said AJ. "I also want to examine my pictures of the pottery in the cave some more while you're here."

"Have you been able to study the murals yet?" asked Amzi.

"Not enough, but I took more pictures of them recently—I left them over at the museum. I did see a few similar symbols in some places. I'll send you copies to study, too, after you go home."

They pored over the pictures of the pottery and AJ's older collection of murals together. "Look at the cat's eye symbols," said AJ. "They remind me of the stonework on the houses and walls we saw at Kuelap. And so many of the other symbols on the pottery and the murals look alike, yet not quite—it's confusing, and tantalizing."

140

"Yes," said Amzi. "It could be, you know, just the difference in the particular artist, or slight changes in style over time. Maybe they even had different fonts, like we do in ours. Some of them look a bit like Donna Gerard's copies, too."

"I took all the college courses I could think of, and I've read all I could get my hands on," said AJ, "but I still feel so inadequate."

"Don't be discouraged, you'll figure it out—*we'll* figure it out," said Amzi.

Lila gave them each a back rub. "You two are exhausted, staying up so late." She had studied AJ's pictures, too, but they were too complicated for her. Graphology hadn't been a burning interest to her, so she hadn't tried to educate herself on these details. *I hope AJ won't have to stay too long in this place.*

Meanwhile, AJ showed them some more of his recent work. He had read about the important tactic the Incas used, their banishment of any writing systems of the mountain tribes, especially the one called quellqa. By destroying every bit of it they could find, they effectively prevented the conquered people from communication—and rebellion.

AJ read aloud to them from his paper: "The Incas substituted the quipu, a device consisting of knotted, colored strings, which was nearly impossible for anyone except official readers or interpreters, quipucamayoqs, to decipher. The quipu was used in conjunction with Inca memorizers, to supplement it when they had to send more complicated messages. Thus they had very tight control over their subjects.

"But there was one tribe that held out much longer than the others—the Chachapoyas. The Incas gave them that name, meaning 'White Warriors of the Clouds,' or 'Cloud People,' because they lived in the highest cloud-enveloped elevations of the Andes, and were ferocious in defending their settlements, highly trained and deadly accurate in the use of the sling. The Incas actually feared these warriors, who were ready to die rather than be enslaved. They partially conquered them after about 20 years, but even then, they feared the Chachapoyan shamans who were reputed shape-shifters, able to take on the form of wild animals and pronounce horrible curses. Their mummies were said to be able to rise up and inflict a horrific death upon anyone who disturbed them."

"I've found so much about them that's really mystifying," AJ commented, "It sounds as if they understood the value of psychological warfare, too. I'll bet they circulated those rumors."

Then he continued reading: "For centuries, since they'd been nearly wiped out and their writings obliterated, no one, even now, knows what the Chachapoyas had called *themselves*."

"That's something I'd really like to learn more about. I wonder if we could figure it out?"

"It seems that they were a peaceful people—most of the time they only wanted to be left alone—but they'd always exhibited an ingrained vigilance against attackers. Some researchers think the Chachapoyas were afraid of attack by the Wari tribe, who were pretty fierce in their own right—cannibals—but others say they think there was a much *older* fear—of what? Or of whom? Where had they come from? Why had they sought the highest, most inaccessible elevations, where they could look out and see any enemies coming, far in the distance? Did some horrible event in their ancient history make them that way?"

AJ, still reading from his paper, was getting excited. "They built fortresses on high ridges all over their territory. The entrances, instead of being wide, grandiose gateways, were tall, narrow passages, gradually pinching closer until only one person at a time could pass through. One huge fortress, Kuelap, on a high ridge overlooking a deep valley, was greatest of all, with walls up to 8 feet thick and 65 feet high. Inside, they built more than 400 circular stone houses with conical roofs. It is estimated that around 4,000 people may have inhabited it at one time.

The Spanish thought they'd seen the last of them in the 1500s. They wrote that the Chachapoyas were taller than most, white-skinned, with many blonde or red-haired people among them, very handsome, and gentle in nature. But diseases such as smallpox, to which they had no

142

immunity, were brought from Europe by the Spanish. It destroyed them, except for a few remaining survivors, who disappeared into the mountains to live in small, isolated settlements, effectively avoiding strangers."

"What do you think, Mom, Dad?"

Lila and Amzi had been sitting, listening intently to AJ expounding his latest discoveries, and it had reinforced their fascination with the Cloud Warriors. The three boys and Daisy had heard more and more details over the years, as their parents recounted their experiences from Peru. They knew that there were some mysteries, though, that were not spoken of. What did Lila and Amzi encounter there that was so secret, and why?

"Well, AJ," said Amzi. "You've done a great deal of research on them. I think you're on the right track. I'll tell you, though, I have a little trepidation about one thing. Though we do want to find out more about the Chachapoyas, I still want to reinforce something—that I'd like you to steer away from Atahuaqa for as long as possible. It has not yet been discovered by archaeologists or the general public, and whether or not it's connected to the Chachapoyas, there are plenty of other ruins and lost cities to explore. You know what I mean—when the public gets into it, there are consequences."

"I understand, Dad. It's important to protect Tica's and her ancestors' remains there. Yes, most of the Chachapoyan ruins and relics are up north, and there really is no reason for people to be poking around down south and finding Atahuaqa."

"Thank you for your understanding," said Amzi. "I think you're doing a great job. Keep us informed on your progress —your mom and I are certainly interested."

~*~*~*~*~*~*~

Chapter 19: Canaanites

Three days after AJ's escape from the cave, Amzi and Lila went home, dressed as tourists, Amzi in a subdued-tone Hawaiian shirt and sunglasses. He had let his beard and mustache grow for those few days, and walked stooped with a cane, to look like an older man—since he now had white hair—blending into the crowd.

AJ hoped to find some clues to new discoveries, and the Internet became an even more useful tool now. A few new articles were appearing online. There seemed to be a reawakening of interest in the Cloud Warriors' origins. He found differing theories and arguments, but no one had cracked the case—yet. To AJ, the different kinds of ancient writing seemed to have some connection with it.

He went back to the museum. They had their own facilities there for making high-definition photocopies and enlargements, making it easy for AJ to copy his pottery and mural photos for Amzi. He sent them off, then sat at his desk to do some museum work, his regular job. All was quiet, so after a while, he began to relax and get back into his primary research. He found a folder with notices updating research on the murals in 2001, with a comment that "Dr. Petersen feels there are more important new discoveries to study, and suggested that we shelve the study of the decorative writing for later consideration." *Did they ever come back to it? No newer dates on the notes. Good!*

Online, he studied again the charts and alphabets of early Greek, Hebrew, Phoenician, and other civilizations' writing. Several characters in different sets of letters were similar, some nearly identical to each other and to characters on the llama skin. At times he felt he was onto something, only to end the day feeling defeated. *What am I missing?*

He took some time off for a tour of Machu Picchu to clear his head, just to get away from the overload of information clogging his mind. But soon he was online again, searching for more articles and ideas. Another website about the Chachapoyas and the mysteries surrounding them had appeared recently. He could see that there still seemed to be two opposing theories of their origins. Some said they were quite sure that the tribe had come from elsewhere, even far away from the Americas. Researchers had devoted years of study to the subject, and suggested these people had come from the east—across the Atlantic, not the Pacific, ocean. But where? Europe? Ideas differed there, too.

In Brazil and Peru, local archaeologists exhibited deep mistrust of any theories of origins from the Old World. The researchers seemed to feel it would diminish the honor of the indigenous peoples to admit that the Chachapoyas were from Europe. It would somehow lessen appreciation of the cultural achievements of native tribes, as if they needed help from outside to create anything worthy of ethnic pride.

These writers resorted to ridicule, not real proof, vehement in their denial that anyone could have crossed the Atlantic in ancient times. They especially insisted the migrants couldn't possibly have made it up the Amazon River to Peru, even if the Atlantic crossing could somehow have been made. Ridiculous! Unthinkable! But AJ noticed that those in denial seemed to have more political reasons than scientific proofs, and wrote in an emotional and mocking style. *That doesn't fool me,* he thought. *To my mind, it sends up a red flag....*

Politics! Bah! I just want to know the truth. Could the Chachapoyas have come across the Atlantic? That would mean they had probably come from somewhere in Europe.

145

The "pro" articles gave as examples the trips of either Celts, Vikings, or Phoenicians, very early seafaring people. There had been numerous relics of ancient Vikings, and even their burial mounds, found in North America. The Phoenicians had a reputation, from long ago, as traders going all over the then-known world, even to Britain and almost the whole way around Africa. Could either Vikings or Phoenicians have reached South America by an Atlantic route?

AJ remembered seeing a documentary about Thor Heyerdahl, sailing a reed boat across the Atlantic from east to west, from Safi in Morocco to Barbados in the Caribbean—and in only 57 days.

Currents in the winds and ocean had accidentally carried other boats across. Was intentional migration possible? He looked at charts of ocean currents and winds. If seafarers started from Senegal or Sierra Leone, just south of the coast of Mauritania, a current could take them to the eastward bulge of South America—Brazil—an even shorter distance than Thor Heyerdahl's journey. It had happened, yes, accidentally. Did they understand, back then, about those currents? Back when? How long ago? Would they do it intentionally? Why?

He contacted his father with his questions. "Dad, I seem to have found something extraordinary about the origins of the Chachapoyas—where they came from. After you and Mom left, I went online and studied more that's been written about them. There seems to be a controversy about it—two opposing opinions."

"Oh? What did they say?"

"One side says they came from across the Atlantic, which would mean, I guess, somewhere in Europe. Kind of like Thor Heyerdahl—remember?"

"Yes, I remember that article in *National Geographic*. I think it was a reed boat. He went from somewhere in northern Africa to the Caribbean."

"Yes, that's it. But I was looking at maps. If they went from southern Mauritania to the easternmost bulge of Brazil, it would be an even shorter distance, and that's closer to the mouth of the Amazon. There's a current in the ocean there that could carry them west, and winds, too. I've studied

146

them. And I found ancient records of it happening accidentally. What do you think? And what people would they be? I've read of both Vikings and Phoenicians exploring in the Americas, and the Phoenicians, they say, went clear around Africa from Gibraltar—things like that."

"What was the other argument?"

"They didn't really offer any proof, just poo-pooed the idea, saying it was a ridiculous theory—that they would've had to migrate up the whole length of the Amazon River, and it would have been impossible."

"Okay, son, I need to tell you something. Remember when we all went to Cuzco, and your mom and I spent several days with Umayo at Atahuaqa?"

"Yeah, Dad, you never told us what you were doing there, but I figured it was another one of those secret things."

"I'm sorry, son, but Umayo didn't want us to talk about it, then. Maybe he'll be more forthcoming now, but you'll have to be careful. Anyway, he had asked me to help him move Tica's and Maupi's remains, because of the earthquake damage on the mountain. He had made sarcophagi like those up at Kuelap for them."

"What? Really? Where... how...? Ohhh, now I remember those pictures you and Mom were looking at in the brochure at Laymebamba... I didn't know how to connect it..."

"I know, it's pretty shocking. I helped him move them to a ledge at the back of the city, just below a wall overlooking a valley. Your mom was allowed to come along to witness it, because of her part in retrieving the pink emerald."

"Hmmm.... Okay, but how does that fit in with what we were talking about?"

"While we were there, we noticed pictures on a part of the wall. They showed ancient *ships!* We asked Umayo where the ships were from, and he said something like 'Kane-an-im.' To us, that sounded like 'Canaan.'"

"Dad.... "

"What, son?"

"Isn't Canaan another word for Phoenicia?"

147

"We thought of that, too. I wasn't sure what to make of it at the time. Then Umayo clammed up and didn't seem to want to talk about it, and you know how it is—you don't push Umayo! But I wanted to see if you came up with the same ideas. Sorry to keep it from you, but I thought you might find additional information, coming from a different angle."

"Hmmm," said AJ. "I would've liked to have known about that, but I do see why you did it. If you'd just told me straight out, I might not have looked up some of the sources I found. I'll look into it further and get back to you. I wonder if I could ask Umayo about that? Probably not. I sensed that reticence in him when I almost asked too much, you know, when I first met him."

"Yes," said Amzi, "there is something there that they are reluctant to discuss. Maybe it's just an ingrained attitude toward the 'outside' that makes them naturally that way. Please be careful. If we get too pushy, he might become angry and turn against us. He's been a good friend for a long time and I'd be really sad to see our relationship damaged."

"Is there anything else you haven't told me?"

"One thing. When your mother and I were looking at the ship pictures, and Umayo said 'Kane-an-im', he took off his hat, and said, 'You have seen.' His hair was snow white—I was shocked—couldn't remember if it had been, before that. I remembered it used to be reddish brown. Then later, we were so upset after Daisy's abduction that we didn't try to find out more."

"Oh, that's why you and Mom were talking about Umayo's hair at Leymebamba? Dad, I keep thinking about the Canaanites being seafarers—traders—and the name, "Phoenician," was given them by the Greeks.

"I know, son. Hard to wrap your mind around, isn't it?"

"Dad, do you think I could ever see those ships?"

"Well... you know, Daisy saw the wall, but it was a totally different circumstance, and she mostly noticed the sarcophagi, not the ships. Umayo didn't want her to talk about it except within our family, and you know she never liked talking about that time, anyway. You would have to be in a really close relationship with Umayo for him to trust you that much, I think. It was over twenty years before he told *us*. I don't think I could tell you how to get there by yourself, either. There are so many switchbacks and hidden passages, and the trail is purposely kept faint."

"Hmmm, I think I'd better not try," said AJ. "I nearly blew it already, asking too much too soon. If he knew (and I have a feeling he would) that I was sneaking around behind his back, he would be really angry. Okay, I need to look into some more information—see what's available."

"I'm glad you're so good at using the Internet," Amzi said. "I was never good at that type of thing—kinda wish I had learned, but at my age, it's pretty late to start. I think I'll just stick to email."

Early one morning, a couple of days later, AJ got a call from Umayo: "I have something for you."

"Oh? What..."

"Remember, when we were talking, I mentioned an Inca site? Come out today if you can, and I'll tell you about it."

AJ wolfed down a breakfast of humitas and fruit juice, and went to find Rafa. Umayo was waiting, as usual, by the beaten track in front of Vilcatambo. They began their usual walk up the road, where they could not be overheard.

"I have some information that we can give the archaeologists that will keep them busy for a time," Umayo said. "I know where an ancient Inca settlement is hidden. It's not big, but it will be an interesting 'find' for them. I am going to guide one of the young boys from the village here, to 'happen' onto it, and get a ride with me to Cuzco. He can tell them about it."

"That's a really good maneuver. It should keep them occupied away from Atahuaqa, and I can study into other things, meanwhile."

"Yes. Have you found anything significant yet?"

"I have. It seems that some people think the Chachapoyas came from the Atlantic, and up the Amazon to Peru. Others are adamant that it couldn't be possible. But the proof seems—"

"Ah, keep digging," Umayo said. "I'm sure you will find what you are looking for."

AJ looked at Umayo as they walked. *What does he know, and why doesn't he just tell me? Maybe he's like Dad, wanting me to come by the information by a circuitous route? Is it that important to learn it that way? Sometimes it's so frustrating; makes me feel dull-witted.*

AJ traveled back to Cuzco, puzzling things out in his mind. *Umayo seems confident that I'll be able to find what I'm looking for. I guess I must be on the right track.*

The next evening, Dr. Holcomb called AJ at his hotel. "Great news, Mr. McGuire. I think we have a new discovery! A young native boy has stumbled onto a site in the mountains. We're sending a party out soon to examine it."

"That's really exciting," said AJ. "Is it a pristine site, no meddling huaqueros?"

"As far as I know, only the young boy saw it, while chasing a runaway alpaca, he said. He knew it was something we would be interested in, and we gave him a small reward for telling us discreetly."

AJ could hear the delight in the older man's voice. *I almost feel guilty for leading him on like this. He's a good man—I just want to steer him a little to one side.*

"That's good. I'll be interested to hear what you find," said AJ. As he hung up, he smiled. *Umayo orchestrated that well. Now I'd better get busy....*

Reassembling the pictures, AJ studied the murals with more understanding. Then, after more searching on the Internet, AJ found another article. At a place in eastern Brazil, along a river called "Paraíba" was a rock with a sizeable area of mysterious incised symbols that looked like writing. It had actually been well-known to the local natives for hundreds of years, but with renewed interest, it was now spotlighted by researchers. It was on a big rock along the side of the river, and locally, it was called Pedra do Ingá, the Rock of Inga. Native legends told of large men with red beards making it. Attempts to decode the carvings had been made for decades, all unsuccessfully. The photos supplied with the article showed a tantalizing puzzle of pictographs and symbols, along with dots and lines. Some looked very much like the ones AJ had been studying, but others did not. *Were they all made by the same people?* The natives' name of the river, "Paraíba," it was said, meant "bad for boats." AJ studied maps of the area. The Paraíba flows down to the east coast of Brazil, ending about 1200 miles from the mouth of the Amazon.

Hmmm, AJ, musing, rubbed his chin. *Red beards? Large men? That sounds like Vikings....*

~*~*~*~*~*~*~

Chapter 20: Ancient Writings

AJ spent the next week searching the Internet and poring over all the books and articles he could find, and came up with only a few more items on the subject of the Chachapoyas, but nothing really new. One of them was a tongue-in-cheek theory about possible crossings from Africa over to the Caribbean, and didn't show much documentation. Another also agreed with the trans-Atlantic theory, but gave examples of authentic ancient records, and recent discoveries of artifacts much farther south, on the coast of Brazil, and inland, up the Amazon River.

Some of the finds were of Celtic origin, and others suggested Phoenician derivation. *I wonder what that means? thought AJ, I guess they were both explorers—but at the same time? At first I was thinking 'Viking,' but the Celts came first, and were probably exploring closer to the same time as the Phoenicians. What was I thinking? The Vikings came much later. What were Phoenicians doing in the Americas?—just exploring, or looking to colonize?*

He tried to organize his notes into a time line, but any recorded history of South America in ancient times was scanty at best, especially in the wild Amazon. How long would it have taken them to migrate up the Amazon to the Andes? Some researchers had ventured guesses, from a few years to nearly a thousand. Not many records existed on the conditions of travel in the Amazon at that time, except a recent discovery of an ancient shipyard along one tributary, containing artifacts made of Phoenician bronze. Some said they were planted—a hoax.

And the Earth is flat, thought AJ.

Continuing his search of the Internet, he came across something astounding. He found a site he'd somehow missed before. It reported a letter that had been written in the 16th century to the Portuguese King João III. It told of 300 Indians that had come up the Amazon in dugout canoes. They had escaped slavery from a Portuguese land owner at the mouth of the Amazon on the Atlantic coast, and had arrived at an important ancient trading crossroads in the south part of the Chachapoya region in the Andes of Peru.

AJ sat, staring at the screen. *They did it! They really did, and it didn't take hundreds of years—for those Indians. But for the emigrants - - did it? If they came from across the Atlantic, being from somewhere in Europe, they probably didn't know about the Andes, to keep going, hoping to reach them. These newcomers were probably just concentrating on escape—from whatever it was, maybe the Romans, as other writers have speculated—and in no hurry, once they found safety. Looking behind them, not ahead—who knows how long they took? The 300 Indians, being natives, probably knew of the mountains' existence, especially if they had once been part of an extensive trade network. So they might have intentionally headed there—kept going—in one long trip. What really happened? Did any other early records exist?* He continued his search, and found that the Conquistador, Francisco Orellana, had traveled eastward down the Amazon to the Atlantic from eastern Peru in 1542, in a brigantine the Spanish had built near the western end of the Amazon. He had with him 70 men. It took them eight months.

Orellana wrote that he had encountered well-organized Indian tribes. Some of them were warlike native women, who reminded him of the Amazons of Greek mythology. He was so impressed with them that he named the great waterway, "River of the Amazons." He reported also that he'd met light-skinned European-appearing natives in the middle of the Amazon region. *Celtic descendants? I wonder if Umayo would tell me anything about this. He seemed to intimate that I was on the right track. Maybe if I first ask him about the writing.....*

AJ called Umayo and asked to meet with him at Vilcatambo. Umayo seemed, as usual, to be anticipating his call. *Does he read my mind, or what?* thought AJ. He found Rafa, and they arrived at the village later that day. AJ met Umayo in the road outside the village entrance.

He stammered nervously, "Umayo, I... I seem to be bailing with a bottomless bucket here. I really need your advice and help. I just cannot figure out the messages on the murals. I have studied several kinds of ancient writing, even sounds to go with symbols, and there are some similarities, but not enough to tell me if I'm on the right track. And even if I figure that out, I've realized, I don't know the *language* to put with it—the *words*."

Umayo listened quietly as AJ went on about his difficulties. *The time is growing short. I feel sure now, he is the one.* "I will help you," he said.

AJ was taken aback. *That was easy*, he thought. He didn't know what to say. Then he realized he was standing there with his mouth open. "Oh... Well, thank you, I'd really appreciate it. I know I must seem too inquisitive, but I have been so frustrated, and I really want to understand why this seems to be something involving my family, and that there is something else important for some reason, but unseen. I don't want to pry into your privacy, yet I feel this need to understand because the messages seem to be pointed toward my father and our family, but I cannot figure out why."

Umayo studied AJ's face, gazing into his eyes with that dark, smoldering look. "I have known your father for many years, and he has always been trustworthy with those things that were revealed to him. I, too, feel there is a reason for his involvement, and I know he has raised his children to be respectful. I appreciate it, but I caution you, it is easy to overstep."

AJ lowered his gaze. *Oh, no—did I blow it again?*

"I can assist you. Let me see your research."

Feeling a little shaky, AJ went back to the car, and pulled out a briefcase bulging with papers and maps. He laid out some of them on the hood of the car. Briefly, he showed Umayo the copy of the llama skin, as well as charts, symbols and characters of various ancient civilizations' writings.

"You are overwhelmed by so many symbols," Umayo observed.

"Yes, you're right about that. I'm just trying to collect as much as I can, to see if anything rings a bell."

"Your people have a saying, about not seeing the forest for the trees?"

"Ha! That seems appropriate right now. What am I missing?"

"A few key things. Come. I have something to show you. Bring the llama skin copy."

AJ put his case back in the car, saving out the copy of the llama skin. They walked over to the village, and through the narrow front entrance. "I wouldn't want to risk the spy seeing you, but he is gone for the day," Umayo explained.

AJ felt excitement coursing up through his body. *I'm actually going to see inside the village!* He took special care not to gawk at everything, trying to walk purposefully. *Don't blow it*, he thought to himself. *Just be businesslike.* As they passed through the village wall, many small, round, stone houses, with conical thatched roofs, came into view. *I never would've thought about this before I read all those articles. It's like a miniature Kuelap.* He followed Umayo to one of the houses. Inside were several people.

"This is my wife, Brynna," said Umayo, gesturing toward a handsome woman. She had reddish blonde hair streaked with white at the temples. She looked quizzically at Umayo, but nodded a greeting. "This is Pacay, my son, and Aiden, his friend." He gestured again. "Gene McGuire, a trusted friend."

They were all unusually tall and fair-skinned, the two younger adults' hair were shades of blonde.

AJ inclined his head toward them, with a clumsy greeting. His heart was racing as he remembered hearing that people of some of these isolated villages were called

Gringuitos by the other tribes because of their light complexions and sometimes Nordic appearance. They were a curiosity to the Andeans, "Gringuito" meaning a little gringo, a foreigner, a term stemming from "gringo," used in Spain as early as the 18th century. "Nobody knows how they got here," said one researcher.

Brynna and the young men said something in Quechua and went outside, leaving Umayo and AJ alone.

"You asked what you were missing," said Umayo. "It helps to know some ancient stories and traditions that have been passed down by the historians of the tribe, and have *never been discovered* by the archaeologists and experts. Look here, and here..." He pointed to parts of the llama skin drawings that AJ had brought in with him. "If you know the right clues, it will reveal itself. The language you seek to understand is an ancient form of Quechua. The People—the Chachapoyas, and other tribes of the Andes, used a writing system derived from one called *quellqa*. It had been used for thousands of years, even before the People arrived, but it was banned and destroyed by the Incas, in order to subdue all the tribes under their rule."

"Yes!" AJ felt breathless. "I remember reading that the Incas did that. Wait—what? Are you saying that your tribe is Chachapoya? And your tribal name is 'The People?'"

He was stunned. *The Chachapoyas! Why ever did I take so long? I knew, but I couldn't believe it.* His head was swimming with too much information at once.

And the writing! "But what exactly was this quellqa? Was it successfully destroyed, or is there any of it existing today?"

"You can find it if you know what you are looking for. Different cities had slight variations in their styles of quellqa, but it was always necessary to make it very decorative, with flowers and pictures, to be sure that no Inca would recognize it as writing if they happened to see it. The penalty was death if any were caught using it, so it was only used on walls of secret locations, and camouflaged to look like decorations."

He pointed to the llama skin characters. "As you know, this message was found in the women's rooms in

156

Atahuaqa, where no men were allowed. Tica knew of it. The story of our people and the secret of the pink stone was shown to her there, and being warned in a dream, she used the stone in her escape from evil priests. That was the night Atahuaqa was invaded by the Incas. Later, Tica and her assistant, Maupi, were killed—buried alive—as they hid in a cave during an earthquake, and their bodies had been hidden there ever since."

How does he know all this? thought AJ excitedly. *And what else does he know?*

"Your mother and father helped me move Tica's remains to a proper place at Atahuaqa last year when all of you came to Peru." He looked down for a moment. "I'm sorry your sister went through such suffering."

"Thank you. My sister is fine now." A shiver went over AJ, as he remembered being trapped in a cave, too. "Hmmm, my folks didn't tell us how they were helping you. I assumed it was not my business at the time," said AJ.

"I appreciate your respect. But I think you can know more, now. I just had to be sure, but you have shown discretion in your activities here."

"So there was an Inca attack, and later an earthquake?"

"Yes, and their remains were safe until the nortéamericano Gerard and his wife took the emeralds. It was a pain to Tica's spirit all those years, waiting for the halves of the special stone to be reunited and returned. Finally, circumstances were in place, and your father was chosen to bring it all about. Then, the recent earthquakes made the ground unstable at the cave-in site, so we had to move Tica's and Maupi's remains."

AJ trembled, as if an ancient vibration were coursing through his very bones.

"So! Let us see what we need to do," said Umayo. "since you are to help bring a conclusion to this matter."

"One thing I would like to understand," said AJ, "is, how did those murals predict the return of the pink emerald, and even the mode of escape of my family—in 1993? Is there some kind of prophecy or time-travel involved? It seems unbelievable and amazing."

157

"You nortéamericanos," Umayo tossed him an amused glance, "are always dumbfounded at the magical things that happen here. We are used to it. But, putting that aside, just try to, as you say, suspend your disbelief. Yes, there is time-travel involved. It is a talent passed down from the ancient holy man who gave Tica's ancestress the stone. She had saved his life, and it was a token of gratitude."

"You know that story, too?" AJ exclaimed. "Oops, I mean, of course you know! It sounds like a wonderful story." *Calm down, you're getting giddy.*

Umayo smiled again. "Yes, maybe some day I will tell you more, but right now we are losing sight of our objective for today."

"Oh. Yes, that's true. Uh, where were we?" AJ's mind was doing loops.

"Your next step, I think. " Umayo turned to look across the room. "You wanted to understand the messages, and find the origin of our people."

"I would appreciate so much, any help you can give me," said AJ, humbly.

"I have something here that you will find interesting." Umayo bent over a small trunk. He removed an ancient-looking cloth that covered the top, and lifted the lid.

AJ stifled a gasp.

~*~*~*~*~*~*~

Chapter 21: Tanitay and Time Travel

157 AD – Tanitay, eager to become a historian for the tribe, arose early the next morning after her talk with Andoti, to bathe and ready herself for her interview with the Chief Shaman at the temple. She dressed in a simple brown woolen tunic, with a necklace of small emerald beads, and pulled her long golden hair into a braid down her back.

Her mother hugged her and smiled proudly. "You will do well, daughter," she said.

Tanitay and her mother made their way through the misty streets of Ayatambo, between the round houses. The pathways were bordered by low walls built of stones arranged in a cat's eye design—long, narrow stones arranged in a diamond shape with a center stone prominent in the middle, set within the simple rock background pattern.

The temple loomed in the distance. Feeling a little shaky as she left her mother, she walked to the entrance, where Andoti waited to escort her. They entered, and listening to the minor strains of someone playing a panpipe, walked down one of the shadowy corridors, lit only by small oil lamps in niches.

Andoti showed her the way to the Chief Shaman's reception chamber.

"Welcome, young Tanitay," said Ake, "You have come at an early hour, a good sign of devotion and reliability."

Tanitay shivered, partly because of the cold, but this was a stressful experience, too. "Thank you, Great One," she said, bowing her head. "I have brought an offering of lúcuma fruit. I hope I might be allowed to serve the tribe in keeping the Memories."

Ake invited her to sit on a padded bench near the fire, and asked her some questions about her life, her desire to be a historian, her love for her people and her home. He showed her a kind of writing, called quellqa, that was being used in the Andes, and had been in use for thousands of years among the scattered tribes, long before the arrival of the People.

"It's very beautiful and interesting," said Tanitay. "I knew the memories were kept in the historians' minds, and passed on to the younger generations that way, but I've never seen this, this ... quellqa ...before. How does it keep the memories?"

"We find it very useful. We still recount the memories in speaking among ourselves, but we have trained people called scribes, too. They use paint and brushes to set down the memories onto smooth cotton cloth, and on wall paintings to be hidden for future generations if anything happens to silence the historians' voices."

He showed her a room where the scribes were at work, and unrolled a length of painted cloth for her to see. "This is one way of keeping the memories. If you learn to make characters, or letters, you will then learn to put them together to make words, then stories. Soon when you look at them, they will speak to you in your mind. You can choose which kind of historian you'd like to be, by memorizing or by writing," he said. "Or, if you are deemed an artist, you might learn to paint our stories on walls. I want you to go home and think about it, and come to see me in two days' time."

Two days later, Tanitay again readied herself for an important day.

Her mother made up a snack of fruit and goat cheese for her to take along, a little parting gift, knowing she might not be back for a while. She hugged her daughter one last time. "Come visit us when you can." She allowed herself a few tears only after Tanitay had started off down the path. *It is a good thing,* she thought, *and we still have her brothers and sister with us.*

Tanitay presented herself at the temple entrance, and was shown in. She knew the way this time, but her legs felt shaky, going down the cold torch-lit corridor. Ake smiled as she entered. He led her to a large room where some boys were sitting on mats at low wooden tables, getting ready for their lessons. She found an empty mat and slid into place.

Tanitay had decided to learn the quellqa writing, and was given some large dried leaves of the jabillo tree, used for practice work with small brushes and dark ink. The brushes were made of animal hair inserted and glued into the tips of the feathers of large birds like condors or parrots. She glanced nervously around, and the boys looked at her with curiosity. She was the only girl, but no one said anything. *I'll just do what they do, she thought. Maybe they will get used to me.*

An elderly man walked to the front of the room. All the students, including Tanitay, rose and inclined their heads respectfully, then sat down again.

"Greetings, young ones," said the man. "I see we have a new learner. What is your name, please?"

"T-T-Tanitay," she mumbled. She could feel her face reddening.

"Greetings, Tanitay," said the man. "I am Breckin. You are welcome to study with us." He looked sharply at the boys. "You will help the new learner, if needed."

"Now, we are looking at a new symbol in our system of characters." He went on to show how to draw a vertical zigzag line, using a thin, smooth board with a rabbit hair brush dipped in a thin black paint, and made it very large so all could see. He hissed the sound "s," associated with the letter, which looked like a snake, and said the character could also be used for the word, "amaru." He propped the board at the front where everyone could see it, and walked slowly toward the back, observing the students.

Tanitay watched what the boys did, and imitated their actions as they dipped their brushes and made small

161

imitations of the large picture. She saw that they made rows of the symbol, practicing to get it just right. She made a shaky one on the first try, then became less nervous as she learned to handle the brush, and worked more smoothly.

"Very good, young Tanitay," said a voice behind her. Breckin had been moving silently about the room, checking everyone's progress. "You may take another leaf now, to learn the letter we worked on yesterday." He had brought a small flat piece of wood with a different symbol on it. "This is the symbol for the sound, 'ka'...." It looked like a little tree with three branches pointing upward.

Soon Tanitay had caught up with the class, and was developing a beautiful style in her own writing.

She was given a sleeping pallet in the women's quarters of the temple, since she was the only girl in the writing class at this time. The boys were bunked in a large room elsewhere. She already knew some of the girls, as they had grown up together in the village. These girls were in training to become priestesses. The children of the People lived with their own families until they were ready to choose their future occupation. Any who chose to follow his or her parent's occupation stayed home to be taught by their mother or father until adulthood. Others were sent to live where they would be taught their new vocation.

After a week at classes, Tanitay was adapting well and knew her way around the schooling area of the temple. She had made friends, and began to feel comfortable in the daily routines. One day at mid-day mealtime, she went outside to eat her kinwa cakes, hummus, and a tumbo fruit. As she sat on a large stone overlooking the valley, a boy from another class came to sit nearby.

"Hello, my name is Qircamo. I'm learning to paint, and some day I'll show our history on the walls." He unwrapped his lunch.

"I'm Tanitay. I'm learning the writing."

"I saw you in the class. Do you like doing the letters?"

"Yes, I'm studying to be a historian. I want to set down the stories of the People, so they will never be lost."

"I do, too. It's a good feeling to make pictures of things that happened long ago. When I make the paintings, it makes me feel as if I'm there, watching it happen."

"It's important that the stories live on," said Tanitay, "even after we are gone. It's like talking to our descendants, far into the future."

"Have you heard that some of our shamans can go there?"

"Go - - where?"

"The future. Maybe it's a vision. Or, I wonder, do they really go there?" Qircamo got a faraway look in his eyes as he sat there. He had forgotten to eat.

"Yes, I heard whispers about it. I don't know how they do it - - if they really do."

They sat, musing, for a while. Then it was time to get back to their lessons.

As time went on, Tanitay found that Qircamo was growing obsessed with the idea of time-travel. He spent hours listening at the fireside of the elders as they discussed healing herbs and other interesting activities from their own work. Time travel was sometimes brought up in hushed tones, yet Qircamo was able to squirm near enough in the dark without being noticed, to hear what they were saying. He learned that they used certain leaves, seeds and roots as potions to bring dreams and visions that were like actually going to a different place and time.

"Tanitay," he said one day, "I think I will soon be ready to try it."

"You mustn't try such a dangerous thing by yourself," she told him. "I'm afraid. If you do the wrong thing, it could bring great evil, maybe death."

"I won't try it until I am sure, but I have heard them tell their experiences so many times, I think I know how. Already I have secretly tried some of the healing herbs they mentioned, on myself and my animals at home, and they work very well."

"But it could be really dangerous. What if something goes wrong?"

"That's why I'd like you to be with me when I do it. Just in case I need your help."

"But Qircamo –"

"You are the only one I trust."

One night, when Tanitay was cleaning up her area after the evening meal, she heard a "Hsst!" from the dark doorway.

It was Qircamo. He called Tanitay out to the garden, away from the main temple. "I want you to help me try this," he held up a small bag. "I have seeds of kakawi, some special herbs, and the dried red pods of a ruqutu plant. I am going to burn them in a brazier and breathe in the smoke. This is what the shamans do in a healing ritual," he whispered. "But they also use it for time-travel. I heard them talking again last night."

"Qircamo! I'm scared. I don't think you should do this."

But Qircamo was determined. He struck sparks from a flint into some dried moss tinder and kindling, and soon had a small fire going under the little brazier. He crushed the dried seeds and pods in a bowl. After mixing them with the herbs, he carefully put some in the brazier, a little at a time. A thin string of smoke began to spiral upward.

Tanitay sat across from him, the little flame flickering light on her face. "Qircamo, be careful," she said. *Maybe I should stop him, or run and tell someone. Or should I? Is it that bad a thing?* She tussled with her feelings. She liked Qircamo, and didn't want to get him in trouble.

He looked across the fire and smoke at her. His eyes betrayed a little fear, but he was still determined to go ahead with it. He leaned forward and moved the smoke toward his face with a fan he'd made of parrot feathers. He breathed in....

Tanitay didn't even realize she was holding her breath. She watched in fascination as his eyes took on a dreamy look.

He sat, staring, his eyes not focusing near or far. Then his gaze began to move—he seemed to be watching something, looking right through her. His eyes widened, and he sucked in his breath sharply.

164

"Stop!" yelled Tanitay. She kicked the fire, and it went out. A little smoke still rose, but she blew it away.

Qircamo froze, then seemed to awaken. He blinked, looking around as if trying to see something he'd been watching, then shaking his head because it wasn't there anymore. "What happened? Did you do that? Why?"

"You frightened me! I'm sorry. But you looked scary, as if you were watching something that wasn't there!"

"I was. I saw men in shiny metal clothes, riding on big animals like dogs. It was weird, but I didn't feel afraid, really. I wish I could have watched longer."

"I'm sorry," Tanitay said again. "It was just too scary for me to see you that way. Maybe you should get someone else to help you."

"No, Tanitay. I trust you, and no one else. I'll quit for this time, but I do want to try it again soon. I promise I will talk to one of the men, though." He cleaned up the debris from the little fire, and picked up his brazier and materials. "You believe I did see something, don't you?"

"Yes, but ...should you? Isn't it forbidden?"

"No one has told me not to, but they don't know how much I've heard. It's all right, I'll think about it."

Qircamo did talk to one of the older shamans, admitting that he had tried the more advanced methods of using healing herbs, with good success. He then confessed that he had attempted the methods for time travel that he'd heard about, and that he'd had a vision of men in shiny metal clothes and hats. They were riding on big beasts. He'd never seen animals like that before, so he called them dogs.

He asked forgiveness, and stressed that he only did it because of his strong desire to become a shaman and help his people. He was taken before the council, and an intense session of questioning followed. After a long discussion, the council decided that he had a special talent that should be recognized, and he should be given further instruction.

He took Tanitay aside the next day. "I am to be trained for special duties," he said excitedly. "I explained to them about my vision, and they think I have a stronger spiritual connection than most. No one else has seen the vision of the men riding dogs, and they want me to paint my visions."

Tanitay was more relieved than excited. She had been worried that he would be shunned by the tribe, or even executed.

Several months later, Amancay, the wife of the chief shaman, Husiy, became dangerously ill, and none of the medicine men could do anything to bring her out of it. She had gone into a deep sleep for several days.

Husiy decided to try one more thing. "Call Qircamo."

Now, Qircamo felt uneasy. *How can I help Amancay if no one else can?* He looked over all his collection of herbs. *Do I have anything that the others haven't tried? What to do?* He felt a heavy weight of responsibility—this was important, and frightening. He went into the jungle to sit in his special place for meditation, and built a small fire to burn some herbs, inhaling the smoke and taking on a trance-like state. He saw *chacruna*, an herb that had been tested before as a tea, but not in very strong doses, as it seemed to bring a person close to death. *Should I try it? She is asleep, but still breathing, so instead of a drink, I'll need to make it into smoke to breathe in.* He meditated again, and the answer came to him. *Try it.*

He gathered dry leaves of the herb in the nearby jungle, crushing them a little in his mortar and pestle, and brought them with his brazier to Amancay's bedside. She was still unconscious. He didn't tell the others what herb he had. He made a small fire and soon had a little smoke curling up, which he slowly fanned over the woman's face as she lay motionless.

After she took about ten breaths, her eyelashes flickered. A few more, and she opened her eyes, then sat up and looked around. She was weak, but had no more fever.

Husiy sat, sorrowing, dreading to hear the news that his wife was gone. A young girl came, smiling, to tell him to come. His heart was fluttering with apprehension as he entered the hut, and he nearly fainted to see his beloved wife, sitting up and drinking a rejuvenating tea that Qircamo had brewed for her. Husiy showered Qircamo with gifts, and raised him in rank that very day.

166

Over the years, Qircamo's knowledge and talents grew, and he became a great holy man of the tribe, and his wife, Tanitay, helped record his visions on the temple walls, developing a beautiful ornamental style of quellqa that looked like decoration, framing the pictures he painted of the sights he'd seen. They passed these talents on to their children.

Tanitay also became a great tribal historian in her own right, recording in her special style of quellqa, on rolled lengths of cotton fabric, the oral stories that had been told for generations: stories of Akbar and Tanith, Anat and Ewan, Ysabel and Eppo, and many others. She often sat and dreamed about the Great Migration from sunny lands across the Sea of Darkness, and adventures of the People along the Great River.

Chapter 22: Traitors at Kuelap

In the year 1223 AD, the great fortress city of Kuelap was well advanced, but additions and reinforcements were always under construction. The main wall was gargantuan, 65 feet high in some places, 10-20 feet thick, made of worked-stone rectangular blocks, closely fitted by the highly skilled stoneworkers. The entrances, one on the west side and two on the east side, were tall and narrow, with corridors decreasing in width as they penetrated into the wall, until only one person at a time could enter. This was a characteristic of their ancestors' walled Celtiberian cities in northern Iberia, traditions preserved for generations by their tribal historians.

Behind the walls lay a community of hundreds of small, round, stone houses with conical thatched roofs, built on raised foundations, the familiar hallmark of the People. Each house had its own water and drainage system connected to an overall network of channels from mountain springs. Every family kept their own homes clean and presentable and their beloved ancestors safely tucked into the walls or under the floors. Some ancestors were placed in caves on high bluffs. The most highly venerated leaders, whose remains were interred in upright, painted sarcophagi, were placed on high ledges, a place of honor. These were set near the city, facing east, keeping watch as they looked down on the Utcubamba Valley.

The practice of interment was done according to the historians' records from the time of the old sunny lands of hundreds of years before, with the mummified bodies bound in a fetal position, inside caves, houses or sarcophagi. The Celts had practiced cremation back in Iberia, keeping the ashes in ceramic urns, which were also interred in caves. But the indigenous people of the Andes were horrified by the thought of cremation, and to mollify their anger, the Celtiberians took on the practices of their partner tribe, the Kena'anim.

Rapau, great Chief Shaman of the People, a distant descendant of Tanitay and Qircamo, walked along the edge of the wall, looking down through the mist at the Utcubamba River, winding through the valley. Condors circled out across the sky at the same level as the wall, sailing in and out of the clouds. Rapau was troubled. New priests from somewhere across the gorge had arrived recently. They had claimed to have superior new ideas, questioned Kuelap's time-honored traditions, and thus disrupted the tranquility of the community.

In recent years, a new tribe, the Incas, had arisen in the south, growing by subjugating the leadership of other indigenous tribes, insinuating their way in, or conquering some by straight-on attacks. The Incas had become feared enemies in the Andes. They had tried several times to overcome the People, but superior skills with the sling, passed on down the ages from the ancient Celtiberians and Balearic soldiers, had forced them back. The Incas called the People "Warriors of the Clouds," or "Chachapoyas."

The Cloud Warriors did not fear death, and were so ferocious that the Incas feared them. And the Cloud Warriors let the rumors circulate that their mummies, if disturbed, could cast horrible spells worse than any death.

Kuelap was a thriving city, having grown from a colony planted many years before, from settlements like Ayatambo, after they grew too large to be supported by their surrounding farms. There were other settlements on high ridges all around the extensive Chachapoya region, but none as large as Kuelap. Rapau had been thinking that sometime in the near future, another band of colonists should be sent out from Kuelap, to found a new village.

But now these troublemakers had come. They looked and dressed like Chachapoyan priests, in cotton tunics, colorfully embroidered on the edges. At first they seemed to fit in and were accepted by the population, but after a few months they began to propose new ideas, and challenged some of the old leaders. The People had always sought peace and valued privacy, but they were not pushovers when bullied. Would there be trouble?

The new shamans, Akuchi, Umaq, and Tupa, asked for a meeting of the People. "We will remedy the problems of the residents of Kuelap," exclaimed Akuchi, speaking before an assembly one day. "Our magic is strong, and our healing power comes from Inti, the Sun." The People knew that Inti, the Sun God, was the god of the Incas. Were these men true Chachapoyas? Had they actually come from a faraway Chachapoyan city, as they'd claimed?

"Traitors! Enemies!" came a voice from the crowd. An elderly man, Alliyma, stepped forward. "Akuchi—you are trying to weaken us by undermining our way of life!" He stood defiantly at the front of the crowd. "You are not fooling us. We know Inti is the god of the Incas. We rely on the healing power of Pachamama, the Earth Mother, through Yorano, our powerful shaman. Let us continue in peace, and allow our people to grow old without being confused by a new way."

Llipya, the leader of the suburb, South Kuelap, stood. The citizens took one step back, bowing slightly. "I am in favor of the new way," he said. "If someone wants to try it, let them. And let the leaders receive their just due."

Yorano, standing near the front of the audience, glared at Llipya.

"I will prove our great power," said Akuchi. "I have here a walking stick. See what my magic can do." He threw it down, and it became a snake, hissing loudly, its tongue whizzing out of its mouth as it glided like liquid toward

Yorano. The crowd gave multiple cries of alarm as they shrank away in horror.

Yorano jumped back, but threw down his own rod, and it became a snake, too. It hissed at the first serpent, which turned away, slithering back to Akuchi. Yorano's snake followed, catching the other one by the tip of its tail, and bit off a hand's length, gulping it down and hissing.

The crowd gave a collective gasp. Akuchi grabbed his snake and it became a walking stick once more—but a hand shorter.

"Evil! Evil magic!" shouted Akuchi. "Take that man away!"

Confused temple guards hesitated, then dragged Yorano away through the throng. Since Llipya didn't counter the order, they were not sure whom to obey. Yorano was still glaring back at Akuchi as he and the guards disappeared into the temple, his snake following.

Llipya and Akuchi paused, looking around nervously. "We must take immediate action," growled Akuchi under his breath. "This Yorano is too powerful with his *evil* magic." He gave Llipya a significant look that seemed to have meaning.

"Please, Akuchi, do not give cause for an uprising. Yorano is well-loved by the People, and his magic has always been used to help the sick and troubled," pleaded Llipya lamely. Llipya was usually a good leader in most respects, highly regarded because of his rank, but he became faint-hearted when challenged by this new show of aggression.

One who observed among the audience was a young priestess, Aife. She had been watching the new priests and had heard them privately talking among themselves of subversive plans. *Yorano is in great danger*, she thought. *He is too outspoken. We need to find a better way around this situation.* She had special feelings for Yorano, and knew he had stronger magic than most—she had sensed from the beginning that the new priests were jealous and anxious to get rid of him. *What are they going to do to him?* She couldn't sleep that night.

The next day, Aife observed Llipya sporting a new white tunic and a distinctively designed gold chain around his neck. *Where, I wonder, did those come from?* she thought suspiciously. Being a priestess, she was able to find the room in the temple where Yorano was being held, and bribed the guard to let her in.

"Aife! What are you doing here?" whispered Yorano. "You will bring great trouble on yourself and your family."

"We must talk," she said. "*You* are the one in great danger. Llipya could have you executed. Akuchi and his friends would love nothing more!"

"I know, you're right." He sat on the ground. "But I couldn't let them introduce sun worship—Inca worship! The Incas are becoming powerful and threatening. It would be the beginning of the end for Kuelap and our freedom. We must do something."

"I will go to see Rapau, the chief of all our shamans. Maybe he can give us an answer. I don't think he approves of these interlopers either." She thanked the guard and slipped out through the dark passages.

Aife ran as quickly and quietly as she could, taking a zigzag path through the shadowy back streets, almost the whole length of Kuelap, to keep from being seen heading for the chief shaman's house. Breathing hard, she rapped a bronze rod on the hollow piece of wood at Rapau's door.

"Around here," someone said. Rapau was sitting in his prayer garden at the side of the house. He was fanning a twirl of smoke from a small fire, to inhale it.

Aife bowed, and, still puffing, took the seat Rapau indicated.

"What is happening?" asked Rapau. "You are very upset."

"Great one," she began, still breathing hard, and told him what had happened.

He was not surprised. "I have been thinking, and praying for an answer," he said, shaking his head. "I knew these men were trouble when I first saw them. I suspect that they were sent by our enemies, the Incas, who are beginning to grow in power. I have sent a spy to collect

172

information as to where they actually came from, but he hasn't returned. These Incas were a smaller tribe, but they have developed schemes to gain access to leadership among the unsuspecting. We must not let it happen here."

Aife was relieved to hear that he was already aware of something subversive going on. But what could they do? Rapau instructed her to go home and wait. An answer would come.

She went home, but when she could, she stealthily followed Akuchi and the others, to see what they might be up to. Sometimes she could hear what they said:

"We must get rid of this Yorano," said Umaq. "He is the only one who is really blocking our way."

"But the People love him," said Tupa. "We have to be careful. We don't want to make him look like a hero, and turn everyone against us."

"I have an idea," said Akuchi. "Umaq, can you catch a poisonous snake, and a harmless one that looks like it? We will see if Yorano can withstand a bite, to demonstrate his power." He winked, and Umaq nodded. He knew the old trick.

A few days later, Akuchi again called a meeting of the People, and had Yorano brought forward. "We are willing to compare magical abilities with Yorano," said Umaq, "In a test to see who has the real power, Pachamama, or Inti." He had Yorano taken up onto the higher staging area, so everyone could see.

"We have here a poisonous snake," Umaq said, as the crowd moaned. He opened a large clay jar, and took out of it a large snake, but unbeknown to the crowd, it was a harmless look-alike species. He handled it gingerly, and let it bite him, to no effect. "See, it cannot harm me."

"Now," said Akuchi, stepping forward, "Let Yorano try." Akuchi, too, produced a large clay jar, took off the lid and tipped it, stepping back carefully as another snake, that looked almost like the first one, slithered out toward Yorano.

The crowd gasped.

Yorano took a deep breath, and bent to pick it up. He quickly grasped it behind its head, but it wrapped around his arm and managed to bite him. He staggered back a step.

A collective moan went up from the crowd.

Then Yorano held the snake high in the air. He walked, eyes blazing, toward Akuchi, who was still holding the jar, horrified, looking as if he were about to faint. Then Yorano stuffed the snake head-first back into the jar. "Take this thing away from here," he said, and walked out through the crowd.

The People were silent, watching him go. Then they turned back to Akuchi. "You have proven nothing," said the elderly man, Alliyma.

"You have not heard the last of this," said Akuchi.

A month went by. Yorano was allowed to go back to his place in the temple, but he knew Akuchi and his henchmen would try to think of something else. He sat with Aife at his hearth, discussing possibilities as they roasted suri grubs on long sticks over the fire.

"I thank you every day, Aife, for your help. If you hadn't heard their plans about the snakes, we wouldn't have procured the right herbs for me to take for the antidote."

"And you would be dead now," she said, "but it may yet happen. I can't go everywhere they do, so I don't know what next to expect. I have kept Rapau informed of what I've heard."

"I think we need to leave," said Yorano. "There is need, I know, for a willing group of colonists to found a new settlement. We could take our friends with us."

"Do you think we should? I hate to leave Kuelap in danger of enemy priests gaining control, bringing in their sun-worship. What is next—human sacrifice?"

"Rapau is still the great leader over all, and I have confidence he will be able to defeat these interlopers, now that he knows what they are up to. We can wait a little longer, but I think there will be another confrontation soon. It may be more violent, or it may be something devious, something to undermine the People's respect of our leadership." He put his hand on hers. "I am thankful for your help, Aife. Something will happen soon."

Aife followed the priests discreetly to a meeting place one day, listening as they talked among themselves. What she heard chilled her blood. They were planning to accuse Yorano of plotting against Rapau, an offense resulting in public execution in a painful and humiliating manner—by the Inca method of impaling. They were discussing ideas, but hadn't decided all the details as yet.

Aife ran and prostrated herself in front of Rapau, telling him what she had heard, and of her plan to gather a group of families who had already been talking of leaving, to plant a new community. Many of those who opposed fighting the new ways could go, and Yorano would be safe. This would relieve both the overcrowding and some of the conflict at once. It would give the rest of the People more time to regroup and resist the evil ones.

"I will consider your plan," said Rapau. "I do want to avoid bloodshed if I can. I harbor no ill will towards Yorano, but he is as adamant and outspoken as Akuchi, and Llipya is no help. It might be the only way. Go, and gather your friends."

The next day, Aife picked her way cautiously from house to house, talking to all those who she knew might be willing to pull up their households and migrate to a new location. Several large families had been worried about what was happening in Kuelap, and were ready to go if asked. In a secret meeting, leaders of the new group discussed their plans and made sure to include people with a good variety of skills among them, for a new start.

They had a llama caravan ready to depart in a few days.

~*~*~*~*~*~*~

Chapter 23: AJ's Mission to the Amazon

Umayo reached into the trunk. AJ could see several things inside, wrapped in embroidered cloth. Some might have been boxes, but others were shapes not immediately identifiable, possibly ceramics. Umayo picked out one, and unwrapped it carefully. It was an old-style piece of pottery—intact, unmarred, beautiful. Decorated with spirals and cat's-eye designs, it had stylized snakes around the rim—and some of the characters that Umayo had pointed out on the Llama skin. He turned it to display a painting of an ancient sailing ship with many oars and a horse's head at the prow. He turned it again, showing, on the opposite side, a ship displaying a Celtic dragon figurehead.

"This may be one answer you are looking for, young AJ. You have been wondering if the stories were true. Yes, the People came across the Sea of Atlantis, and migrated up the Great River, the one you call Amazon."

AJ couldn't speak for a minute. His knees felt rubbery. He looked around quickly for a place to sit down, finding a low stool. "One of them looks like a Phoenician ship," he said finally, "but the other looks - - is it Celtic? How old is that piece?"

"Oh, it's very old." Umayo turned it lovingly in his hands. "It has been in the family for hundreds of years. It was made so that we would not forget." He seemed far away in his thoughts.

"It's beautiful," said AJ. "Could I take a picture of it? I understand, if you'd rather I didn't."

"Maybe, at another time." Umayo wrapped it up again. "I'm not quite ready for that. I want to help you, but it has been kept away from the outside world for so long. You know what I mean, I think." He returned the small pot to the trunk and closed the lid.

"Certainly, Umayo, I understand. But why - - is there a reason you wanted me to see this particular piece?"

"I want you to do something for me."

AJ returned to Cuzco with his head abuzz. So many things were circling in his brain, he felt his head would explode. Umayo had asked him to look for something—in the Amazon.

When Umayo had suddenly seemed to shift from his attitude of suspicion and wariness to one of cooperation, AJ had been taken by surprise. He had an incredible mission now, to find an ancient artifact in the Amazon. *It might as well be an arrowhead in Central Park,* he chuckled to himself incredulously—he was to go to Brazil, to that ancient Phoenician shipyard he'd read about, and find a bronze axe head. The thought of it made his heart flutter in his chest.

He called Amzi at Spurwink, using a pay phone that wouldn't be bugged. "Dad, you'll never guess where I'm going now."

"What? Where?"

"Brazil. Umayo asked me to go to Brazil, somewhere near the Amazon River, to find something for him. Remember I told you about the ancient shipyard discovered recently? It had Phoenician bronze bolts and nails, in petrified wood. Umayo thinks there's a bronze axe head there. How could he know that?"

"AJ, you know I've always said I didn't question the way of the Ancients—and I find that Umayo has a connection beyond the parameters of the modern world."

"I noticed that, Dad. When I went out there to talk with him again, he actually brought me into his house! I told him

177

what I had found, but couldn't figure it out, you know. He had a piece of pottery there, like those pieces I found in the cave, only it was intact, like new. And it had a painting of a *ship* on each side. One was an old Phoenician ship and the other looked like one of those dragon-headed Celtic ships—he said it was made so that the People would never forget. Dad—this proves what the articles said is true!

"But since he showed me that much, I think he feels I owe him a favor, too. So he asked me to find this axe—how in the world am I going to do that?"

"AJ, I think the only way to find out is to *go there*. Just start, and I think somehow you will be shown the way. Don't ask me how I know—things just happen in South America."

"He said something like that to me, Dad. He said magical things happen here, and they're just used to it, as if it's commonplace."

"All I can say is - - go with it, AJ. If Umayo thinks you can, then he probably knows."

"Hmmm, okay. I feel like I'm floating where I can't touch bottom, but I'll look up everything I can about the area, and hope I can find my way by asking the locals, once I get close."

AJ stayed up late that night in his hotel room, looking up everything he could find about archaeological discoveries in the Amazon, most especially re-reading the one he'd already seen about the ancient shipyard. He studied the description of the general location, and downloaded a map of the area. The article didn't give an exact list of artifacts found, but it was an ongoing study, and visiting researchers could obtain permission to observe. There was a mention of bronze nails and bolts, but no axe.

Finally, by 2 a.m., he felt he was as ready as he would ever be. He went to bed and endured a few hours of restless sleep and wild dreams. Some things seemed to make sense until he woke up, and then they seemed ridiculous. He finally gave up and took a cold shower, then contacted Dr. Holcomb when the museum opened in the morning, explaining that he had to take some time off to explore a possible lead.

"Oh, have you found something interesting?"

178

"I don't know. It could be something, or nothing at all," said AJ truthfully. He didn't have much confidence that he would find what he was looking for. *Umayo will be discouraged with me if I fail,* he thought glumly.

He went online again, looking for information about travel in the Amazon—boat routes, and places to stay near the ancient shipyard area, which didn't have a name. Icaratambo looked as if it might be fairly close, and had a small airport. The only effective way to travel, once on the Amazon river system, was, of course, by boat. He found that many kinds of boats, from giant cruise ships down to small canoes, made up constant river traffic.

Most of the advertised accommodations were for riverboats designed for tourists, and they warned travelers not to expect a reliable schedule. They gave a list of suggested items to bring along: snacks, mosquito spray, salt pills in case of heat exhaustion, a toothbrush and basic essentials like that. He packed a small bag and a backpack with his laptop, binoculars and camera, and took the long flight from a small airline in Cuzco to Manaus, Brazil.

For the first hour, he gazed down, deep in thought, reviewing his adventures and things he'd learned, as the plane droned along over the vast green jungle below. At first the rainforest blanketed high foothills of the Andes, then the terrain flattened along the Madeira, a major tributary to the Amazon. *Wow, it goes on forever and ever. How in the world am I going to – No! I've got to stop thinking that way. Umayo has never failed to understand what's going on, and he knows a lot more than he lets on. Something, or someone, will tell me how to proceed.*

He didn't see much variation in the land below—flat, green, with the coffee latte-brown river winding like a great snake, on and on. Here and there he could see riverboats, large and small, each with a whitish wake behind it, and sometimes there was a town or village, with small boats pulled up along the shore. He tried reading for a while, then gave up, relaxed and nodded off.

He awoke as the plane landed at the airport in Manaus. Not sure what to expect, AJ was surprised to find

Manaus to be a modern, bustling city. Travel-tired, he took a room in a nice hotel near the airport, and stashed his gear. It felt invigorating to take a walk, and he soon found a restaurant. He hadn't realized how hungry he'd become, sitting all that time on the plane. He ordered a steak with grilled vegetables and baked potato. *No telling how long it will be before I'll see something like this again. I'm glad I don't have to wear dark glasses all the time, now, but I'll probably need them, traveling on the river.*

After a night's sleep, he had a good nortéamericano-style breakfast of waffles, eggs and bacon, checked out of the hotel, and returned to the airport. A smaller plane was available for a two-hour flight to Icaratambo. The trip would be shared with a few local-looking people. From Icaratambo, he would have to find the archaeological site, the ancient shipyard, on his own. Would it be difficult? He would have to ask around. On landing, he collected his luggage and studied the small town in the distance. Some of the people at the airstrip looked like tourists, others like native residents.

I'm glad I studied Spanish, but I wonder if I'll understand the local language and accents, especially if it's mostly Portuguese? Well, here goes.... He asked a few people, but no one was familiar with the area he sought. He was directed to a waiting tuk-tuk, three-wheeled taxi, and they trundled along the dirt road into town. The driver was friendly, but had no information for him.

The hot, humid air was stifling. He found a bed and breakfast, booked a room, and put on his backpack to carry a few small, more expensive items, like his laptop, binoculars and camera. *I don't know if they have a theft problem here or not, but it's a totally strange place to me, so I won't take any chances.* He picked up a bottle of water at the entrance. It felt good to get out and walk with long strides outdoors.

Arriving at the dock area on the river, AJ could see many sizes and styles of boats, some fairly large, down to a number of native canoes. He asked around about getting a boat to take him to the shipyard site. Most didn't know what he was talking about, but one man, Tomás, spoke up:

"Senhor, I know the place you speak of. There is a boat that goes in that direction. Follow me."

AJ accompanied Tomás to a port building near the dock area, to book a boat trip past Urucurituba, a small town on the Madeira, the tributary over which he'd flown, the mouth not far down the Amazon. The boat had not arrived yet, but was scheduled to leave in three days—maybe. *I could have left my wristwatch at home,* AJ noted. He had learned that all the riverboats took several days to several weeks between destinations along the rivers and tributaries, and passengers slept in hammocks onboard.

"You can buy a hammock at the market over here," said Tomás. "Come with me."

People are helpful here. Yes, they would be expert at handling river traffic. He followed Tomás to the riverside market, and selected a nice, colorful hammock for about $8.00 U.S. money, and a set of tying ropes for it. He had already bought a bag of biscuits and snacks to go along with his toothpaste, toothbrush and other necessities—only a bare-bones selection, traveling light. He gave Tomás a generous tip, and started back to his lodgings. Along the way, he observed native kids having a great time playing in the river, free of all cares, while women washed clothes in it nearby, talking and laughing with each other.

AJ turned in for the night at the bed and breakfast. He had learned early-on to use mosquito repellent, and now placed a net over his bed. He could hear music from somewhere, and people talking. The tropical air was muggy, even into the night, but by morning it was a little better. He went for a walk after his breakfast of coffee, humitas, and *picarones* (deep-fried sweet potatoes). The town was lively and colorful. He saw several churches and other buildings painted bright colors. Large, painted statues, almost cartoon-like, stood in front of some of the churches or at other strategic spots. Traffic was made up of pedestrians and people riding bicycles or motorbikes, and always the little tuk-tuks. He could hear music with a friendly beat, wafting out from different places as he walked by. With plenty of time to see the sights, he took another path around the outskirts of the town. The jungle had been cleared far back to provide a good distance from varmints. He could hear monkeys and birds calling from the trees, and the air was heavy with the scent of jungle decay and flowers.

He found another marketplace selling travel goods, where he bought some bottled juice and chips, then went back to his room to study his travel brochures and archaeology information again. Here, he was still able to get onto the Internet with his laptop, and tried to find more details about the shipyard discovery, but there wasn't much. He did find the name of a researcher, a Dr. Martin Bowie, who was connected with the site. *I wonder if he'll be there when I get to it, if I get there.... Well, why not? Everything seems to be working out so far. I've got to think more positively.*

He compared pictures of ancient ships he'd collected of Phoenicians and Vikings and Celtic peoples, and noted that some Celtic tribes were fond of using dragons on their ships, jewelry, and other articles. *Yes, that was silly, thinking 'Viking' when I should have been focusing on 'Celtic.' Hmmm....*

He went down to the docks the next morning, and no one seemed to expect the boat that day, so he ambled around the town again, observing local life—families, merchants, tourists, and some just hanging out, watching the tourists. Children ran free everywhere, wearing faded but clean clothes, probably hand-me-downs. He was impressed by the dedication of local boys playing soccer. No matter that their ball was home-made or their field bumpy and dotted with tufts of grass, they played with fervor and laughed joyously.

AJ walked on.

People sure aren't in much of a hurry here. But I was warned, it's no surprise. Got to learn to slowww down. He spent more time on his laptop, but ended up watching cat videos. Another walk, enjoying the scenery, local cuisine and music. He strolled along the river and gazed, spellbound, as a spectacular sunset filled the sky with fiery colors and gradually faded. *I've been missing some things, with my nose in research all the time.* He ambled back to the darkening streets, stopping to listen to music now and then.

Finally, on the third day, AJ figured he'd better be ready in case the boat came, so he packed up everything and checked out of his room early. He made his way down to the docks and found a comfortable place to wait.

After a while, he heard someone whistle, and noticed people becoming alert, pointing upriver and gathering their belongings. The riverboat had been sighted in the distance. This one, tall and glistening white, was considerably larger than the others at the dock, with several levels. Around 11 a.m., it was only an hour later than boarding time was scheduled. It seemed the very air was refreshed with expectation. Arrival of a big riverboat was an exciting event, stirring up the town's monotonous routines.

He hurried to get in line, as Tomás had advised him to try to be among the first to get on the boat and set up his hammock near the front, on the second level. "That's the best spot," Tomás had said, "away from the toilet and kitchen—not so many insects or as smelly. And you don't want to sleep on the upper, open deck. That's where the bar is, toward the back, and where the musicians play."

Already late, the Queen of the Amazon wouldn't be open for boarding until noon, which AJ heard was actually considered quite punctual. It was tiresome waiting to board, but he was afraid he'd lose his place in line.

Just when he was thinking of paying someone to bring him something to eat, the crew let down the gangplank. He and the other passengers in line shuffled along, loading. He was able to get a fairly good spot on the boat, and tied up his hammock, stashing his travel bag underneath. He hung his bag of snacks from the ceiling hook, safe from ants. *This will be my lodgings for a while. Hurry up and wait some more.* He tried to relax and enjoy his surroundings, but it was difficult to get with the slow schedule of things. The boat was scheduled to leave in a couple of days, so he would have to find some other pursuits—he decided to start a journal. He could use his laptop for writing, and for reading over his previous notes, but the Internet was out of the question. The boat had a charging station for batteries, but it was in high demand, always several people waiting their turn. He had bought a couple of small books to read, and was finally able to calm down and concentrate on them.

Lunch was served on the boat, an ample plate of food—a choice of chicken or beef, beans, rice, or pasta. One of the passengers told him that dinner would be the same. A concession stand on the boat sold drinks and snacks, but they were expensive. Breakfast would be fruit, biscuits, sometimes an egg, and coffee with milk. He learned that this would be the fare on most days unless someone caught some fish, but the food was good in any case. Later, he noticed the muffled sound of cackling below, toward the back of the boat. *Wow, the chicken, at least, will be fresh....oh, maybe that's for the eggs.*

Finally he saw that the captain was getting ready to start up the boat. The engines came chugging to life, and musicians climbed to the top level and began to play.

"I hope you like the music," said Gordo, the man in the next hammock. "It's *raggaeton* (Brazilian popular music). They like to play all day and far into the night, as loud as they can." Some of the people began smiling, swaying, and singing along.

"Hmmm, okay...." *I wonder if I'll be able to sleep?*

As if reading his thoughts, Gordo said, "Don't worry, you can nap at times during the day if you lose sleep at night. Musicians have to sleep, too. After a while you'll get used to it."

The boat began to move, swinging out into the current of the Great River. The sun was beating down on acres of brown water, the air warm and sultry, and AJ was surprised at how quickly he began to feel at home on the boat.

The shore slipped away into the distance. He gave himself over to the ease and comfort of river life. *I might as well,* he thought.....

~*~*~*~*~*~*~

Chapter 24: Queen of the Amazon
and the Madeira Maid

AJ settled back in his hammock, and began to watch the people around him—men traveling on business, families, tourists. Children played games, women chatted, doing each others' nails and hair. Men huddled together to talk or play cards. He conversed with some of them now and then, his knowledge of Spanish serving increasingly well as he caught on to the local Portuguese language, laced with native lingo. The people corrected him good-naturedly.

Evening came, and he savored the dinner provided. Beer and sodas were sold at the back of the boat. After a molten sunset, darkness began to descend on the river.

The Queen of the Amazon chugged on through the night. Occasionally, they saw other boats passing in one direction or the other, bright lights blazing, colorful music blaring away. If they passed close by, it seemed the musicians of each boat played in competition with the other, producing a brief cacophony, all in good fun. At times, heat lightning sent a sudden brilliant flash across the sky, and now and then the shore was revealed by the flicker of fireflies. Standing by the railing, AJ scanned a sky full of brilliant stars, the Milky Way dusted across it.

Later, as he relaxed in his hammock, a feeling of loneliness overcame him. *Got to go back to Spurwink as soon as I'm finished with this...mission,* he thought. He found sleep difficult at times, with the loud, sometimes passionate music from above, but at the same time he began to find delight in the new beat and melodies. *I guess this is my mini-vacation,* he decided.

He went up front to talk with the captain, Teodoro Rodrigues, called Captain Teo. "Beautiful out here at night," he said, to start conversation.

"Yeah, it can be," said Teo. "I like it. There's things you haf'ta get used to."

"Like what?"

"Sometimes it c'n eat you alive. Just haf'ta watch out."

"Hmmm."

Teo shrugged. "Caimans and toothy fish and all. An' the 'skitoes."

"I'm learning. I brought bug spray."

Teo's face creased slightly with a grin.

Bet that sounded stupid, thought AJ.

They chugged on into the night, the front searchlight casting a beam back and forth over the surface of the water as Captain Teo watched for floating logs and sand bars. Now and then, pairs of eyes reflected back when they came nearer the shore and shined the light in that direction.

"What's that?" AJ asked, pointing at some paired sparks of light.

"Could be jaguar, or monkeys or lil' wild cats. Never can tell in the dark."

AJ began to wonder how he would figure out where to go. Tomás had seemed confident that he was recommending the right boat to take him there, but AJ had begun to feel a little overwhelmed at the vastness of the area. *Does Teo know about this place?*

"I'm looking for an ancient shipyard out here somewhere," said AJ. "Any idea where it is?"

"Oh, that." Teo shrugged. "Yeah, th' scientists come and go. Say it's really old."

"Will this boat take me there?"

186

"Part of the way. It's not on my usual run, but a friend a'mine goes. I c'n hook you up with 'is boat."

"Okay, thanks."

"Tell you when we get there."

Back to the hammock, to think. The music stopped about 2 a.m.

Morning came, sunny and heating up quickly. Captain Teo was asleep, and the co-captain was at the wheel. Here and there, the boat stopped at small settlements, loading and unloading passengers and all kinds of supplies, sometimes taking a day or two in each place. It was the highlight of the week for each village, the people flocking down to the river's edge in a festive mood, greeting relatives or saying goodbye, picking up packages or loading cargo to be sent on downriver.

AJ noticed some passengers tossing bulging plastic bags onto the water, and people paddling out in canoes to retrieve them, giving thanks to the throwers. "What's going on there?" AJ asked a woman standing next to him.

"They're giving their used clothing to the poor. Sometimes it's the only way they get new things to wear."

AJ watched the jungle with his binoculars when they traveled near shore, and could glimpse monkeys swinging in the trees, and colorful birds he'd never be able to name. He looked down at the brown water, and watched fish and caimans underneath reflections of the clouds. Now and then a boto or two, the playful pink river dolphins, leaped out of the water, or swam alongside the boat, looking up with a friendly eye and funny little smile. In shallow areas, giant water lilies floated, their pads five or six feet across, with huge flowers, eight or ten inches wide.

"Those big leaves can hold up the weight of a man," a woman was telling some children. "The white flowers have just opened today, and the darker pink ones have been pollinated. They will turn even darker pink, and sink under the water to make seeds."

She must be a teacher, thought AJ.

"It's pollinated by a special kind of beetle," she continued. "The flower traps it with its petals while it covers the beetle with pollen, then opens, and the beetle flies to the next flower." The children nodded and wrote in their notebooks.

After two days' travel, the boat turned up a tributary, the Madeira River. Even this was a large river, and they had several days to go before getting to their destination. They stopped at Urucurituba for a day, taking on a few new passengers. Ready for a change of diet, AJ found a small native restaurant in the village. They sold spicy meat with rice and roasted vegetables for dinner. He bought some more biscuits and snacks to take with him.

Soon they were on their way again. AJ wondered how much farther it would be. After a long, quiet afternoon, the boat headed in to a landing at yet another small, nameless village. "Here's where you mus' switch boats," said Captain Teo to AJ. "Your route turns off here. There's the boat I told you 'bout." He pointed to a little riverboat, the Madeira Maid, that looked a bit worn around the edges, and sported a thatched roof. "I know th' captain, Dom Calder. He'll take good care of you."

AJ folded up his hammock and collected his belongings, climbed down from the larger boat and carried the bundle over to the smaller vessel. He looked around at the people, the village, and the distant jungle as he picked his way over the muddy beach. Once on board, he introduced himself as a researcher associated with the museum in Cuzco.

"Ah!" said Calder, "You are wanting to see the shipyard of the Ancients." He studied AJ thoughtfully as he looked up from working with some ropes, then smiled, revealing a missing tooth. "I'll be taking you right to it, up a tributary to the north. I'm picking up another researcher farther on, who is also going there. We'll wait for him when we get to my village. It'll take a few days to get to the shipyard, and you can sleep on the boat while we're there, but I'll have to make the return trip after three days."

"I think three days should be enough," said AJ. *I hope so. I wouldn't like to have to wait for the next boat out.* He tied up his hammock and stowed his bags.

Captain Dominicus Calder was an older man with longish, dark gray hair and a stubbly beard, but he was strong and wiry, with tanned, leathery skin and a ready smile. He had emigrated from the UK many years before, anxious to get away from the high society and stuffy atmosphere he'd grown to despise. He'd taken to the lifestyle of the Amazon at first contact, and never looked back.

"You'll want something to eat." Calder said, matter-of-factly. "I have some beans cooking and some bread. I'll dig around in the cooler and find us a couple of beers. You might as well settle in for the rest of the day."

AJ was surprised to find the beans to be deliciously seasoned, and the yeasty, aromatic bread was obviously home-baked.

"I enjoy cooking," said Calder, "but I don't have time or supplies for anything fancy."

"It's great. Where did you get the bread? It's wonderful."

"My wife has a clay oven, inherited from her mother. She runs a little café at our village, where you'll want to eat. We'll get there tomorrow."

After another day's travel, AJ observed that this tributary was becoming noticeably smaller—he could see both shores, but still far off. Calder brought the boat in to a little settlement, and a small crowd of people came out, happily welcoming him. "This is my village, and my family, here," he indicated a smiling group at one side. "And this is my wife, Carina. She will feed you well."

Carina stepped forward and motioned toward a large thatched hut with an open front. "Welcome to our café. You must be hungry. Dinner is almost ready." She turned and waved to those who were waiting, while AJ and Dom debarked and followed her. They sat together at a larger family table and benches at one side. Carina joined them after serving the others, sitting close by Dom.

AJ was delighted, and overfed by the time dinner was over. The meat was artfully seasoned, home-grown vegetables grilled or roasted, fruit gathered from the jungle,

189

and that good bread... "You are a fabulous cook," he said to Carina.

"Between us, we do very well." she motioned toward the garden areas. "We grow most of our own food, and make whatever else we need from local materials. What we earn with the boat and café pays for any extras."

Dom showed AJ the rest of the village, a comfortable little community of wood-and-thatch houses, some on stilts, accessed by ladders. A few were built as houseboats along the shore. Most had verandahs or porches with the ubiquitous hammocks strung in favorable locations to catch a breeze or avoid the sun. Kitchens were open-air spaces, each shaded by a high thatched roof. Most of the stilted houses had pens of chickens or pigs underneath.

This isn't half bad, thought AJ.

Calder took him for a walk in the jungle, which had been cleared away from the village and their gardens to keep varmints at bay. Parrots and other birds of all colors and descriptions flashed their wings in the dappled sun, and monkeys swung from branch to branch, picking fruit. Huge butterflies fluttered among high branches hung with orchids and other flowers, which scented the air. A large praying mantis obliged to walk across AJ's hand from one leaf to another. *Yes, this would be a wonderful place to live...for some people...for a few years....or more....*

After freshening up in the bucket shower, AJ slept well in his hammock that night, and was awakened early by Calder.

"We'll catch some fish for breakfast," he said, handing AJ a net. "Carina is firing up the brazier." He led the way to a secluded pool that must have been his favorite fishing spot. He showed AJ how to cast the net, and soon they had a pile of silvery jaraqui fish flopping in the basket. "Some use bow and arrows, some use fishing lines. I like the net."

The air in the kitchen was pungent with mingling aromas from the cooking spices as well as the chicken pen. *I could get used to this,* thought AJ, and the tasty food soon overtook his sense of smell.

190

The older children had gathered fruit from the jungle, rounding out the breakfast menu of fish, manioc pancakes and roasted plantain, with a choice of cocoa or coffee.

AJ was almost reluctant to leave when the time came. He was pleased, however, to finally meet the researcher for whom Calder had been waiting, a Professor Dayton, who arrived from another site he'd been visiting.

"Call me Greg," he told AJ. "Out here, 'professor' sounds rather stiff." He was in his mid-30's, with a pleasant round face, glasses, and light brown hair. He smiled, and asked about AJ's purpose on this trip.

"I, ah, came to see the archaeology site near here. I'm a researcher from the States, studying in Peru." *I should have been ready for that question. I'm getting lulled into the swing of river life.*

"Oh? Where are you based?"

"Cuzco. The museum there. I heard some tantalizing reports about this discovery, and wanted to see it for myself."

"You won't be disappointed. My colleague, Dr. Bowie, and I have found amazing things there. The wood is mostly petrified, native to the Amazon, and some of it is held together by bronze nails and bolts."

"Yes, I read about that," said AJ. *Don't say too much. He may reveal something about the axe head. It's odd they haven't made a big deal about it—if they've found it.*

"I'll show you around when we get there."

"That would be wonderful. I'm a little out of my element here."

The old boat backed into the river, then turned upstream. AJ and Greg, the only passengers for this special trip, settled back for the ride. AJ had a gnawing worry in the back of his mind: *Even if I find this axe, will I have to steal it? Is that what Umayo expects me to do?* The jungle was a little closer now, but the river was still large by most standards. *Big enough for Phoenician ships?* wondered AJ. *Yes, could have been.* He looked out across the brown water and tried to imagine the sight, as it would have looked a couple of thousand years ago, and it made him shiver.

The next two days were uneventful but never dull, with so many birds and animals to see and hear, and each of the men telling about their own adventures, trying to top each other in genial competition. Before the third day, they were good friends. That afternoon, Dom told them the shipyard site would be just a little way yet, so they put some of their gear into their backpacks. AJ could leave his other luggage stowed on deck.

"Ah! Up ahead," said Dom after about an hour. AJ strained to glimpse the distant camp. Some government-green tents had been set up on the shore, and a small, modern-style river boat was tethered to a wooden walkway built as a temporary pier. Two men and a woman stood on the muddy shore, watching the approaching party.

As soon as their boat was tied up, Greg and AJ clambered out to meet the trio as they came to meet them on the pier. "This is Dr. Bowie, and two of his student assistants, Margie Conner and Joe Hampstead," said Greg. "This is AJ Darrow, a researcher from Cuzco."

Small talk and pleasantries took up a few minutes, and then came more serious discussion. At this point, AJ felt that an explanation would be in order.

"I have to tell you something, in case you should ever want to reach me at Cuzco, I go by an assumed name there because of a problem with the Shining Path terrorists, in the Cuzco area." He explained briefly about his and Amzi's brushes with the Sendero Luminoso, and how his 'Gene McGuire' moniker was his way of escaping detection.

They smiled, knowingly.

"What is your particular interest in this site?" asked Dr. Bowie.

Wow. Now I've really got to watch it, thought AJ. "I've been studying different tribes and history of the Andes and the Amazon basin. I recently read an article online about this discovery, and, well, I just had to see it. I'd really like to see the bronze artifacts, if I may."

"It is most curious," Dr. Bowie turned and motioned for them to sit at a folding table. "The makeup of the bronze itself is exactly the same as that which we find in the Old

World sites. The workmanship of the bolts, nails and other pieces is like old Phoenician artifacts I've seen near Parnaíba."

"What kind of wood have you found? Have you found anything else, in the three weeks since that article was published?" They positioned folding chairs and sat down, facing each other.

"The dock construction is of native mahogany and other woods, some petrified, but a lot if it has rotted. It's been here a thousand years, maybe two. As you can see, there," he said, pointing, "most of the remains are under water and preserved in mud, not visible to the casual observer. It's a wonder anyone stumbled onto it. But we can tell from the style of construction that it was made during the advancement of Phoenician building expertise."

"Wow, that is interesting," said AJ, Greg nodding agreement. "Now, from your professional point of view, what would you say that indicates?"

"Well, to make a professional judgement, to be politically correct, I'd say the jury's still out, but personally," and he winked, "I'm inclined to think there's something *to* this notion about ancient Phoenicians being here," said Dr. Bowie. "I mean, how could you doubt it?" He studied AJ's face, and seemed satisfied with his smile of agreement.

Dr. Bowie rose and motioned for AJ and Greg to follow him into the tent, where they examined the latest finds. *No axe.*

AJ climbed into his hammock on the boat that night with his mind racing from one thing to another. *I can hardly believe I'm really here, where the Phoenicians built the shipyard—where they lived, hundreds...maybe thousands of years ago. And Celts, too? And they were Umayo's ancestors?* It was hard to sleep.

The next day, AJ was bending over one of the portable tables, watching Margie as she carefully cleaned a piece of decomposing wood, and waiting with his camera to take a picture. The goo of ages clung like tar, and it was difficult to tell where mud ended and soft, rotted wood began. Greg and Dr. Bowie had shown him the bronze artifacts, which were exciting in themselves. They found, even as AJ looked on, a chisel, also made of bronze, with a decaying wooden handle. *But no bronze axe*, he thought. *Where should I look?*

He felt a gentle tug on the side of his shirt. He looked down, and discovered a small Amerindian boy looking up at him with dark brown eyes. He was light-skinned, with blonde streaks in his light brown hair. Barefoot, he wore ragged shorts and a faded blue T-shirt.

"Hello," said AJ. "Who might you be?"

"My name, Umayo."

AJ dropped his camera.

~*~*~*~*~*~*~

Chapter 25: Finding Kanmi's Axe

AJ hardly realized he had dropped his camera, but the boy stooped quickly to pick it up, and handed it back to him.

"Sorry, senhor... Okay?" He pointed at the camera in AJ's shaking hands.

"What? Oh—yes," said AJ, absent-mindedly looking at it, "It's fine." *What? Umayo? How did this boy get that name? He's kind of blonde, too—what....*

Margie was watching. "Looks like you have a new friend," she said, smiling. "He's been hanging around for weeks, but always kept his distance before. Cute kid!"

"Uh, yeah," said AJ. By the time he had recovered his senses, the boy had run off into the jungle and disappeared.

"Those natives. Just curious, I guess," said Dr. Bowie, coming out of the tent. He was cleaning a bronze bolt.

"He had blonde hair," AJ stammered, still in a daze.

"Yes. Some of the natives around here do. I think their ancestors may have encountered white explorers from somewhere. It happens." He shrugged, and turned his attention elsewhere. Dr. Bowie was an older man, with graying hair and a short white beard. He had a habit of squinting at things, and getting so absorbed in his work that he tuned out things going on around him.

Get ahold of yourself. It's probably a common name around here. AJ still couldn't shake the feeling that something significant had just happened. Would he see the boy again? *Why did he come to me and not the others?* It was hard to concentrate on anything else, so he made the excuse of feeling the heat, and retired to his hammock for a while.

The next day, AJ still hadn't shaken off his feeling that there was more to the little boy than coincidence. He took a walk into the jungle several times, softly calling, "Umayo?" But no one came. He didn't even see a hut or village. *Did I dream it? No, they saw him, too.*

"Be careful, AJ," said Dr. Bowie. "It's not advisable to go too far into the jungle alone."

But he had to find little Umayo. He had only one more day before the boat would return to civilization. Finally he saw the boy, sitting on a branch, high in a giant, leaning tree. AJ stood at the slanted base of the huge bole. "Umayo. Hello!"

Umayo smiled and slid down the trunk. "Hello." Hesitantly, he edged closer, looking furtively back toward the shipyard site. "I show you something, Senhor?" His deep brown eyes had a smoldering look.

"Yes," said AJ. "Show me."

The boy climbed back up, a little higher past the branch where he'd been sitting. He reached into a hole in the trunk, and pulled out something wrapped in a big leaf, then tucked it into his waistband and slid to the ground again. "For you." He handed it to AJ.

"What? Uh...thank you." AJ hefted the heavy object. He unwrapped it. It was bronze, very old, the head of an axe. Pitted with age, yet cleaned and polished, probably by little Umayo, it had a beautiful primitive engraving on both sides, of a deer's head with antlers slightly projecting.

"You trade?" The boy pointed at AJ's watch.

"What? Oh—yes! Yes. We trade." He took off his watch and gave it to Little Umayo with no hesitation. It was a nice watch, but AJ didn't care—he could buy more watches. "Where did you get this?" he gestured.

"Water." The boy pointed back toward the shipyard.

He must have found it—in the shipyard? Did he steal it? Or did he find it before the people from the Outside

196

came? AJ was perplexed, but electrified. *This must be the one Umayo—"Old Umayo"—wanted me to get for him. But how—?* AJ wanted desperately to question the boy, but language was a barrier. He felt, briefly, as if he *should* give it to the scientists—it *was* their site, after all. *But this is what I made all this long journey for, and it must have belonged to Umayo's ancestors. Well, they didn't mention missing any axe.* He stuffed it into his deepest pocket.

Little Umayo stood, smiling, turning the wristwatch over and over, admiring its golden glint in the dapples of sunlight.

"Better not tell," AJ whispered to him, putting his finger to his lips. "Keep. Secret." He made motions of hiding and putting something away. *This could get him—and me—in a kettle of trouble.* On an impulse, he bent and hugged the boy, who gave a short gasp of surprise, but then he wrapped his small arms around AJ's neck and squeezed.

Little Umayo climbed the tree to stash his treasure, then slid down again. He smiled beautifully at AJ. "I go," and he vanished into the jungle without a sound.

Early next morning, Captain Calder was up, puttering around and getting the Madeira Maid ready to go. AJ was still in his hammock.

"Breakfast!" called Calder, offering coffee and biscuits. "We'll get a good start today. I'm anxious to get back." He grinned, sipping his hot drink.

"Me too," said AJ. "Say, is there a way I can get back to the Amazon faster? Say, a small plane somewhere?"

"Sure," said Calder. "Right on our way. There's a guy, Diogo, with a little air strip, not far from my village. He'll take you directly to Manaus if you want."

"That would be great," said AJ. "I enjoyed this trip, but I'm getting the itch to get back to my home now."

Calder smiled and nodded, looking down at his cup. "Know the feeling." He looked up. "Hey, come back some time. We'll be here."

AJ's return was pleasant, even though it was not as leisurely. He was bursting to tell his parents of his

197

adventures. He wanted to show them the axe. *But I must take it right to Umayo. At least I can take detailed pictures of it to show my folks. Good enough for me.* He waited until he had a private hotel room at Manaus, then took good digital close-ups of the axe head from all angles, with a ruler alongside for comparison. The next morning he left Manaus on a small plane.

Back at Cuzco, he went first to his hotel room to freshen up and unpack. Then he called Umayo. "I'm back," he said. "I have something for you."

"That sounds wonderful, Mr. McGuire. Come as soon as you can."

Early the next morning, AJ found Rafa, and they arrived at Vilcatambo while the mists were still drifting. He met Umayo at the roadside, out of sight and earshot from the village. They embraced briefly, along with the usual light back slap.

"Here it is," AJ brought out the axe head, still wrapped in the big leaf.

Umayo unwrapped it slowly, reverently. "Ahhh," he murmured. "Kanmi's axe."

"Who?"

"Kanmi—an ancestor of mine. He was working on the dock when he lost it." Umayo caressed the deer antlers with his thumb as he gazed at it, transfixed.

"*What?* How long ago?" whispered AJ, feeling the familiar shock again.

"Oh ---" Umayo seemed to suddenly realize what he had said. "Forgive me. It is an old family thing. I think you'd call it an 'heirloom.'"

"May I ask how old it is? And how did you know it would be there, waiting for me?"

Umayo smiled, then looked down. "You may ask, young AJ, but... I have no way to explain it. Do you get my meaning?"

AJ nodded. "My father was always saying, "I never question the ways of the Ancients."

"Yes. I appreciate your understanding. You have done a great thing for me. I want to give you something." He reached into his pocket and took out something made of

198

gold. It was half of a beautifully wrought buckle—a crocodile, actually a caiman, with emerald eyes. "I wish I could give you the whole thing, but the other half was lost, long ago. Some day it may be found. It is a reminder of our life on the Great River. Now that you know a part of our story, this small token will summon your memories of us."

They embraced briefly again. AJ was overcome with emotion, but Umayo, too, spoke hoarsely. "You are like a brother to me now."

AJ went back to his hotel. More than ever, he was bursting to go home. He called Amzi. "I'm back, and I have so much to tell you."

"We were beginning to wonder what happened to you," said Amzi. "We hoped you weren't lost in the Amazon jungle."

"And no one would ever have found me. Believe me, you could vanish in a thousand different places out there, and no one would know where to look. It took a lot longer getting there than coming back. I didn't know exactly where I was going at first. Then, when I was ready to return, I found a small airstrip, and the pilot knew right where to go."

"We're just glad to hear from you. Well, did you find anything exciting?"

"Wait 'til I tell you! I don't even know where to begin. Actually, I think it will be better if I come home for a short visit."

The next morning he flew to Lima, then the flight to Miami and back home, where he rented a car at the Baltimore airport. He had almost forgotten what it was like to drive. He was weary of all the travel, but it was so good to come up the driveway to Spurwink, and see the timeworn house waiting like an old friend. The front steps and porch looked to AJ like arms open wide. *Now I feel completely at home,* he thought.

His folks, his brothers, and Aunt Melanie immersed him in a warm welcome. They were all eager to hear everything about his adventures in both Peru and Brazil. Daisy was away at school, but Elfie and her family crowded around to hear the tales, too. Viola, the cook, furnished a big dinner of the ever-favorite spaghetti with all the trimmings, and lingered at the doorway to listen.

By the time AJ had recounted a couple of hours' worth of stories, he was exhausted, but just happy to be home with family all around him. He would tell his parents the more confidential details later, but at last, he could totally relax with people he loved, with no reason to worry about who was watching him, and why.

~*~*~*~*~*~*~

Chapter 26: Aife's Escape, and the Pink Emerald

1275 AD -- The Incas were growing in power after beginning as a small, insignificant tribe, gaining influence by insinuating their ways into unsuspecting tribes of the Andes. People from different settlements were indoctrinated and sent to infiltrate host villages, gradually impressing the inhabitants with the beliefs and principles of the Inca way, weakening their defenses.

Trouble had been brewing at Kuelap between the malicious priests of Inti and Yorano, a talented and beloved shaman of Pachamama, endangering his life. Aife, Yorano's priestess friend, overheard them plotting to frame him for treason against the chief shaman, Rapau, a crime for which Yorano could be executed.

Aife, knowing Rapau had been thinking of sending out colonists, gathered a large group, which included Yorano, and with Rapau's blessing, they all left Kuelap, heading south through the Andes with a pack train of llamas. For many weeks they traveled the trails of the high ridges, camping, searching for the right place to establish a new settlement. They had with them a shrewd scout, Crevan ('Fox'), who was an expert at finding hidden places, or creating them. They pressed on, trying to find a safe new home as far from Kuelap as they could. Avoiding most villages and cities, they found help at certain stops along the way, places where their people from Kuelap had had trade relationships in the past. They longed for rest, and peace.

Scouting ahead, Crevan had returned with a warning when they neared Cuzco. Knowing the Incas were there, they needed to find a location safely far away from them, and well concealed.

Aife had another reason to avoid capture. Yorano had given her a precious stone, a pink emerald, for saving his life and having the cunning and courage to help him and others escape the danger they had faced. In a secret ceremony, he had imbued the stone with special powers giving invisibility to any female owner, and it was to be passed down to her female priestly descendants through the ages. If she were captured, or the stone stolen, it would mean loss of a great secret power. If she used the stone to escape, she could not take Yorano with her.

Yorano and Aife were married along the way, in a simple service dictated by urgency as they continued on their escape route from Kuelap.

They ended their journey nearly as far south as Cuzco. Crevan had discovered a wonderful hidden canyon, cradling the small Yanabamba River, several days' journey out northeast from the Cuzco area, where they could build the new settlement, high above the stream. He created an ingenious way, a camouflaged, difficult trail, to discourage strangers from locating their new sanctuary. They had among them a master stone mason, a descendant of Huarwar, and young, trained men who were eager to begin construction.

They changed the name of their tribe to Pahuaca, to disguise their Kuelap origin from strangers. Crevan, with his helpers, spent the rest of his life creating and maintaining secret tunnels and hidden pathways in the surrounding mountains, while workmen cleared land for their new settlement. They gradually developed terraced farmlands below the main walls. Lookouts were posted on the high ramparts overlooking the valley to the southwest, ready to give the alarm if approaching enemies were sighted in the distance.

1276 AD - About a year after the Pahuacas had settled down to building their new city, which they named Atahuaqa, Yorano had a vision of civil war in Kuelap, with bloodshed and fire. In a few weeks, a runner was intercepted by a Pahuacan lookout on the main trail along the Andean ridges, with a message for Atahuaqa. He told the lookout that Kuelap had suffered a great conflagration in an uprising of the two factions, between worshippers of Inti and those of Pachamama, and many were killed. A part of Kuelap had been destroyed by fire, but at last the evil priests and their followers were overpowered and killed or ousted.

The Pahuacas continued to build Atahuaqa, high above the Yanabamba, and life was peaceful for several generations. New murals were painted at major points of the city, some purely for decoration, showing historic events or persons. Others in more concealed areas, inside temples and tombs, illustrated important genealogies and information that needed to be protected and carried on through succeeding generations. Yorano, as the first chief shaman of Atahuaqa, had chosen Tanitay's style of decorative writing because, camouflaged with flower and animal symbols, it could easily be mistaken by the casual observer for mere decoration. Yorano's gift of time travel and prophecy was passed down as well. It was the distinctive secret of Atahuaqa. Some of the other cities had their own styles of quellqa, and all varied in their ability to give hidden meanings.

In 1351, Huaca was born, and grew up to be high priest. His wife was Davina, a descendant of Aife and Yorano. A priestess, she inherited the pink emerald.
In time, several children were born to Huaca and Davina -- two boys: Umayo, Amano, and in 1375, a girl, Tica. Of the three children of Huaca and Davina, their daughter, Tica, displayed the strongest desire to join the priesthood. She began training when she was a young teenager, living in the

temple under the supervision of her parents. Amano became a farmer, and Umayo made fine pottery.

One day, Tica came to her father and asked permission to go outside the city confines. "Pucu is missing," she said. I'm afraid a jaguar or other animal might kill her. Please, may I go looking for her? I will take one of the temple dogs with me."

Her father understood how much her white llama meant to her, but cautioned her about dangers to watch out for. He knew that she had been in the jungle before, but he was glad she would have a dog with her for protection.

"I'll be really careful," she promised. "I don't think Pucu will go far." So she hurried out from the walls of Atahuaqa, excited at the feeling of adventure, but concerned about her pet. It was a beautiful pure white llama, and Tica had given her an old Amazonian name. Tica came across a faint trail up the mountainside near the city walls, and began to ascend, calling softly for Pucu. At the top of the trail, she came to a bald hill, but could see no llama, so she called the dog and turned back.

On her way down, she noticed a dark place in the shrubbery. Leaning closer, she realized that it was a small cave. She pushed back the vines that hung over it, and threw a rock in, to see if any animal might be inside, but heard nothing, so she entered. After she was inside, her eyes became used to the gloom, and she had an idea. *What a nice little cave. I think I'll keep this secret. I might need it some day. She gathered some dry firewood, and cleaned the little chamber to be habitable. Yes, this might be fun sometime, or even a good place to hide. Father always says it's good to have a place to go in times of danger.*

On her way home, she found Pucu, grazing in a small meadow. "Oh, Pucu, you naughty girl! You could have been the dinner of a jaguar. Let's go home."

When Tica was nearly fifteen, her mother contracted a jungle fever. On her deathbed, she told Tica the story of the Pink Emerald, its powers of invisibility to female owners, how Yorano gave it to Aife, and onward. Davina gave her daughter a special necklace of green emeralds and blue lapis, with the pink stone, now a 100-year old heirloom, prominent in the center. "Guard it with all your heart," said Davina. "It may save your life some day."

After her mother's death, Tica was taken by Davina's assistant into the special rooms for priestesses and their female attendants. Here she was shown the painting on the ceiling that told the story of the pink emerald. Her best friend, Maupi, was to become her personal attendant.

Tica's father, Huaca, was now her teacher and mentor. He felt increasingly concerned as he saw the atmosphere of the priesthood taking on a negative feeling of aggression. Some of the priests of Pachamama were talking of the way of Inti.

The weaker, more unstable priests had listened to a new teacher who was very persuasive. He and his two cronies had arrived a few months before, traveling from the north. Huaca suspected that they had been banished from Kuelap after another attempted takeover.

Politics among the priesthood became increasingly charged with ambition and deceit. Then Huaca had died under suspicious circumstances, and the new high priest, Taikan, stepped in. He was tall and powerful, a jealous and evil man who coveted adoration from the people, and wouldn't allow any of the priesthood to be seen in public to display more wisdom or power than himself.

After inheriting the pink emerald from her mother, Tica had often studied the story of it, painted in a mural with decorative writing on the ceiling of a small alcove of the women's rooms in the temple, where only the priestesses and their attendants had access. She had never had occasion to try becoming invisible, but kept the jewel close by at all times, often wearing it hidden under her robes.

After a few years, Tica began having premonitions and foreboding dreams, from which she awakened in the dark, gasping for breath and sweating.

Maupi came quickly to her side. "What is wrong?"

"I have had another dream," panted Tica, "I know the gods are warning me—of something. I see strange people, armies of them, overrunning our houses, our fields, our temple. I see fire and smoke and blood. I should tell someone, but the priests won't believe me. It has been forbidden that I speak out to the people. I don't know what to do."

"Yes, I remember when you first spoke to the priests," said Maupi, "how they laughed and patted you on the head. They had no dreams themselves, and they mocked you as an upstart—an ignorant girl, they said—too young to be a real priestess."

"I know we will have an invasion by the Incas, and soon. I think I will have another dream and more instruction before long." Which she did, the next night.

"Watch that one," Taikan had told his top guard, Chulpa, "and see that she doesn't do anything foolish, talking about all her dreams and warnings. She must stay in the temple, away from the people."

Tica had only one ally, her assistant and girlhood friend, Maupi. They each set aside a kind of backpack of emergency provisions, as the dreams instructed. Awakened one night by a more urgent vision, Tica and Maupi snatched up their belongings and headed quietly for the back of the torch-lit temple.

Chulpa, skulking in the shadows, lunged at them, breaking the cord around Tica's neck, but she was able to wrest free while grasping a few of the stones, especially the precious pink one. She grabbed Maupi's hand, and using the power of the pink emerald, the girls became invisible.

While Chulpa, confused, thrashed about looking for them, they escaped into the night. The moon, full and high, lighted their way.

"Come quickly," whispered Tica to Maupi, "I know a way of escape." They ran for the mountain that rose in back of the temple. Where the ground ascended underfoot, Tica and Maupi stopped for a moment to catch their breath. "Do you remember, Maupi, when my white llama, Pucu, was lost, and I went to search for her?"

"Yes, you were gone for a whole day, but you found her. Your father was worried that you had become lost, too."

"I found more than the llama, Maupi. I found this pathway up the mountain, and while exploring it, I found something else. Come see." They continued up a trail that was overgrown from disuse, and well hidden.

"Here," Tica pointed at a dark place. "Look under the branches and ferns. What do you see?"

Maupi bent down and looked at a dark hollow in the moonlit undergrowth. "It's a cave! Can we get in it?"

"We'll clear away some of the branches and go in." Tica began pulling away tangled greenery. "I kept it secret from the day I found it. I knew I might need it some day." They entered the small chamber, setting down their burdens. Tica produced fire sticks from her pack, and lit a small campfire, using the dry wood and tinder she had gathered when she was there before. There was evidence of animal inhabitants of the cave in ages past, but nothing had lived there recently. They unloaded their bundles by the firelight, and set up a camp, being very quiet and wary of every noise.

Later that night, they huddled together outside the mouth of the cave, shivering as they looked down the mountain to see their beloved city being invaded by an army of Inca warriors. They stayed hidden, listening to the cries and sounds of destruction from below. Tica wondered if her brothers had escaped, but there was nothing she could do.

They found comfort in their friendship that had grown over the years, and now even more since they only had each other. No one was looking for them now. Using the power of invisibility, they made forays into the village for food, blankets, and a few cooking pots and utensils. The invaders didn't know of their existence, and the two young women plundered the Inca invaders at night, a little here, a little there, to avoid attracting attention.

Tica made a new cord for her necklace by braiding a few strands of her long dark hair. She threaded it through two oblong green emeralds, with the round pink one in the center. Tica wondered why the gods allowed only her and Maupi to escape. *Were we spared just because we were young and innocent? Was Taikan in league with the Incas, a secret agent in their plan? How many others of our people survived?* She could see a few of them, at times, being treated as slaves by their Inca captors. She wondered about her brothers. *Were they among the survivors still living at Atahuaqa? Would the memory of our tribe die with them?*

The two girls found life lonely and uncertain. Living in the cave for several months, they wondered if they should stay there, or try to find another gathering of their people somewhere.

Later, Tica was finally able to find out that Umayo had escaped the invasion on that same night, and was staying with other refugees in a makeshift settlement in a hidden canyon. She sent a message to him, revealing where she and Maupi were living. He brought them food, but said it was too dangerous for them to try to live in a city at this time, with an increasing number of Incas traveling about.

One night, a powerful earthquake destroyed the cave and the city, killing the two young women and many of the people below. Where the cave collapsed, a depression opened up, and dust rose through the moonlight. Soon all was silent except for a distant rumbling, as monkeys and birds settled down.

The ruined city was not rebuilt, and the few survivors who had taken shelter nearby traveled to other settlements, where they were absorbed into the population. The jungle slowly covered the streets of Atahuaqa, climbed the walls, and eventually swallowed the whole area. Colorful macaws and toucans watched over it from the trees. Monkeys and tarantulas clambered over the carved stones.

Another watcher returned at times. Umayo was determined to protect the burying place of his beloved sister, and the remains of Atahuaqa.

~·*~*~*~*~*~*~

By 1475, the Incas had conquered most of the other tribes of the Andes, but the People at Kuelap had held out for a good 20 years longer. Known for their fierceness in battle and expertise in using the sling, they were not afraid to die in order to preserve their freedom. The Incas respected them, and called them Chachapoyas, "White Warriors of the Clouds." They finally succeeded somewhat in conquering and dispersing the Chachapoyas, but never totally subjugated the People. The Incas feared the Peoples' shamans, and were convinced that Chachapoyan mummies could come alive if disturbed, bringing down horrible curses on their enemies.

Whether or not they believed this themselves, the Cloud Warriors encouraged the legend to spread throughout the Andes.

After the Incas had warred against Kuelap and taken away many into their culture, some of the People remained at Kuelap, never totally conquered. In 1532, these holdouts were persuaded to join forces, briefly, with the Spanish, and helped destroy the Incas' power, but then the Spanish double-crossed the Chachapoyas, treating them harshly. Many of the Andean tribes who were not killed in battle perished under their conquerors' cruel treatment, or died from new infectious diseases to which they had no immunity. This nearly wiped out the Cloud Warriors, as well. Some escaped into the mountains and built sanctuaries in nearly inaccessible locations, keeping to themselves, as was their age old custom, living in small, isolated villages.

From 1532 it was downhill for the Incas until they were themselves totally conquered in 1572. Their descendants still live on in the Andes regions, along with the Quechuas and other smaller surviving tribes.

The remaining Chachapoyas, called *Gringuitos* by other tribes, still avoid civilization as much as possible, choosing to preserve their privacy and secrets.

~*~*~*~*~*~*~

Chapter 27: Secrets of Atahuaqa

Late summer, 2014 -- AJ took a few days at Spurwink to relax and recuperate from his long journey in the Amazon. In the back of his mind, he was feeling little jolts of anxiety, thinking he should get back to Peru. "I guess I'd better quit playing hooky," he announced one evening after dinner. "I'll be leaving in the morning."

Lila and Amzi had spent as much time with him as they could while he was home. With his recent discoveries, the secrets of Atahuaqa seemed to loom in the near future. What would their adventurous son find? Amzi often wished he could go back to Peru, but that would double the chance of the Shining Path becoming aware of any Darrows' presence in Cuzco—AJ needed to attract as little attention as possible until his purpose was fulfilled.

AJ landed in Cuzco the next day, and reported to his job at the museum. He had plenty of interesting stories to tell Dr. Holcomb and the others about his trip, without ever mentioning the bronze axe head. The ancient shipyard site was no secret, and they were fascinated to hear about the latest discoveries there and to see AJ's pictures of his trip and the artifacts the scientists had found. It was exciting to announce that while he was at the shipyard, Dr. Bowie's team had discovered the remains of a bronze chisel with the nearly decomposed remains of a wooden handle.

The archaeologists had some news items themselves, about the new Inca discovery they were working on. The Inca site was a smaller settlement, but it would be enough to keep the scientists busy for a few months.

Meanwhile, AJ had more questions for Umayo. He called and went out for a visit. "Umayo, I've been thinking about some things that I don't quite understand.

"What is it?" Umayo asked. "Have you found something new?"

"No, not yet. It's just something you said... I'd like to understand better. You said your people were Kena'anim, and Celtic. May I ask... would you tell me more about that?"

"Ah, yes, I thought you might wonder how that came about," said Umayo. "I'm sorry it was so misleading at first. I knew your parents would deduce that 'Kena'anim' sounded like 'Canaan' and think of 'Phoenician.' But I didn't want to complicate it just then, with both. It is actually quite simple.

My tribe, the People, is two tribes—actually three, with the Brazilian native element—melded into one. The Celtiberians were Celts from Northern Spain, and the Kena'anim from Islands in the western Mediterranean, the Balearics. We banded together to escape our enemies from the Old World—it was the time that Rome was destroying Carthage, and we knew they would be coming for us next. We could not let them take our freedom as they had done to our kindred.

After we arrived in Brazil, the New World, our ancestors intermarried through the years, as we migrated up the big river. Some of both Celt and Kena'anim men married native Brazilian women. We became one big tribe. I know all these stories because I am the chief tribal historian of the People."

"So, the Cloud Warriors came from across the Atlantic as two nations, and combined with the Brazilians into one, here in South America. Is that the great secret, or is there more?"

211

"That is part of it. We kept our origin secret because the indigenous people of the Andes didn't like us making it known. They felt we were trying to say we were superior to them.

When more Europeans, Spanish this time, arrived, they came as cruel conquerors. They deceived the masses into assuming the conquistadors were gods—then treated the native people as if they were sub-human animals—destroyed their culture, smashed their artwork. We didn't want to be associated with the Spanish in that way. We would rather get along with our neighbors than subjugate them. All we cared was to be left alone, in peace. Later, we did join with the Spanish for a time, in order to rout the Incas, who were even worse."

"You say that is 'part' of the secret. What else is there?"

"Ah, young AJ, if you consider consequences, I think you can figure that out yourself. You know why the pink stone had to be protected from modern civilizations. Other things, too, must not be discovered and put to use by the wrong factions. It could destroy the world."

At this, AJ flinched, as he began to imagine the magnitude of the consequences. *What if Hitler's henchmen had been able to time travel? Or if their female spies could be invisible? Or what if any country's spies had those abilities? Or even common criminals! Would it keep changing history? The whole world would get so messed up, history changing and people disappearing or new ones appearing....* his mind was doing loops again.

Umayo watched AJ's face going through changes as he grasped the implications of the revelation. "Now that you know, young AJ," he said quietly, "you must not let anyone else discover it—except your father, of course."

"Oh yes, I understand, and I will keep it safe, you can be sure."

Umayo was quiet for a time. *I must pass on a few more things. I think the time has come.* "You have done well, young AJ. I think it is time you hear a few of the stories you have wondered about."

AJ shivered. *What am I about to hear?* He stood holding his breath expectantly, not wanting anything to distract Umayo from such an important disclosure.

"Let us sit," said Umayo, motioning the way to a bench outside the village walls. "My people know many of these stories, and I have passed all of them on to my son, Pacay, as he will be the chief tribal historian after I am gone. But I know you are deeply concerned, and your father has done so much in helping our cause, I want you to know."

Umayo told him some of the stories, ancient tales of the People, the crossing of the Sea of Darkness to Brasil, the adventures of Anat and Ewan, Ysabel and Eppo, and many of the others. He told of Kanmi, how he traded shrewdly for the axe that had been brought from the Old World, and how he'd lost it on the dock in the battle with the anaconda. He gave AJ a brief history of the building of Ayatambo and Kuelap, and the split off to Atahuaqa, and some of its history down to Tica's time.

He didn't explain the secrets of the more recent magical happenings—the transference of Qhawa and Missy, how little Umayo found Kanmi's axe in the Amazon, or how Amzi had acquired certain magical abilities—but he gave AJ an overview of how things were done.

I hope I can remember all this. I wish I had brought a recorder. Then he realized that such a device would be about as welcome at Vilcatambo as a camera.

After several hours, they said goodbye for the night, and AJ found Rafa asleep in the car. He apologized as he slid into the seat, but the driver shrugged, seeming unconcerned, and started up the engine without comment. They took a hair-raising trip over the crude track back to Cuzco, the old car's dim headlights barely piercing the mist and dark. AJ gave Rafa an extra-large tip when they arrived.

AJ returned to his hotel room feeling exhausted by the weight of his new understanding. Right away, he opened his laptop and typed up all he could remember of Umayo's disclosures, working far into the night, having heard somewhere that the average human mind forgets a great deal of what it hears within a short time. He called Amzi the

213

next morning, and told him briefly of his latest discoveries and Umayo's stories. He was bursting to talk about it, but not wanting to utter even a word aloud about the secret things over the phone—he knew Amzi had guessed much of it anyway, from his long association with Umayo.

Now, what to do? It seemed, since he had the origin of the Chachapoyas nailed down for certain, and knew what the guarded secrets were, his main goal had to be to nudge the archaeologists away from making dangerous discoveries—finding Atahuaqa. But for how long? Would it be just a matter of time before someone stumbled upon the hidden city?

When AJ returned to the museum, he was careful to display great enthusiasm over the latest work on the Inca settlement, and Dr. Holcomb was delighted to fill him in on the details. They had discovered some beautiful artifacts, and interesting mummies. AJ fought to keep his attention glued to the finds being shown to him, and to exhibit amazement at appropriate points of interest.

Working at his cubicle in the museum a few days later, AJ noticed a new girl working a few desks away. She was nice looking, with dark red-brown hair and brown eyes. She kept looking at him, then down at her work, some kind of paperwork.

After a while, she came over. "Hello, I'm new here. My name is Cattnia'" she leaned closer and whispered – "Señor blue eyes!"

"Uh, what? *What? No!*"

She laughed and said softly, "Don't worry, I won't tell!" And walked away quickly.

AJ felt a cold chill, then panic. *Who is that? What does she know about me, and how? Why?* He had been very careful, in public, to wear his shaded glasses at all times.

She was back at her desk. She looked up coyly, and put her finger to her lips, then smiled, and went back to her work.

AJ was flustered. *What is this all about? Blackmail? A threat? Or was she just flirting? Have I seen her before? Where have I seen her?* He had been too focused on his research to notice any local women that much. He realized he was sweating.

She returned. "You look so much like your father," she whispered, her eyes twinkling. She was looking around to make sure no one else could hear.

He stood up. "How do you know my father?" he whispered hoarsely. "And where are you from?"

She didn't have to look up at him, being quite a tall young woman. "I saw you and your parents when you were caught in that cave near the farm," she said. "I thought your family seemed so close, and very nice people."

"Oooh, now I remember...Uh, well, I remember your family—that *was* your family, right?"

"Cousins, actually. I was there visiting with them, but I was born at Vilcatambo. Grandfather Umayo told me who you were when I mentioned that I saw you at Vilcatambo. He encourages us to get out and acquire a good education, but insists we always come back to our own people. I've been studying archaeology at the University, and started working here to gain a little experience."

"Would you...ah, would you like to go to dinner with me so we can talk?" AJ, even at 21, was the studious type, not highly experienced with dating. He was still nervous.

"Oh, yes, that would be nice. I do think we have some things to talk about. You may call me Catt." She gave him a sideways glance, brushing back her hair and looking mysterious, as she returned to her desk.

They found a restaurant that offered private tables, out of earshot of others. Cattnia seemed more vivacious and provocative than any of Umayo's people AJ had ever met. He had to admit, he was intrigued.

They looked over the menus. "I will call you 'Gene,' if you want, I know the reason you are keeping out of the spotlight, so to speak – the Sendero Luminoso. That's why I said right away that I wouldn't tell."

"That's a great relief. I wasn't sure what was going on. I'm sorry, I'm kind of a nerd, I guess. I've been deep in research here. I don't remember seeing you before."

215

"That's okay. I haven't been around here much. I've been working at other places in Cuzco and going to school. But I found your family and your father's story so interesting, I wanted to meet you."

"I must say, I'm surprised you are so outgoing. Most of your people are very reserved."

"I guess I was always the odd one in my family. Going to an outside school has made me even more so. I just like being free to have good friends and interesting experiences."

"I hope I don't seem like a wet blanket, but I want to make sure that no one else here knows who I am, except Dr. Holcomb."

"Oh, don't worry. I don't plan to say anything." She made the zip-lips sign, and winked.

"Thank you. You gave me quite a scare. I'd like to be able to finish my research here without getting kidnapped— or worse."

Catt's expression became serious. "Yes, I know about your sister. That must have been hard on your mother— well, all of you. I'm so glad it turned out well. So, I suppose you will eventually be moving back to the States?"

"Yes, I'm not sure when, but I won't be able to stay here indefinitely, and all the rest of my family is back there, of course."

They finished their dinner of ceviche with causa and roasted vegetables, and AJ took Catt back to her apartment in Cuzco. "I'm glad of the opportunity to meet you," she said. "Thank you for dinner. Maybe I'll see you at work again?"

"Could be." AJ gave her a guarded smile as he turned to leave. "Good night." He still wasn't sure what to think of this development. *What is her real motive? She didn't ask me anything specific about my research. Is she just a friendly girl, or is there something else?* He didn't sleep well that night.

The next day, he didn't see Catt at work. He occasionally stopped his own work to look around, sometimes taking a short walk through the building, but didn't find her anywhere. He began to wonder if he'd dreamed the whole thing.

It was Monday, two weeks later, when he saw her at the desk where she'd appeared before. She glanced up and caught him looking her way, and smiled. She motioned, a little finger-wave, so no one else could see.

~*~*~*~*~*~*~

Chapter 28: Fall of Atahuaqa

One morning, a few weeks later, AJ received a phone call at his desk, from Dr. Holcomb. "Gene, I have some news. Please come to my office," he said, and hung up.

AJ, with curiosity and more than a twinge of premonition, hurried to the adjoining building, and Dr. Holcomb's office. As he entered, he was startled to see a gathering of his archaeologist friends, standing around the desk, smiling.

"Mr. McGuire, I wanted you to be in on this! It's a stunning discovery! A lost city, several days out east from a little village called Vilcatambo. You will want to be with us when we go to explore it."

AJ stumbled, and nearly dropped the shaded glasses off his face. His heart skipped a beat, and felt like a weight in his chest. *They must have found Atahuaqa! No! It can't be. It must be a different one. Calm down. Listen to them....*

The professor was talking, making plans. "...then we'll have to get a preliminary expedition together, so it will be a week or two." –He turned to AJ–"I'll let you know, and you can accompany us..." He smiled, then noticed that AJ's face had gone pale. "What's wrong? Are you all right?"

"Oh—yes, I'm sorry, I've been having a problem with-- (gasp!) Sorry, I need to take a pill. Excuse me, please." He started for the door, then looked back briefly. "That's really great news. I'll be waiting to hear more!" Then he hurried out, lurching down the hall to a restroom where he could splash cold water on his face. *I've got to be careful. Mustn't blow my cover. Think! Think!*

Back at his workplace, he made a passing excuse to coworkers of not feeling well, as he hurried out the door and escaped to his hotel room. He called Umayo.

"Hello, Mr. McGuire," said Umayo. Has something happened?"

"I'm afraid so. Have you seen any strangers around your village, or going by, lately? I think someone has discovered something. We need to talk."

"Yes, come as soon as you can. Be careful, though, that you are not followed."

AJ and Rafa arrived in the early afternoon. Umayo met him in the road, as usual, and they walked up the hill together, talking where no one could hear. AJ told him of the announcement, and the plans for an imminent expedition.

"I am not surprised," said Umayo. "We always knew that some day, some person would stumble upon Atahuaqa. We need to prepare."

"Prepare? How will you prepare?" AJ's voice squeaked.

"Calm yourself, please." Umayo didn't seem worried, or even excited. "We must go to Atahuaqa before they get there. There is something I want you to see."

"I'm sorry. I guess it scared me, coming so suddenly. I should have been prepared for this to happen. I'm glad I was there to hear about it."

"Yes, it is good. Do not fear, young AJ. As your people say, it will all work out."

They talked some more, and devised a plan: AJ would discover an "urgent" reason to go home, just before the archaeologists were to leave, and he would stay away until just before the expedition actually left, returning secretly to meet with Umayo. The scientists would travel more slowly, and it would take them at least three days to get to the site. Meanwhile, AJ and Umayo would take a shortcut to Atahuaqa and arrive ahead of the scientists.

219

"It will require close timing, and we must not let them discover you coming back afterward, and realize that you were there when you said you'd be gone."

"Why not go now? It makes me nervous, thinking of them getting there, maybe before we can get out?"

"Do not be stressed, young AJ. The time is not right, yet. It will be done as it was always meant to be."

What does that mean? Umayo doesn't seem to think anything bad will happen. Maybe I'm worried for nothing, but I'll keep close tabs on what the archaeologists are doing. Worries and possibilities tumbled over and over in his mind, all the way back to Cuzco. It was getting dark by the time he entered his hotel room. He tried to sleep, and ended up taking a sleeping pill.

He monitored the office memos and listened to water-cooler talk, into the next week. After eight days, he heard that the expedition would be leaving Wednesday or Thursday of the following week. He quickly called Dr. Holcomb before he'd think that AJ had heard the departure date, telling him something urgent had come up, and he needed to go home. He mustn't let Dr. Holcomb realize he was purposely avoiding the trip.

Dr. Holcomb's voice betrayed disappointment. "I was just about to call you. We'll leave next week, about Wednesday or Thursday. Are you sure you can't come?"

"Oh, I'm sorry." AJ tried to sound surprised. "Family emergency. I won't be able to go with you this time ... maybe on a second trip?"

"Really? I thought you'd not want to miss this."

"Yes, I'm really anxious to hear what you discover, but I need to go home. I'll be back shortly, though, and maybe I can see your discoveries then?"

"Very well. Please call me when you get back. This may be a big breakthrough, and there will probably be plenty for you to see anyway."

AJ called his folks, and told them only that he had some news, and had to come home to talk about it. He caught the first flight to Lima, and then home via Miami. He had too much time to reflect, on the plane, worries tumbling

220

through his thoughts. *I wonder what Umayo has in mind—he seems to have had a strategy in place for a long time for just such an occasion. He knew that someone might discover Atahuaqa, so it wasn't a big shock to him. Will he try to prevent them somehow? What's there that they shouldn't see? What can he do? Destroy something?*

Amzi was waiting to pick him up at the Baltimore airport. They discussed the discovery on the way home to Spurwink, both wondering what would happen, and what Umayo had planned.

Lila was anxious to hear all about it. The three of them had a long talk after a pizza dinner that night. "I think Umayo doesn't mind so much if they see the front part of the city," she suggested, "but I wonder if the thing he doesn't want them to see is the sarcophagi, and especially the ships?"

They looked at her. "Yes, I believe you may be onto something," said Amzi.

"It does seem that the secret of the Chachapoyas has to do with their origin—but it also has to do with their power of time-travel, and of invisibility via the pink emerald," AJ speculated. "All I know to do right now, is to wait until it's time to fly back to meet Umayo, so that's what I'll do. I'll keep in touch, and let you know how it goes. Yachay will let me know when it's time."

The call came Wednesday.

AJ returned to Cuzco late at night, and slipped out of the airport without being recognized. He took a room at a different hotel so no one would notice him, and called Yachay for an update. One of Yachay's people was employed at the museum, keeping watch.

"They are still set to go, leaving the museum early on Thursday," said Yachay. "It will just be a small party, to check out the first reports and look it over, so they can make plans."

AJ met Umayo at Vilcatambo before dawn, prior to the archaeologists' trek. Umayo repeated his plan to get to Atahuaqa before the expedition arrived.

Why? wondered AJ – *what can we do? We can't keep them away now. What is Umayo planning to do there? What good will it do for us to get there just before they do?*

221

The archaeologists' expedition departed from the museum, picking up llamas and native porters on the way out to Vilcatambo. The party was guided by the man who made the discovery. Yachay called AJ and Umayo to let them know the museum people were on their way.

Okay, thought AJ, *they'll take a good three days to get there, but Umayo and I had better get going. I wonder how they found it.*

All went as planned. On the second day, Umayo and AJ were well on their way, taking an alternate trail. Umayo knew several approaches to Atahuaqa, most of them extremely difficult to navigate, purposely made that way anciently, by Crevan, "the Fox." They scaled steep bluffs, thickly grown with spikey agaves and other stickery plants, squeezed through tunnels and climbed narrow steps cut into rock cliffs. AJ's legs and arms were bruised from rocks and bloodied by razor-sharp thorns.

"This is not the way I took your parents," said Umayo, when they paused for a rest.

"No foolin'!" said AJ. He couldn't imagine his mother traversing some of the hair-raising ledges and swinging bridges. *Some trail,* he thought.

On the afternoon of the second day, Umayo stopped, waiting for AJ to catch up. "It isn't far now. I don't think the others are very near yet—they are very slow." A hint of a smile crossed Umayo's face. "We can get to it through here." He motioned toward a tangle of vines that looked impenetrable, but he knew just how to part the foliage, taking hold of a certain branch that opened up the mass like a door. Behind it was another tunnel, the rock carved to look like a huge mouth in a frightening face. AJ shivered as they went through, but the coolness of the cave was a relief from the hot sun as they walked in the dark, dripping shaft.

And there it was.

They entered Atahuaqa, squeezing through a cramped side portal, and passed the temple and ruins of round buildings to the back wall, then through the back passageway. As they broke out into daylight, AJ caught his breath as the sudden dizziness from the heights surprised him on the narrow ledge. Umayo showed him the row of sarcophagi.

"They look like the ones we saw at Kuelap," said AJ. "Of course!" He felt foolish somehow. "Those two new ones... are they..."

"Yes, Tica's and Maupi's. This was our mission when your parents came to help me."

AJ stood, stunned. *Chachapoyas,* he thought. *It's almost too real—of course it's real! They've been hidden in plain sight for hundreds of years, but it took me so long to believe it. And Tica—she's right there on that ledge. Am I dreaming?*

Then Umayo motioned for him to come back to the wall where the ships were painted. AJ felt breathless as they came into view. *How many people ever get to see such a thing?* He couldn't stop staring at the painting. *Yes. Ancient Phoenician and Celtic ships, with square sails and some with rows of long oars. That's how they came....* He could imagine them, two thousand years past, skimming slowly up the ancient Amazon, sails unfurled, men rowing, and Umayo's ancestors surveying their new homeland. He trembled inside.

"Did your father tell you of this?" Umayo asked.

"Only recently. Thank you so much for letting me see it. It's wonderful!" He edged closer to study it. "May I take a picture of it?"

Umayo looked at him for a moment, his face expressionless.

Oh, no! I've really done it this time. They don't like photography.

"Yes, the time has come. Yes, take your picture, and show only your family."

AJ brought out his small digital camera and took one picture. He wished he could ask to take more, but.... best not to push it. *Maybe later.*

"You must go back now," said Umayo, his dark eyes smoldering with emotion. "You must avoid the archaeologists' knowing you were here. They have found Atahuaqa, as we always knew they would. They mean well, but there are things they must not discover." He embraced

223

AJ with the familiar back-pat, and stepped away. "Your father has been a great friend to me—to us. And you, young AJ, I will never forget you."

They heard a far-off rumble ... thunder?

"And you have been a great friend to our family," said AJ, confused. "Wha... are you going away? Will we see you again?"

"Go. *Now!* Hurry to the gates." Umayo took off his hat. It was the first time AJ had ever noticed him looking timeworn... tired. The breeze ruffled his snowy hair. He looked out across the valley as AJ, bewildered, turned to go. Another rumble sounded, *like a truck going over a bridge....*

AJ hurried back through the ruins. As he came away from the front gateway, he could see the archaeologists coming, far off down the mountain. *I can't let them see me here,* he thought, as he picked his way toward some jungle cover. Just then the ground began to move, shaking at first, then seeming to roll like ocean swells. The rumbling grew louder, accompanied by hollow cracking sounds deep underfoot. The ground buckled and tossed, knocking AJ to the ground.

Umayo! AJ turned to look back. But Umayo wasn't there. The whole back part of Atahuaqa was *gone*—the mountainside had caved off into the chasm, and a massive column of dust rose like a mushroom cloud, higher and higher into the sky.

"Nooooo!" screamed AJ, his voice drowned in the powerful roar. He realized with shock -- Tica, all the sarcophagi—and Umayo—were now dust at the bottom of the chasm!

The archaeologists were pointing and yelling to each other. AJ could see they had taken cover on the hillside about half a mile away. At that point, they hadn't yet caught sight of the city, but could see the column of dust rising from the mountainside.

It's as if Umayo knew it would happen, thought AJ, shaking violently. *He and Tica are beyond the reach of the outside world now.*

Was that their plan?

He hurriedly found his way back to Vilcatambo, avoiding the expedition by hiding until they'd passed by, as they hiked up for a cautious look. Their broad trail was easy to follow, even at night, where they'd hacked their way through the jungle. He didn't stop to sleep, and only paused briefly to pick some fruit in the jungle on the way, to keep up his strength. *I need to notify Umayo's relatives of his death. Will they blame me for his being there?* Running helped relieve the pain of his grief.

When AJ reached Vilcatambo, Umayo's son, Pacay, came out to greet him, and was not at all surprised. "I'm glad you were not hurt, Mr. McGuire. My father left something for you." He unwrapped something he was holding in his hands—the ceramic pot with the ships on it.

AJ's hands trembled as he took the sacred family heirloom from Pacay. "You knew—*he* knew?"

Pacay motioned toward the wall. "Come and sit." They moved to a bench where they could talk. He began to tell AJ some more about Umayo. "My father was the leader and chief historian of our tribe. He has passed that honor on to me, and I have been training for many years. He said that you and your family will always be friends to us, and he felt that the more important details of our heritage should be known by a trustworthy family outside of our tribe—your family."

Now AJ thought about Umayo telling the story of the Inca attack back in Tica's time, and how she and a few others escaped, and then the earthquake.

Pacay said Tica had come to Umayo in a dream after the first, the ancient quake that had ruined Atahuaqa, and had later drawn him back to where she and Maupi were buried. Some of the other Chachapoyan survivors of the quake, including Umayo, had regrouped and established Vilcatambo where they lived quietly for about 600 years, many generations. "Umayo lived on," said Pacay, "gained a modern education, and sometimes traveled to different parts of the world, knowing some day he would be there to save Tica's remains and all the rest from the outside world. At

225

Vilcatambo he lived as a potter, and made the piece you hold as a reminder of our journey from the Old Countries.

"He was angered at Orrin Gerard, but watched over the rings, with help from his network of friends, keeping track of where they were, mostly in Peru for many years. Then, in the '80s, the rings began to move through different channels to the States. In early 1975, Tica told him of your father Amzi at Cuzco. He contacted Amzi, supposedly on museum business, building a friendship with him, but didn't tell him about Tica at first. After a time, working together, they became as brothers."

"Do you mean...how do I say this...could I ask... how old was Umayo?"

He saw in Pacay's eyes the same dark, smoldering look. "Yes, he was Tica's older brother. He was not a shaman at that time, but dedicated his life...helped the family and survivors so much.... he was given the gift of long life. He had many years to train as a tribal historian, and developed great abilities. He had several families during those years. My mother, Brynna was his last wife. I have begun to train my son, Ronan, as a tribal historian."

The archaeology team made their way cautiously up the mountain to look at the entranceway of the city. "Take care, there," said Dr. Holcomb, as one of the younger archaeologists forged ahead, "we don't know how stable the ground is, and some of those rocks may yet fall." He was looking nervously at one of the giant boulders overhanging the trail. They came near the front portal of Atahuaqa and approached the tall, narrow entranceway which still stood, now only a facade, where they could look through and see the dust still boiling up from the abyss.

"What if we had come an hour before now!" said one of the men, wiping sweat. "I will carry this day in my memory forever." His friend laid his hand on his shoulder, and nodded agreement. They retraced their trail back to Cuzco as fast as they could manage.

AJ came to the museum the day after they returned, and had no problem acting stunned—he still was.

226

"Well, Gene," said Dr. Holcomb, grimacing, "You missed all the excitement."

"I'm not sorry I missed *that* kind. I hope no one was hurt?"

"Only our expectations. We were all revved up for a great discovery, but now it's too dangerous to go near there for a while. Can you imagine? Most of the city caved off— just dropped right into the valley, before our very eyes!"

AJ's face reflected the grim memory. "I think I can. I've been in earthquakes before, and I didn't like it." His stomach roiled at the thought of Umayo's last moments. *He knew ... He must have prepared himself....*

"Oh, yes, I almost forgot. You were in that cave...."

"Yes. I might have made a great discovery, there, but I escaped with my life, and that's good enough for me."

That night, AJ in Cuzco, and his parents at Spurwink, all shared the same dream, Umayo and Tica, in the pink mist, smiling, holding out their hands. "Do not grieve for us," said Tica. "Our bones are dust on the wind, and the wind blows where it will."

Yes, that was their plan all along. The secret powers of Atahuaca are protected from evil knowledge. The People are finally safe from being poked and prodded and put on display by the modern world, like those at Laymebamba.

They are free.

~*~*~*~*~*~*~

Chapter 29: Grief Shared;
Heading for Spurwink

AJ went to his job at the museum feeling like a zombie, unable to focus on anything. His bones ached. Nothing seemed interesting anymore. He grieved for Umayo as if one of his own brothers had died. He couldn't make himself think about artifacts or mummies or history.

He looked over at Cattnia's workspace. She had come in late, and had dark circles under her red-lidded eyes. He remembered she had called Umayo "Grandfather." *They must have been close.*

When it was getting near lunchtime, AJ rose and walked over to Cattnia's desk. He wasn't hungry; figured she probably wasn't either. "Catt, would you like to go for a walk?"

She nodded, and set aside her work. They left the building and walked along a path where the woodsy landscaping offered a little privacy.

"I know you are feeling a lot of hurt, losing Umayo. I am, too" said AJ. "We had grown close in the last few weeks and months. I miss him terribly—he was a great man."

She looked at him, with tears beginning to flow. "AJ," she whispered, choking up, "he was such a wonderful grandfather to me. He raised me after my parents died in an accident in Cuzco. He taught me so many things..." She turned to him, and he gently took her in his arms. She laid her head on his shoulder and sobbed, and his own eyes were stinging with tears. His throat hurt.

"He wasn't actually my grandfather, but it didn't matter. I have never known anyone who understood... so much."

They held each other for a long time, feeling a comfort neither had realized they were aching for. Then Cattnia moved away a little.

"I'm sorry," she said. "I hardly know you. But you seem to understand more than anyone else I know. I have some family back at Vilcatambo, but I've grown detached from them in the last few years. Grandfather Umayo..." she choked up, "...was all I had." She turned away as her face crumpled in agony.

AJ put his arm around her again. "I think I know what you mean. He seemed to know so many things, understand just what was going on—when I hadn't a clue."

"The others at home act as if it were meant to happen. It was his mission in life to protect Atahuaqa, and die with it. He fulfilled it, they say, so all is well."

This was something AJ had been shocked to hear implied, first from Pacay. He was tempted not to believe such a thing could be true. He felt he didn't know Pacay well enough, though a friendship seemed to be growing between them after Pacay had shared the stories with him. *Other things have always turned out to be true—could it be?* Suddenly it seemed as if the whole world focused in on AJ and Cattnia, but it was all a blur of pain.

They returned to work, both pretending to be absorbed in their jobs, for the rest of the afternoon. AJ had called his parents to tell them about the quake and Umayo. They didn't talk much about it—there weren't any words.

The next day, he sat at his desk, fiddling with papers. *I don't know if there's anything left to do. Why am I still here? A good question. Why am I still here? Should I tell Dr. Holcomb a certain portion of what I've found, enough to satisfy him, and let that be it? I could leave, then. Maybe my mission down here is finished.* He looked over at Cattnia.

She looked depressed, wooden, as if she were just going through the motions.

AJ put together a proper scientific report, a summary of what he'd found at the different sources, from the Internet and the papers he'd studied at the museum, and his own experiences at the shipyard in Brazil, omitting the part about Kanmi's axe. His conclusion was interesting in itself. He wrote that he felt, personally, that the Chachapoyas had come from somewhere in Europe, that likely they were, as some had suggested, both Phoenician and Celtic, and mixed with Brazilian natives, the fact borne out by DNA studies. He gave no more proof than what he'd discovered in other researchers' findings. He called Dr. Holcomb, then went to see him.

"Well, I must say, this is very intriguing," said Dr. Holcomb, after skimming over the papers. "I had hoped we would find more conclusive evidence, something tangible, but this is a big step in that direction. Are you sure you don't want to stay and do more research?"

"I'm sorry, but home beckons, and frankly, I've run out of places to research, at least for now. Maybe I'll be back, at some future point. More discoveries may come—who knows? But right now I feel I'm spinning my wheels. I don't want to waste your time, either."

"I'm sorry to see you go, but I understand. Give your father my fondest regards, and the rest of your family, too."

AJ felt a bit of heaviness lifted, though it certainly was not all gone. He went back to clear his desk and pack up his things. He looked over at Cattnia. She looked forlorn. *She's lost between two worlds,* he thought. He walked over to her desk.

"Oh, I just don't feel well today, I'll be better soon." She looked down.

But he could see that her eyes were still red. *This is no place to be so alone.* "Let's have dinner and talk again. Would that be okay?" he asked.

As before, she nodded and put away her work, then accompanied him out of the building. "I'm not sure what I'm going to do with my life," she said as they walked. "I thought maybe I could have a career in archaeology, but I've lost interest, these days. Maybe it will come back."

AJ was quiet as they walked a little farther. "I'm going home," he said. "I've just realized I don't have much to do here anymore."

Cattnia looked at him, startled. She knew she had no reason to feel abandoned, but she did. "I'm sad to hear that." She caught her breath, uncertain of what to say.

He stopped and turned to her. "Catt, would you like to get away for a while? Would you like to come with me, even just for a couple of weeks, to clear your mind, and be able to think, without worrying about work? My family has a big house, and I'm sure there would be a nice room where you could stay, and have privacy. No commitments, no pressure."

She stood, looking at him. "I...I don't know....let me think about it... ... ... yes!"

What am I doing? thought AJ. *What will the family think? This is so sudden. But I know they'll understand— they always do.*

Catt got some time off from work, and they booked their flight to the States. They sat together on the plane, and AJ let her sit by the window so she could look down. "This is my first really long flight," she said. "It should be interesting."

"I've been getting used to it, lately. I've been traveling all over between Peru and Brazil, but, exciting as it is, I always love going home. You'll love my family, Catt. And I know they'll love you."

It's doing her good already, to get into totally new surroundings. I feel better, too. I think it will be a healing journey, and ... who knows what else? ... Hmm ... Where did that thought come from? He had called his parents to let them know he was coming home for a while, and bringing a friend—a Chachapoyan girl.

Hanging up the phone, they were astonished at first, then looked at each other with realization. "He's old enough, and by now I'm sure he knows what he's about," said Amzi. "I wonder if it's serious. He didn't say anything to you, did he?"

231

"Not a word. Maybe he's like his father, a fast worker," she gave him a jab in the ribs.

"Ha! You chased me so fast, I caught you," he said, and they both laughed.

By the time AJ and Cattnia arrived, there was a nice room ready and waiting for her. She had observed Lila and Amzi at the family farm near Vilcatambo, but she was looking forward to really getting to know them and the rest of the family at Spurwink. Viola whipped up a welcoming dinner of causa, roasted vegetables, and a nortéamericano touch—fried chicken.

Catt spent hours in her room the first couple of days, but gradually began to come down more often to visit with Lila, Elfie and Melanie, and to take walks with AJ. He had explained to the family about the sudden blow she had received with Umayo's death, and her family not understanding her pain. She was greatly comforted by the warmth and support she'd found at Spurwink.

Gradually, she began to take part in the family's activities. She liked the spaghetti and other dishes Viola made, and observed the sewing ladies' activities when they came for their weekly sessions at Spurwink.

She was amused by Danny and Ben's friendly humor. Brightened at the sight of their small alpaca herd, she was learning the names of the animals when she came across Ben's favorite white alpaca. "What is her name?" she asked, petting the nuzzling beast.

"Oh, that's Pookie," said Ben, "I don't know why I named her that, she just seemed to be "Pookie," and the name stuck."

"Ah, I think I know why," said Catt. "An old Amazonian name is 'Pucu'. It was the name of Tica's white llama."

There was a moment of mutual amazement as the boys' and Catt's gazes connected.

AJ, Amzi, and Lila took long walks together, reminiscing about times with Umayo. So many things seemed to work out in a strange, mystic way—was it the influence of the Ancients?

232

Frequently, AJ and Catt sat and talked in the gazebo. It was getting late in the summer, autumn leaves coloring up. She watched the squirrels busily searching for acorns. This was all new and foreign to her, but she was beginning to relax and feel a little better, and so was AJ. *It was a good idea for me to come home, and good for Catt to get away, too.*

Lila and Amzi noticed the two in the gazebo, and were reminded of those times when they sat there together, too. "She's a pretty girl," said Lila, leaning against Amzi. "The Chachapoyas have such a serene, gentle look."

Two weeks flashed by. Catt began to think about packing to leave.

"You can stay as long as you like," said Lila. "We've enjoyed getting to know you."

"Oh, I've taken advantage of your hospitality so much already, I don't want to overdo it."

"Come for a walk, Catt," said AJ. "One last time, at least." He gave his parents a meaningful look over his shoulder as he escorted Catt out the door.

"Are you thinking what I'm thinking?" said Amzi to Lila.

"Let's wait and see," said Lila with a smile. "I think something is brewing."

AJ and Catt walked along the road to Ravenwood, strolling in silence for a while. The brilliant autumn leaves were beginning to fall. Birds were migrating in the sky overhead. The two came to the town park, and finding themselves alone there, sat on a bench together.
"Catt," AJ began, "I know you've been brought up to feel you should live at Vilcatambo all your life, and be a part of your family's culture. I was wondering, how strong a tie is that?"

"It's a strong tie. Most of our people keep their home base there, even if they temporarily live outside like I did, to get a higher education." She looked down, as if afraid to look AJ in the eye. She felt her heart beating faster.

"Do any of your people ever...uh, decide to live elsewhere, move away to another country? Is it forbidden, or...."

"What are you asking, AJ? Are you asking if I would live somewhere other than Vilcatambo?" She was looking at him now, at his startlingly blue eyes. She could hardly breathe.

AJ took her hand. "I've dated a few girls, here and at college, but I find more and more that I have nothing in common with them. They are only interested in TV, social media, clothes, celebrities, whatever—you get the idea. I have never felt as close or comfortable with any of them as... as I do with you."

She looked down at his hand holding hers. "Yes, and so?"

"Cattnia, will you marry me?"

She was silent for a long minute.

Oh, no—it's too soon. I blew it, thought AJ.

"*Yes,* AJ. I would love to marry you!" She wrapped her arms around his neck and they kissed, a lingering, warm kiss that melted their hearts together as one. Then she drew away. "But... but I must... *we* must... ask Pacay for permission."

AJ's heart sank a little. What would Pacay think? *He seemed understanding and friendly when I was with him. But maybe this is a whole different kind of thing.... would this seem to be a betrayal of Pacay's trust—of the Tribe?*

"Don't worry, AJ," she said. "Pacay has been inseparable with Umayo for a long time. They were very close, and thought as one."

What would Umayo have thought? AJ worried. *Would he have felt it treachery to take his Cattnia, this special girl, away from Vilcatambo and their culture?* "I guess the next thing to do is ask him."

They walked back to Spurwink and made their announcement, of their intentions, at least, and were smothered with hugs and good feelings.

One week later, AJ and Cattnia would take another long flight—south, this time, to Peru.

~*~*~*~*~*~

Chapter 30: Home on the Amazon

The growing household at Spurwink had no problem accepting Catt into the family – they all loved her. She had felt drawn to AJ and his parents from the time she'd observed them at her cousins' family farm after the quake in Peru. Watching Umayo's growing affinity and respect for him had encouraged her.

She and AJ drove to Baltimore to find a jeweler, where AJ bought her an engagement ring – a green emerald set in gold, with a small diamond on each side. "I think it goes well with that beautiful glint of red in your hair." He smiled as he slipped it on her finger.

Lila had taken her aside one day and asked her to come out to the gazebo for a chat. She told Catt how she had come to love Amzi, and that her mother had died at about that time. Because of that, she could better understand Catt's mixed feelings of joy and sadness. She could see the pain in Catt's eyes whenever Umayo was mentioned.

"I just want to make sure you know your true feelings for AJ," Lila said. "I know I could have been swayed at my time of great grief, but I was certain that Amzi and I were meant to be together. He was so kind and comforting to me when I needed him. I know AJ has deep feelings for you...."

"Oh, Mrs. Darrow...."

"Just call me Lila, honey."

"Lila, it is true that I have such sadness in my heart. Grandfather Umayo was the great person in my life, and AJ seemed to be the only one I knew who truly understood. My own family avoided talking about his death, and seemed to feel it was expected, and that we shouldn't feel great shock or sorrow. I know it is our way, our culture, but I can't help my feelings." Her eyes were brimming with tears again. "I have somehow felt a magnetic attraction toward AJ and your family ever since that day at the farm. I couldn't stop thinking about all of you, and then... when Atahuaqa..." Her lip began to tremble.

"You can't help feeling pain when your heart is raw with grief," said Lila her own tears welling. "AJ must have known that getting away for a while would help. It did for me." She gave Catt a warm hug, and told her the whole story of the rings, her mother's death, of marrying Amzi and then their mission to take the rings back to Tica at Atahuaqa.

Catt had heard parts of it before from Umayo, but after putting it all together, she felt even closer to the family.

AJ and Catt boarded a plane for Miami after a week of close family talks. AJ donned his shaded glasses again as they neared the Cuzco airport. He would not be in the country very long this time, but he still needed to be careful, for his own safety, and now Catt's, and by association, all who lived at Vilcatambo.

Pacay had told him earlier that the Shining Path informant was gone from the village. Umayo had given Pacay all authority to control the affairs of the tribe there, and Pacay was tired of everyone having to walk and talk so carefully. He 'discovered' the spy's activities one day, and sent the guy packing. This failed enemy agent would probably have to flee the country to avoid punishment by the Sendero Luminoso. Good riddance!

And now, AJ and Catt had returned together—with unexpected news. Initially, Pacay was surprised at this turn of events, but he knew Cattnia, and although it was a bit unconventional to allow modern-day nortéamericanos into the tribe, it had been the ancient way of the People, intermarrying with other races. And AJ, after all, was a special friend. Pacay thought about it, and came to realize this could be part of that pact he had been told to make with AJ—to have this chosen 'outside' family guarding their secret, the secret of Atahuaqa. "Yes," he said, "I believe it is fitting. I believe Umayo would have given his blessing. Your family will now be part of the People, AJ, and we will be part of your family." They shared a brotherly embrace and a firm back-pat.

The wedding took place two weeks later. AJ had called the family at Spurwink to tell them how it would be done according to tribal traditions, and that they would hold a second ceremony for the Maryland folks when they returned. "I wish we could take pictures, but..."

"Yes, I understand," said Lila.

Meanwhile, AJ was given a place in one of Umayo's round houses while being instructed in the way of the People. Pacay taught him even more of their history and culture. It was difficult for AJ to sleep at night with the realization that he was living in Umayo's home village, seeing things that Umayo saw and used in his lifetime. He lay on the sleeping pallet, wondering if Umayo had lain there, looking at those walls, with clothes, tools, musical instruments and other things he might have used, sitting on shelves or hanging from pegs as he might have left them. It still seemed like a dream, and gave him jolts of excitement to think of it. And then to be married, himself, in their tribal wedding ritual... felt like an echo from ancient times:

Catt was a dark-eyed beauty, her hair glinting red highlights under a crown of jungle orchids. She wore a long, graceful white tunic of finely woven alpaca wool, painted and embroidered with colorful flower motifs. It had been handed down in her mother's family for generations.

AJ was dressed in Chachapoyan wedding garb of white embroidered and painted alpaca wool, loaned by

Pacay's family. *I wonder if Umayo ever wore this?* thought AJ as he dressed for the event.

Pacay explained that these wedding garments were heirlooms, having been carefully preserved by generations of parents of brides and grooms, and they were several hundred years old. Each family had its particular symbols and styles of embellishment, within the Chachapoyan traditions, which were a combination of the Celtiberian and Kena'anim, forged down through the ages into their own distinctive style, with some added Andean touches. The same held true with the ceremony:

Members of Catt's and Umayo's families joined hands in a circle in the center of the village, surrounding the bride and groom, who were barefoot, symbolizing closeness to Mother Earth. Cattnia smiled, her eyes full with tears of joy, as the residents of Vilcatambo called friendly taunts to the happy couple.

Several musicians joined in playing traditional melodies on their panpipes, and a Celtic musician added to the beauty of the ritual, playing an ancient-style lyre. AJ's and Catt's hands were clasped together and a ceremonial piece of embroidered linen was wound around their hands by Umayo's widow, Brynna. The village holy man presided with nuptial vows, the age-old ceremony brought down through generations on the great migration from the Amazon to the Andes, a combination of Celtiberian, Phoenicean and Brasilian traditions.

AJ and Catt embraced, kissed, and then AJ lifted her high above his head, turning slowly as she laughed and spread her arms wide, coming down into another embrace. The crowd cheered and made loud, joyous music with flutes, drums and panpipes as they danced around the couple, chanting.

They held a great feast, with the whole settlement contributing and partaking of the bounty. Many partook a little too much of the wine, made from jungle fruits, but it was amiably overlooked on this occasion of great celebration.

Awakening the next morning, blue eyes and brown eyes united their gaze as the dawn light of their new beginning streamed in.

"Did you have a dream?" she whispered.

"You too? Was it Umayo?" ... she nodded. "Yes, I had the same...."

"I feel so much better—he looked happy for us."

"I thought so, too. ......"

AJ and Catt had agreed to stay at Vilcatambo for a month before going back to the States. It might be a long time before they could visit again. They were happy together, even though the poignant reminders of Umayo were all around. They resolved to just acknowledge the sad fact and try to deal with it, each in their own way, finding comfort in each other. They were welcomed wherever they went in the village, and AJ was made to feel part of the community. He learned some new skills, lending a hand with neighbors' daily tasks, finding materials in the jungle, learning to make his own tools, even learning to use the sling. Starting at his age, he couldn't expect to achieve the skill of a Chachapoyan slinger, but with practice, it would be something he might use...some day.

Pacay spent some time with him most days, repeating the stories to help him memorize them, and AJ filled a notebook with them as well.

"I'll never be able to remember as much as a true tribal historian," he said, but I'm happy to know a good part of the history—it's amazing."

Catt, as well, spent hours making household items she would probably need in her new home, practicing with the drop-spindle inherited down the generations of her family. It was a special heirloom, archaic and time-worn, brought along from the Old Country as the People migrated up the Amazon. She could almost feel their presence as she worked, inspiring her to make traditional heirlooms for her beginning family, copied by memory from things she had grown up with at Vilcatambo. It strengthened her connections with the People and the long, important history

239

of their origins. "So we will never forget," as Umayo would have said.

A month later, they boarded a plane for Lima, and made the trip to Miami, then home to Baltimore and Spurwink. AJ hoped Catt could be happy there. He thought he'd try to find work at the Ravenwood Museum, and maybe she would, too, given her interest in archaeology.

Arriving at Spurwink, they were welcomed with lots of hugs and well-wishing, and excited talk of plans for a nortéamericano wedding, so the Darrow and Spurwink families could take part in it. Daisy had returned from art school with her fiancé, Tony, and soon everyone began to talk about the wedding.

Though AJ and Catt spent most of their time together, there were times when Catt sat huddled alone on a bench under the trees, out by the garden. She had a faraway look in her deep brown eyes, and it worried AJ. He came, softly, and asked if anything was wrong.

"I'm sorry," she said. "I just have to be by myself at times, to think about things and to pay respects to Grandfather Umayo."

"It's fine, I just want to make sure you have what you need. If you want some space, it's here, whenever you feel that way."

It took three weeks for Daisy, Lila and Melanie, along with AJ and Catt, to get the details decided, sending the few invitations and making ready the other trappings for the ceremony.

Catt was intrigued with the preparations for a nortéamericano wedding. She and Daisy went shopping together with Lila and Melanie, and found dresses, veils and bouquets. Catt was satisfied to let Daisy pick out everything else, since she figured this one was more for the Darrow family anyway. She had already had the ceremony that was more important to her, and she treasured those memories. AJ just wanted to be done with it, but to be sure that Catt was content.

Catt settled in as a real part of the family now, and participated happily with the Spurwink sewing ladies, entertaining them with her skill in using her drop-spindle. She regaled them with even more exotic tales of the Andes as she worked. It gave her a way to fill the time as they looked forward to the upcoming wedding.

The big day finally came, and Amzi's parents and sister were thrilled to attend. Danny was AJ's Best Man, and Daisy's fiancé, Tony, was his Groomsman. Aunt Elfie was excited to be Matron of Honor, while Jason, her husband, was pleased to be just an observer. Wilson and Zoe, Spurwink Manor's gardener and his wife were there, and their eight-year-old daughter, Barb, was thrilled to be the flower girl. Cousin Tamara, and Sue, a classmate and friend of Daisy's, were bridesmaids, while Ben played special piano pieces before the ceremony, and his friend Karen sang a favorite song, "Whither Thou Goest, I Will Go," from the Book of Ruth in the Bible. Another friend, Don, took wedding photos.

As mother of the groom, Lila had great difficulty in holding back tears, and Amzi felt honored to escort the bride down the aisle. Lorna and Courtland Darrow were honored guests. It was all done at the little Wexford church where Amzi and Lila had been married. The reception afterward was festive and fun. Catt savored the warmth and humor of the family interactions.

"Too bad Uncle Angus didn't get to see this," Lila murmured to Amzi in a slightly somber tone.

"Well, you know, maybe he did," said Amzi. "I wouldn't rule it out. And Umayo, too."

Lila smiled and leaned on him.

The happy couple took off on their honeymoon, and flew to Scotland, to tour the ancient Darrow lands of Darroch, near Falkirk. "In ancient Gaelic, "Darroch" came from the name "Macdara," meaning "Son of Oak," AJ explained to Catt. "They say there may have been a grove of oaks somewhere in that area."

"I remember the oak trees in Maryland," said Catt.

"Yes, Oakland Manor got its name from the Darrow oaks, and my father had some beautiful furnishings made at the hacienda in Cuzco, designed in oak wood and cast iron in the theme of oak leaves and acorns."

At the reminder of Cuzco and the hacienda, he changed the subject. Too many negative memories surfaced, even though he had never seen the place himself.

They returned after two weeks, taking up an apartment that Melanie had arranged for them in the sprawling Spurwink house.

But AJ and Catt had been talking of their future. He had noticed that even with the scenery of the rugged Scottish highlands as a distraction, Catt still could not shake off her melancholy memories.

She was so bright and mischievous when I first met her. Now she's like a butterfly with a broken wing, thought AJ. *Maybe we both could use a complete change of setting.* The next time they talked in the gazebo, he proposed a whole new scenario—in Brazil. After hearing his ideas, and descriptions of life on the Amazon, Catt agreed that it might be a good thing, too.

They left after a week at Spurwink, flying to Manaus, and then took the riverboat trip, back the way AJ had gone in search of Kanmi's axe. They talked of the future as they gazed at the Milky Way, brilliant in the unpolluted black of the Amazon sky. Memories flooded back for AJ, as they glided along the great river. It had been months since he'd been here. Could it be healing for Catt, a new world to take away her depression? Would they be welcomed? Dom Calder had said, "Hey, come back sometime." Had he meant what he said?

AJ had a fleeting feeling of uncertainty when the little riverboat came into view. Then Dom caught sight of him— his face broke into a wide grin—and all doubts fled away. He was surprised but elated to see AJ—and with a bride! The ride to the little village was filled with excited talk and plans, and Carina was ecstatic to have a new friend.

The whole village participated in building a new house of jungle wood and thatch, each family donating a chicken for the pen underneath. They cleared some land for a garden.

"I love chickens," said Catt. "I helped keep ours at Vilcatambo."

AJ noticed a fleeting shadow of sadness pass across her face at the mention of her girlhood home. "It's a good thing, I think. You will have lots here to take up your time and thoughts."

Catt agreed. She immersed herself in her new surroundings, and worked with enthusiasm.

Soon Dom and AJ were hunting and fishing together, between Dom's boat trips, and Catt helped Carina in the café. AJ had learned many new skills at Vilcatambo, and put them to good use right away. Catt, of course, had grown up with the People at Vilcatambo, and was well-versed in their arts and crafts, including spinning yarn with her precious drop-spindle. As she worked, she often dreamed of it being used by generations of women of the People, making warm clothes for their families in the Andes.

Here, of course, there was no need of warm clothes, nor were there any wool-bearing animals, but they brought in cotton and other fibers, and Catt discovered a new interest in creating fancy bags, clothing, and other items to sell, shipping them out via Dom's riverboat.

Soon she was expecting their first child, and happily looking forward to a new way of life. A boy was born in July of the next year, and named Umayo Amzi Darrow.

AJ sat snuggled beside Catt, gazing down lovingly as she nursed baby Umayo. "All this," he mused "—what happened with my family, your family, the protection of Atahuaqa, even the existence of myself, my brothers and sister—began when my mother accidentally found a ring."

Catt looked at him and smiled, but her dark eyes were simmering again. "AJ, my love, do you really think that was an accident?"

In the back of his mind, he heard the ancient voices echoing:

"Our bones are dust on the wind, and the wind blows free."

Glossary

(I have given the indigenous name wherever possible)

Animals

Alpaca (possibly from Spanish *al* + Quechua *p'ake*) – a smaller relative of the llama, raised for meat and especially their soft, thick wool. (Sometimes mistaken for sheep by the Conquistadors—(*See Special Notes*).

Amaru (Quechua) – snake, serpent or dragon.

Anaconda (originally from Sinhalese *henacandaya*), the name later transferred to a very long, heavy South American boa, a jungle snake that crushes its victims in its coils.

Anhinga (Tupi *áyinga*) – a black, pelican-like, fish-eating bird of tropical and subtropical America, with a long, sharp-pointed beak and long neck.

Arapaima – *Pirarucu* – a huge, armor-scaled carnivorous fish, sometimes as long as 9 ft., can weigh 300 lbs. or more. Its gaping mouth is full of teeth, even on its tongue. Its armor is impervious even to piranhas.

Boto – Pink river dolphins of the Amazon and other rivers and lakes in South America.

Capi-bara (Tupi-Guarani) – Capybara – very large rodents, often 4 ft. long or more; look like giant guinea pigs.

Chinchilla – one of several small rodents (including *cuy* and *viscacha*) native to the Andes that are hunted for meat. Also known for its soft, luxurious fur.

Birds – many birds here go by their modern English names – eagle, owl, parrot. Some names like toucan, condor, macaw, and anhinga, are actually of Tupi-Guarani or Quechua origin.

Condor (Quechua *kuntur*) – the Andean condor is the largest flying bird in the world by combined weight and wingspan.

Crocodile (Latin *crocodilus*) – these were actually *caimans*, more closely related to alligators, but they looked and behaved so much like the crocs they remembered from Africa, the People naturally called them crocodiles.

Cuy, or cavi (Spanish) or cavy – guinea pig, native to the South American Andes, raised for a source of meat in South America, and as a pet most everywhere else.

Horned frog – "horns" and edges on its head make it look like dead leaves when it burrows into a pile of jungle humus with its head sticking out. It waits for small prey to walk by, so it can leap out with its huge mouth open and engulf its meal. It makes a mooing sound at night.

Jaguar (Tupi-Guarani *yaguara*) – the largest American member of the cat family. More compact and well-muscled than the puma, it has a beautiful black and tan spotted coat like a leopard, and some jaguars are very dark, almost black.

Jaraqui (Portuguese) – a small, silvery fish with a colorful striped tail; a popular food fish of the Amazon.

Jurutai bird (possibly a Guarani name) – a brownish nocturnal bird with large yellow eyes, it sings sad-sounding songs at night.

Llama – (Quechua) – a family of South American camelids, related to the smaller alpacas, vicunas, and guanacos. A very important animal in Peru for meat, wool, milk, and especially for hauling freight.

Macaw (Tupi-Guarani) – a species of large, colorful parrot.

Ocelot (Nahuatl or Aztec) – a small jungle cat of Central and South America, it is about twice as big as a house cat, with a beautiful marbled coat.

Pira-na (Tupi and Gaurani) – piranha, a fish that tears through flesh quickly with many sharp teeth. They often attack prey or a carcass in numbers, quickly cleaning the meat off the bones.

Poison dart frogs – several species are used by natives in tropical Central and South America to poison the tips of blowgun darts. These tree frogs are so poisonous that just brushing against their skin can kill an adult human. They are usually very brightly colored, a warning to all.

"See-through" frog – the Glass Frog, several species of tree frog of tropical South American rain forests that have a translucent underside, so you can see the heart and other organs working.

Suri grubs – *Cocotero* – larvae of the palm weevil which feasts upon the aguaje palm. Their large, edible grubs can be up to 5 inches long. Usually roasted on sticks over a fire.

Tapi-ira (Tupi) – tapir. A distant relative of horse and rhinoceros that looks like a combination of deer and pig with a flexible snout.

Toucan (Tupi *tucano*) – a tropical, fruit-eating bird, usually mostly black, with a huge, strikingly colorful beak.

Viscacha – a mountain rodent that lives in the rocky highlands of the Andes. It looks like a rabbit with a long tail, but is related to the chinchilla.

~*~

Plants, Foods:

Agave (see *Chaguar*).

Amaranth – not really a grain, but a staple (seed) food of the Incas, high in carbohydrates, fats and protein.

Ananas (Tupi) – pineapple, the "excellent fruit" of Brazil. (English pine apple) originally meant pine cone,but when English explorers discovered ananas in Brazil, they thought the fruit looked like pine cones, so they transferred the name to the fruit.

Bamboo – in this story, a neotropical woody bamboo native to Latin America.

Batata (see papa) – potato.

Bijao – edible leaves of achira, a kind of canna lily, used in marketplace booths to wrap food to eat out of hand.

Cajá (from Tupi *aka'ya*) – a small, oval fruit related to both mango and cashew – juicy, eaten with the skin on. Tastes like mango. Another name for the tree is Siriguela (derived from Latin *cereola pruna* 'wax colored plums').

247

Callampa – wild edible mushrooms of Peru, served in a dish
called *Capchi* in restaurants. During the rainy season,
lightning strikes the earth and calls up huge callampas.
Some say these mushrooms are a gift from the union of the
gods – the lightning (male) and Pachamama (female).

Capchi – a special dish made with Callampa mushrooms.

Capirona – a jungle canopy tree, grows to 90 ft. It produces good
lumber. (*See also in Medicinal Plants.*)

Cashew – (tree) from a Tupi word *acajú*, or *caxu* – that means
"nut that produces itself," after the strange way it grows one
nut from the bottom of each cashew apple. (Cashew apples
are also edible.)

Cassava or manioc – (see *yuca*, an Arawak word, not yucca, a
different plant), a widely eaten root used for flour, breads,
tapioca, and a fermented drink, *chica* beer.

Chaguar (Quechua, pronounced "*chawar*") agave – a spiny,
succulent plant of arid countries that grows in rosettes with
many sharp-tipped, leathery leaves which have strong
fibrous tissue useful for making ropes, nets, sandals and
sleeping mats. The sap can be made into alcoholic drinks.
The leaves and roots have many medicinal uses, as well as
a sweet, syrupy nectar.

Chica beer (Spanish *chica*, girl or young woman) -- sometimes
called "spit beer." (The starter is traditionally made by
women -- the chewed pulp triggers fermentation.)
Traditionally brewed from manioc (yuca) or purple corn, it
can be made from several other plants as well.

Chili peppers (*see Ruqutu*)

Choclo – a special variety of "giant" corn, with short ears of very
large kernels, grown for eating steamed, roasted or boiled,
with meals.

Cinnamomum (Latin) – cinnamon, imported from the Old World.

Faseloi (Greek *phaseloi*) – beans. Seed was imported from the
Old World.

Guayava (Tupi or Arawak) – guava.

Huayro – a favorite variety of Peruvian potato with a rich
taste, used in causa and other dishes.

Jabillo tree – the tallest tree in the Amazon, it can grow to
over 200 ft. tall. Leaves are as wide as 2 ft. Its sap
is sometimes used by natives for poison darts.

Jabuticaba or bark-fruit – from the Tupi words *jabuti*
(tortoise) and *caba* (place) – "Place where turtles are found."
Plum-size fruit that looks like grapes, growing all over the
bare trunks and branches of the tree.

Jocote (see siriguela).

Kakawi (Quechua) – *Cacao* (tree) – cocoa or chocolate. "Food of
the gods" – natives learned to ferment it and mix it with fruit
juices to sweeten it.

Keras (Latin) carrot – imported from the Old World.

Kickere (Latin) chickpea – imported from the Old World.

Kinwa (Quechua *Quinoa)* – Inca "mother grain" relative of
the amaranth family, the seeds are used like rice or
couscous, very important to the Peruvian diet, high in
protein.

Lentes (Latin) lentils – imported from the Old World.

Lúcuma fruit (Andean) – the (tree) fruit resembles an avocado, but
with orange or yellow flesh. The taste is between maple
syrup and sweet potato.

Mahiz or maiz – maize, corn (native to the Amazon and all South
America, Central America, and Mexico) It has been a vital
food crop for at least 3,000 years.

Pacay – ice cream bean. A tree with large bean-like pods with
very sweet, fibrous pulp surrounding black seeds. The pulp
is used for flavoring ice cream.

Palmito – the only native palm tree of Majorca and the Balearic
Islands.

Papa (Quechua) – potato, also called *batata* (Taino). The
potato is native to Peru, where archaeological evidence is
noted from at least as early as 2500 BC. Early Moche
Indians were fascinated by the strange malformed shapes,
and it inspired weird pottery and art provoked by an emotion
called *mundo hororroso*, an abhorrence of physical
deformities.

Papaya (Carib or Arawak) – a tropical American tree resembling a
palm, with a bunch of large leaves at the top of the trunk.
The large, melon-like fruit is yellowish-orange inside, with
black seeds, and can be eaten raw or cooked, or made into
juice. Incas grew this fruit in Peru.

Peki (Tupi *peki'i*, or Tupi-Guarani, *pyqui)* – a tree fruit with sharp
spines on the inside seed hulls. After the juicy fruit has been

eaten, the seed hulls are dried and cracked open, and the seed kernels inside are roasted and salted, eaten like peanuts.

Pippali (Sanskrit) – black pepper, a seasoning spice imported from India.

Pisa (Latin) – peas, a vegetable garden seed imported from the Old World.

Pitanga (old Tupi *'ybapytanga'*, from *'yba'* [fruit] and *'pytanga'* [colored light red or brown.]) also called Brazilian Cherry and many other names. Small, juicy, deeply corrugated, red or orange fruit, a tree, native to tropical South America. (*See also in Medicinal Plants*).

Quinoa (*see Kinwa*).

Ruqutu (Quechua) Chili pepper – many different kinds of peppers are native to the Amazon.

Singabera, or zingeber – ginger. A well-known spice all over the Old Countries of Europe and Asia.

Siriguela, or Jocote (from Nahuatl, *xocotl*) – a very popular small fruit, grown for thousands of years in tropical America. It is related to the cashew and mango.

Tumbo fruit (Tupi-Guarani *mara cuya*,) – passionfruit. Small, edible, yellow or purple elongated egg-shaped fruit of the passionflower vine.

Uchucuta – Peruvian red-hot chili sauce.

Unio (Latin for *large pearl*) – onion. *Unyun* in Middle English, as Romans introduced it to Britain.

Vainilla (Spanish) – vanilla, a flavoring substance made from the seed pod of the vanilla bean, a vining orchid plant in the Amazon jungle.

Yacon – Peruvian ground apple or strawberry jicama, related to Jerusalem artichoke. Produces large, juicy, edible tubers with texture similar to jicama; flavor is like apple/pear. It has been cultivated for centuries on the eastern slopes of the Andes toward the Amazon, also in Bolivia, Colombia to N. Argentina. Health benefits: weight loss, control of insulin levels, aids digestion, and is high in antioxidants.

Ynchic (Inca, Quechua inchik, Spanish mani)—peanut. An annual vine with yellow flowers and brittle pods that ripen underground, containing one to three edible seeds. The Inca

name means "ground nut." Peanuts originated in Peru and
Brazil.

Yuca (Arawak) – (see *cassava* or *manioc*), an edible root,
(not to be confused with Yucca, a flowering plant of the
agave family.) Used in making chica beer.

~*~

Special Notes:
Some of these were not mentioned in the story, yet are important
parts of the Andes and Amazon.

Alfajor – a famous South American cookie. Caramel filling
between two thin cookie wafers, coated with either powdered
sugar or coconut. (Some kinds of alfajores were eaten
anciently in Iberia and the Middle East).

Brazier – a cooking device used since ancient times to burn
charcoal or other solid fuel for cooking, heating, or for
cultural rituals. Often takes the form of a metal or ceramic
box or bowl with feet, the elevation helping circulate air to
the fire.

Brazil nut – the most common tree in the Amazon is the Brazil nut
tree. They can grow up to 150 feet tall with a trunk up to 6
feet wide. The Brazil nut tree is so common in the Amazon
rainforest because it can grow in many different types of soil
and it is also resistant to the diseases that affect other trees.

Biochar – the famous Black Earth of the Amazon, is made using
special biochar charcoal, with fish and turtle bones, manure,
humus and broken ceramics. The People were taught by the
natives how to make and use it, and they used it later,
terraced, in the Andes. The natural soil in both the Amazon
jungle and the Andes was thin and poor.

Carpássio – large Phoenician trading or fishing ship.

Causa – (Quechua "sustenance for life") a cylindrically-molded
dish consisting of fluffy mashed potato layered with ají
amarillo (Peruvian yellow pepper), tuna or shredded chicken,
and a choice of other vegetable fillings, mushrooms, olives
and a touch of mayonnaise.

Charango – Andean lute-like stringed instrument. Sometimes the
body is made out of an armadillo shell.

Ch'arki (Quechua) – dried, salted meat, it originated in Peru and the Andes. Andean ch'arki was originally sun-dried, salted llama meat. Incas learned to freeze-dry it with their cold dry mountain air and strong equatorial sun. The word was Anglicized in the U.S. as 'jerky,' usually smoked beef.

Drop-spindle – this was an Old World device used from ancient times in spinning yarn, brought with the People and used until modern times, an interesting validation of their origin, as it was not known by Andean natives before the People came. Used by Catt in their home on the Amazon.

Garden Vegetables, etc. – faseloi = bean; keras = carrot; lentes = lentil; pisa = peas; kickere = chickpea; unio or unyun = onion. (These are Latin names, of Old World seeds brought over by the People.)

Humitas – corn dough mixed with lard or butter, and steamed in a corn husk. They can be sweet or savory. *Sweet* humitas are made with sugar, raisins and cinnamon. *Savory* humitas are seasoned with salt, mixed with milk or queso fresco (cheese). Both are sold in their wrappers to tourists on the go.

Inti – Inca God of the Sun.

Jungle fever – any of several tropical diseases such as dengue or yellow fever. (also see Tuberculosis)

Lima beans – named after Lima, Peru (see). Domesticated in the Andes, evidence has been found of them being grown there as much as 6,000 years ago.

Lumber trees, such as: mahogany, kapok (saumama), brazil-wood, rubber, brazil nut and capirona, are native to the Amazon.

Nortéamericano – a citizen or inhabitant of the U.S., especially as distinguished from the peoples of Spanish-speaking America.

Orgle, orgling – one of several sounds made by alpacas. The male orgles while mating.

Pink emerald – *morganite* (see description of its formation in *Gem of the Andes*) – A rose-colored variety of beryl (emerald), used as a gem. As it forms, the usual chemical makeup of green emerald sometimes includes manganese, which produces the pink color instead.

Popcorn – (Aztec *momochitl,* Peruvian Indian *pisancalla*) evidence of popcorn has been found from 6,700 years ago on the northern coast of Peru. A Spanish writer, Cobo, mentioned in 1650 that the Peruvian Indians roasted a certain kind of corn until it bursts. Besides eating, popcorn has been used for clothing decoration and religious rituals.

Puls – hot cooked cereal from ancient times in the Old World, often sweetened with cut-up figs or honey.

Quellqa – (quel-ka) ancient writing system of the Andes, over 5,000 years old, banned by the Incas.

Queso fresco – fresh cheese, mild, soft and slightly tangy.

Quipu – Inca method of keeping records or sending messages – a rope with colored and knotted cords of different lengths attached.

Quipucamayoq – interpreter or reader of quipus.

Sheep and goats – when the Conquistadors arrived in Peru, they found "sheep" being raised by the natives, but these were probably alpacas. (*See the chronicles of Pedro de Cieza de Leon, The Discovery and Conquest of Peru.*) The People, in the story, imported sheep and goats, but when they became established in the Andes, they began to favor the alpacas' wool, and these animals were better suited to the country.

Tectonic Plates – the Nazca and South American plates are two of seven major and many minor tectonic plates, sections of Earth's crust which ride upon the more liquid core of the Earth, rubbing against each others' edges and causing earthquakes and volcanoes. Sometimes they collide, pushing up mountain ranges such as the Andes.

Tuberculosis (see notes above) – ancestors of the People were noted to have had it, showing they came from Europe. It was not otherwise known in the New World before the time of Columbus.

~*~

Tribes, People:

Arawak – indigenous tribe living chiefly in NE South America and anciently in the West Indies.

Carib – a tribe indigenous to northern South America and formerly in the southern Indies.

Celtiberians – ancient Celts living in Northwest Iberia.

Gringuito – "little Gringo" – modern name for descendants of Chachapoyas in Peru.

Huaquero – a grave robber, or tomb robber. A thief who breaks into known or undiscovered tombs and steals artifacts, sacred items, gems and gold, to smuggle or sell.

Inca – the tribe that came to dominate ancient Peru with a highly developed civilization, until the Spanish conquest. It is still very prominent in the country.

Kena'anim – Canaanites, Phoenicians from the Mediterranean area.

Moche – a very creative Peruvian tribe, making artistic pottery and working with gold and silver. They practiced human sacrifice.

Pahuaca –The People of Atahuaqa, a fictional tribe, split off from Kuelap.

Quechua – one of the most prevalent of the surviving South American tribes. The language most commonly spoken in Peru and neighboring countries.

Sendero Luminoso – (Spanish, *Shining Path)* – Communist Party of Peru, a violent guerrilla group that launched its terrorist activities in 1980 and began to decline around 1990.

Shaman – medicine man/woman, healer, or advisor.

Talayotic – ancient people of Menorca, the Talayotic civilization created megalithic "Taula" or stone towers in Menorca's 'houses of the dead.' Long before the Roman Empire, Talayotic people left strange stone structures on the Spanish island.

The People – collective name of the mixed tribe of Canaanites, or Phoenicians, and the Celtiberians, who both mixed with the native Brasilians. (Note: Other indigenous tribes of the Americas also call themselves 'The People.')

Tupi and Guaurana – two of the most prevalent of many native tribes in the Amazon.

Wari – ('we' or human beings, people) more a civilization than an organized tribe. Flourished from 500-1,000 AD in central highlands and coast of Peru, and in the Amazon. Practiced cannibalism.

~*~

Geographic names:

Afrika, Mauharim, Libya, Alkebulan, Besacath – Most of the ancients didn't realize Africa was one huge continent, and named familiar parts of it around the southern shores of the Mediterranean.

Atahuaqa – fictional lost city of Pahuaca tribe in the Andes, where Priestess Tica lived.

Ayatambo – fictional first Andean settlement of the migrating tribe, the People.

Balearic Islands – islands in the western Mediterranean Sea (Mare Hibericum), just east of Spain (Iberian Peninsula). Majorca (Mallorca) is the main island, Anat's home island in the story.

Brasil – Brazil, named after the legendary island, Hy-Brasil of the Celts. Later it became Brazil, named after brazil-wood, a beautiful reddish wood exported to the Old World from the Amazon.

Brigantia – ancient name of La Caruna, at Betanzos, port of the Celtiberians in the northwestern Iberian Peninsula.

Darroch – ancient home of the Darrow ancestors in Scotland.

Gaul – ancient name of the area north of the Iberian Peninsula, including France.

Great (or Big) River – the Amazon River, extends nearly clear across northern South America, mostly in Brazil, the headwaters beginning in Peru. The Marańon and Madeira are two important tributaries.

Iberia – ancient name of Spain, in general, though the whole peninsula is known as the Iberian Peninsula.

Karajiah – location of the famous sarcophagi of the Cloud Warriors, high on a ledge above the Utcubamba River.

Karth-Hadash – one of the ancient names of Carthage.

Kuelap – great ancient fortress of the Cloud Warriors, built high in the Andes.

League – the ancient Roman league was 1.4 miles. (15 *ancient* leagues = 21miles.)

Lima (place) – Spanish corruption of Quechua *Rimaq* or *Limaq*, meaning "to speak" as, a priest. A famous oracle in the Rimac valley before the time of the Incas was known as Limaq.

Machu Picchu – (Quechua *Machupijchu*, Machu "old man" + pikchu "peak") ancient ruins of the Incas, high in the Andes.

Madeira River – a major tributary of the Amazon River, extends to the Andes in Peru. For the sake of this story, I have set the last dockyard of the People on this river.

Marańon River – west end headwaters of the Amazon River in Peru.

Mare Hibericum – ancient name of the Mediterranean Sea.

Mauharim – ancient Mauritania. South of here, somewhere between modern Senegal and Sierra Leone, the westernmost point of Africa is closest to the nearest eastern point of South America. The westward-flowing ocean current and winds can carry ships across the Atlantic from here.

Northern Sea/Sea of Caribs – the sea north of the main body of South America, later (after the time of Columbus) named the Caribbean Sea, after the Carib Indians.

Oakland Manor – fictional home of Amzi Darrow and his parents, Lorna and Courtland Darrow, in *Gem of the Andes.*

Ollantaytambo – Inca fortress and other ruins in the Sacred Valley at the beginning of the trail to Machu Picchu. About 45 miles northwest of Cuzco.

Paraiba (from Old Tupi *pa'ra a'iba*) – means "bad for boats," name of the river in eastern Brazil north of Recife that is very shallow and full of rocks.

Pedra do Inga – the Rock of Inga. A long rock alongside the Paraiba River, about 15 leagues from the sea, carved with mysterious ancient signs and symbols.

Pillars of Hercules – ancient name of the Strait of Gibraltar.

Rainbow Mountain – located about 3 hours from Cuzco at an altitude of more than half of Mount Everest, is *Vinicunca* (Quechua), or "colored mountain." 14 different minerals give it colorful bands.

Ravenwood – fictional Maryland home town of Lila and her family, in *Gem of the Andes*.

Sacred Valley – Urubamba Valley north of Cuzco, between 6700 and 9500 ft. elevation, it includes Ollantaytambo and Machu Picchu.

Saqsaywaman – ancient fortress or temple on the northern outskirts of Cuzco.

Sea of Darkness, Sea of Atlantis – Atlantic Ocean.

Spurwink Manor – the fictional Maryland home of Lila's family in *Gem of the Andes*.

Urubamba River, in valley below Machu Picchu.

Utcubamba River, in valley below Kuelap.

Vilcatambo – fictional small village near Cuzco, where Umayo lived.

Wexford – fictional Maryland home of Uncle Angus and Malcomb Sneed in *Gem of the Andes*.

Yanabamba River, fictional river, canyon, below Atahuaqa.

Characters, with name pronunciations!

Some readers have complained that my characters' names, and also names of places, plants, etc. were almost impossible to pronounce. Sorry, but in order to be authentic, I couldn't use names for natives of ancient Peru or the Amazon like "Joe" or "Sally." I did try my best to pick names from the lists that were the simplest, and to give most of the correct pronunciations here.

Ancient Phoenician/Celtiberian names

Aife (Aye-fee) priestess, and wife of Yorano at Kuelap.

Akbar (Ak-bar) father of Anat.

Akuchi (A-koo-chee), Umaq (Oo-mack) and Tupa (Too-pa) evil priests of Inti at Kuelap.

Andoti (An-doe-tee) shaman at Ayatambo; helps Tanitay.

Anat (An-nat) – 8 year old Phoenician girl on Phoenician ship in 146 BC.

Brigid (Bridge-id) descendant of Druse; Ysabel's teacher in the Amazon.

Breckin – teacher of quellqa at Ayatambo.

Crevan (Cray-van "fox") scout that finds site for Atahuaqa.

Danel (Dan-el) the younger of Anat's brothers.

Dannius (Danny-us) lead explorer for the People who first sights the Andes by climbing a tree.

Druce the Wise (Droos) Celt shaman; father of Ewan.

Elissa (Ee-liss-ah) Anat's friend, (named after the Princess of Tyre and founder of Carthage).

Eppo – husband of Ysabel.

Ewan (Yoo-an) young shaman, husband of Anat.

Huaqa (Hwa-ka) and Davina (Da-vee-na) – parents of priestess Tica.

Huarwar (Hwar-war) stone mason brought from the Old World to help with construction in the Andes.

Inti (In-tee) Inca God of the Sun.

Kanmi (Kan-me) the older of Anat's two brothers.

Maupi (Ma-pee) Tica's friend and maiden assistant.

Mungo – father of Huarwar.

Pachamama (Pock-ah-mama) Earth-mother goddess of the Andes.

Qircamo (Kir-cam-oh) mural artist at Ayatambo, husband of Tanitay; talented at time travel.

Rapau (Rah-pow) head shaman of Kuelap.

Taikan (Tie-con) evil priest at Atahuaqa.

Tanitay (Tan-i-tay) she becomes a tribal historian, using the quellqa writing system.

Tanith (Tan-ith) – mother of Anat, Kanmi and Danel.

Tica (Tee-kah) ancient priestess at Atahuaqa who inherits the pink emerald and dies in an earthquake.

Yamm – Phoenician God of the Sea.

Yorano (Yo-ran-o) shaman who resists evil priests at Kuelap; husband of Aife.

Ysabel (Ees-a-bell) priestess at an early village in Amazon.

~*~

Modern-day names

Amzi (Am-zee) Darrow – Lila's husband, detective from Peru, whose original home is in Maryland. (See *Gem of the Andes*).

Amzi Jr., shortened to AJ: Amzi and Lila's 3rd child.

Angus – Uncle Angus, elderly friend of the Darrow family.

Benjamin – youngest son of Amzi and Lila.

Brynna (Brinna) – last wife of Amzi's friend, Umayo (*Gem*).

Carmella (Car-mel-ah) – friend of Yachay, who spies on the terrorists.

Cattnia (Cat-nee-ah) – AJ's Chachapoyan bride.

Cornelius (Cor-nee-lee-us)– Lila's and Elfie's grandfather.

Daisy – Amzi and Lila's only daughter.

Danny – Amzi's oldest son, Daniel Angus Darrow.

Diogo, (Dee-oh-go) pilot in Amazon – Portuguese name means "a wandering explorer."

Dom Calder (Dom Call-der) – AJ's friend, Dominicus Calder (with wife Carina), in the Amazon.

Elfie – Lila's cousin, daughter of Aunt Melanie.

Lila – first protagonist of *Gem of the Andes*, marries Amzi.

Lorna and Courtland Darrow – Amzi's parents.

Orrin and Donna Gerard – found the pink emerald in 1852; Donna wrote a paper about it. They made the two pink emerald rings. (see *Gem*.)

Micos (Mee-kose) – young thug in the Shining Path.

Pacay (Paw-kay) – Umayo's son.

Qhispi (Kis-pee) – Amzi's head cook at the hacienda.

Rafa (Rah-fah) – the faithful driver for Amzi and AJ.

Tamya – (Tom-ya) Yachay's friend who gathers information on terrorist activities and plans.

Umayo (Oo-my-oh) – Amzi's friend and guide in Peru.

Umayo Amzi Darrow – AJ and Catt's son, named after Grandfather Umayo.

(little) Umayo – young Amerindian boy AJ discovers in the Amazon with the ancient axe.

Wilson – gardener at Spurwink Manor (see *Gem*).

Yachay (Ya-kay) Amzi's head gardener at the hacienda (see *Gem*).

Animal Characters:

Bartleby (bar-tul-bee)– black-and-tan corgi dog at Spurwink.

Chichi (chee-chee) – Ysabel's pet ocelot in the Amazon.

Chitee (chit-tee) – Anat's pet parrot in the Amazon.

Lionel – golden and white corgi dog at Spurwink.

Missy – Lila's long-haired calico cat in *Gem*.

Olga and Igor – the first two alpacas owned by Danny and Ben at Spurwink.

Pookie – Ben's favorite white alpaca.

Pucu (poo-koo) – Tica's pet white llama.

Qhawa (Ka-wa) – family dog at the hacienda with Amzi and Lila (*Gem*), also lived with them in Ravenwood and returns to Peru to save Daisy.

Medicinal plants and trees of Amazon and Peru:

(Note – some of these may be covered under 'plants.' Many are not mentioned in the book, but South America, especially the Amazon is so full of important medicinal plants, I have included some of the more interesting ones here.)

Ajo Shacha – a vine with long, lavender flowers and smells like garlic. Leaves, vine, bark and root used in baths to cleanse a negative spirit and boost immune system. "Magical." Good used for inflammation, arthritis, colds, and general tonic.

Albahaca (basil family) – an herb used in cooking. Also the seed in your eye will clear out foreign material. Good for digestive ailments.

Ayahuasca – a vine used by shamans, who brew the mashed vines with leaves of Chacruna and drink them in a healing ceremony with the patient.

Capirona – a canopy tree, 90 ft. tall, produces good lumber. Sheds its bark yearly, so it is easy to collect and use as a poultice for cuts, wounds, burns, infections, parasites, and to soothe insect bites. Stops bleeding quickly.

Chacruna – (Quechua) – an herb whose leaves were brewed with Ayahuasca and drunk in ceremony by a shaman to enter a spiritual dimension for healing diagnosis.

Chanca Piedra – a small herb, made into tea or extract for tuberculosis, cancer, or gall stone removal.

Chinchona (Quechua *quinina*) – the national tree of Peru. Quinine, to treat malaria, is made from the bark of the chinchona tree.

Chiric Sanango – a shrub with beautiful purple flowers, usually grown near the shaman's house. Helps with rheumatism, chills, fever, colds and flu.

Cocona – (see Wapotok.)

Cordoncillo – a plant that causes numbness, used as an
anesthetic. Chew for tooth pain, or rub crushed leaves on
wounds as a pain-killer.

Croton lechleri tree – commonly known as sangre de drago
(Spanish), which translates to "dragon's blood." This refers
to the tree's thick red latex. Cut the bark and collect the red
latex that seeps out. Apply to a deep wound and stay
motionless while it sets. After a day or two it falls off, leaving
barely a trace. It can also be used for diarrhea associated
with cholera and many other ailments.

Curare – (Arrow poison) a vine. Can be used (carefully) as
general anesthesia and to treat muscular disorders.

Guanabana – a small tree. Nearly every part of the plant is used:
fruit for worms and parasites; leaves to cleanse liver; bark
and roots for liver and heart. Also good for chills, fever,
colds, flu and diarrhea.

Ishanga (Stinging nettle, an herb) – used for muscle and arthritis
pain, eczema, asthma, diabetes, nosebleed and head lice.

Jaborandi – an herb used by the Guarani to treat mouth ulcers.
Also useful for colds, flu and gonorrhea.

Kapok tree – its Brazilian name is samaúma, or in Peru, sama
huma. Rising above the rainforest canopy to heights of up to
200 feet, it can grow up to 13 feet in a single year. It is
supported by buttresses which can extend up to 30 feet from
the main trunk. Many species make it their home—birds,
frogs, snakes, bats, orchids and bromeliads —and
mammals, use its long branches as highways. The seeds,
bark, leaves and sap have been used for centuries by
natives for a large range of maladies such as fever, asthma,
dysentery, and kidney ailments, while the lightweight wood
has been used in carving dugout canoes. Kapok is probably
best known for its "silk cotton" fibers from inside the
seedpods, the world's lightest natural fiber, known for its
thermo-regulating properties, making it useful for stuffing
pillows, mattresses and sleeping bags.

Ku-na-ne-mah – climbing hempweed. Usually burned by a
shaman for an unconscious person to inhale, like smelling
salts. Absorption through the sinus membranes of certain
drugs is almost as fast and effective as being administered

intravenously. (from the book, *Amazonia*, by James Rollins) *(Note: this was in a story set in Venezuela, and the Yanomami tribe, but the fact about <u>absorption by inhaling the smoke</u> should be the same with other medicinal plants used for this purpose).*

Lapacho – a tree. Used to treat cancer, alleviate pain from chemotherapy, and fight infections.

Maca – a bulb root in the Andes, used for calcium, energy, memory, stamina and libido.

Mullaca – an herb used for skin disorders. Antibacterial, antiviral, anticancer.

Pitanga –(old Tupi 'ybapytanga') from 'yba' (fruit) and 'pytanga' (colored light red or brown.) Small, juicy, deeply corrugated, red or orange fruit, a tree native to tropical South America. It has many vitamins and antioxidants, useful against heart ailments, cancer, eye ailments, common cold, and skin conditions.

Samambaia – a fern. Promotes perspiration, relieves psoriasis, reduces inflammation.

Sodo – an aromatic shrub or tree, used to cure addiction, including alcoholism.

Tawari tree – its bark is used in treating cancer, infection, tumors and inflammation.

Tuyuya – (Cayaponia tayuya) – a woody vine. The bark is used as a blood cleanser, and to reduce pain and inflammation.

Wapotok – or cocona. (both are a kind of wild tomato) High in vitamins A and C, fruit useful in cooking, plant parts can also be used to treat burns, diabetes, and skin inflammation.

Wasai tree – has red roots. Great for kidney health, the roots are ground up and used as a diuretic.

~*~

The Author

Jackie McGuire grew up on a goat ranch known as Buzzard's Roost on a mountain in Southern Oregon. Her Aunt Ethel, who worked in Lima, Peru as an interpreter at the American embassy, wrote to her about life in Peru, and advised her to take every opportunity to travel or learn new skills.

Jackie graduated in 1966 from Burnley School of Professional Art in Seattle, Washington and took courses in writing as well as attending several different writer's clubs, conferences, and a critique group while living in Washington and Oregon. She has illustrated several books by other authors, and published *Wife on the Road*, a non-fiction book, in 2017. In 2021, she published *Gem of the Andes*, her first fiction work.

Now residing in the Appalachians of Kentucky, she continues to write and learn new skills.

Coming Soon: *Giant at Boiling River*, by Jackie McGuire

Third in the series, we continue the adventures of AJ Darrow and his friend Dominicus Calder, investigating the rumors of a giant man, or *something*, in the foothills of the Andes near a place called Boiling River. A boiling river? Such a place actually exists in Peru, near Pucallpa, on the eastern slopes of the Andes.

Many legends of giants have been chronicled, down through the ages and all over the world. The Incas told the Conquistadors that giants built the huge stone walls in Peru, long before their own time. Could this be true? AJ and Dom want to find the answer.

About This Book

I have tried to be factually accurate in background details for this story, and the basic premise of the story of the Cloud Warriors. They were an actual mysterious race in the high Andes, set apart by their different appearance and culture, and their origin being a subject of controversy among historians.

Gretchen Brunk and I researched names and places of actual people, and flora and fauna and foods, noting general dates of some actual events in the ancient history of the Mediterranean, Peru and Brazil, and especially ideas of what may actually have occurred back in 146 BC and onward. It is an astonishing study to find recent discoveries showing that the Amazon of ancient times was not just a wild river with a few natives living in isolated villages along its banks, but that at one time, many indigenous towns existed, far back into the rain forest from the river—all interconnected with roads.

Others have maintained that the poor jungle soil could never have supported many people, but we find that these Amazon natives invented a wonderful fertile *biochar* soil, by adding manure, fish and turtle bones, charcoal, and broken pottery.

I chose native names as accurately as possible, according to their specific nationality, in ancient times, for which some readers complain that it's too hard to read them – but would you

265

believe a Phoenician in 146 BC named Joe or Betsy? Believe me, I picked the names that were easiest to read from the authentic lists! When reading the story, I suggest you just figure out your best guess on pronouncing them for yourself – make it simple! (The glossary should help.)

Forgive me for such a huge glossary and special notes section! South America is so full of fascinating things, but I didn't want to cram the story full of lists. Even at that, I've only concentrated on Peru and Brazil. Who knew that so many wonderful foods originated there? Chocolate, vanilla, peanuts, pineapple, tapioca, potatoes, tomatoes, peppers, - - foods we enjoy every day. *I encourage you to read over the* **glossary** *at some point. Who would guess that "ynchic" means peanut?*

Most dates and facts in the story were accurate, though some might have been "nudged" a bit to fit the circumstances – so sue me! This IS fiction! I was thrilled when I read the history of this great adventure and found it highly exciting to try to imagine what it was like to BE those actual people back in that ancient world. It was daunting at first, to think of trying to find any history recorded of the wild Amazon back in 146 BC to 1 BC and onward. But we found that there are actual accounts written by explorers and historians of the times, and others like the Conquistadors—to discover some incredible eye-witnessed events they recorded.

I'm not sure whether the People made trading trips back across the Atlantic very soon after settling in the Amazon, but some think so, and it fits the story. Otherwise, how did they hear rumors that the Romans had looked for them? And how else did the mariners continue trade with their brother settlers in the Andes later on?

Another controversy: Did the People bring wives and children with them? It seems right – who would leave their own families alone and unprotected, with the brutal Romans coming? They wanted to establish colonies in the New World – it seems to me they would bring their families. Some would say it was only men, and they took native wives in Brazil. Forget the old family,

266

just start over when we get there? I don't believe it. But of course there *were* probably some who had no choice.

The main framework of this Chachapoya story, was, of course, inspired by Hans Giffhorn in his book *Wurde Amerika in der Antike entdeckt*, (America Was Discovered in Ancient Times) which unfortunately was only available published in German when we were working on this book. My friend and researcher, Gretchen Brunk, was able to translate parts of it for our study of the subject. Forgive me if you don't agree—I changed some small details to fit the story where needed. You can find several ideas of what really happened, on the Internet and old TV documentaries, but we found Giffhorn's to be the most plausible, citing many years of thorough research in Spain, Brazil, Peru and connected countries, and numerous photos.

Did the Chachapoyas actually come from Europe? I think that part is true. What AJ concluded from his research was what we found – those who believe it true give much more convincing evidence, and many who don't, just poo-poo the idea and make mockery of it. I've usually found that those who ridicule without giving good reason, are just covering up that they don't know what they're talking about.

Braiding the ancient history into the modern adventures of the Darrows made the story really come alive, as we see AJ hot on the trail, assisted by his family's friend, the mysterious Umayo, and the ancient priestess, Tica. Later, as AJ comes closer to discovery of the truth about Atahuaqa, he is sent on a fascinating mission to the Amazon and discovers a new link to that ancient world. As the story unfolded, I had no idea what would happen next, so I hope that reading it will be as exciting to you as it was for me in unearthing and writing it.

Made in the USA
Las Vegas, NV
15 November 2023

80896189R00154